Women and Politics in Contemporary Ireland

WOMEN
AND POLITICS
IN CONTEMPORARY
IRELAND

FROM THE MARGINS
TO THE MAINSTREAM

YVONNE GALLIGAN

PINTER
London and Washington

Pinter
A Cassell Imprint
Wellington House, 125 Strand, London WC2R 0BB
PO Box 605, Herndon, VA 20172, USA

First published 1998

© Yvonne Galligan 1998

British Library Cataloguing-in-Publication Data
A catalogue record for this book is available from the British Library.

ISBN 1-85567-432-7 (hardback)
    1-85567-433-5 (paperback)

Library of Congress Cataloging-in-Publication Data
Galligan, Yvonne.
    Women and politics in contemporary Ireland : from the margins to the
mainstream / Yvonne Galligan
        p. cm.
    Includes bibliographical references (p.) and index.
    ISBN 1-85567-432-7 (hard cover)
    1. Women in politics—Ireland.   2. Women's rights—Ireland.
3. Feminism—Ireland.   4. Women—Ireland—Social conditions.
5. Ireland—Politics and government—1949–   I. Title.
HQ1236.5.I73G35   1997
305.42'09417—DC21   97-8652
                                                                      CIP
Typeset by Ben Cracknell Studios
Printed and bound in Great Britain by Biddles Ltd, Guildford and King's Lynn

CONTENTS

PREFACE

The idea for this book came in the course of my work on a doctoral thesis. As I researched women's relationship with the State in Ireland, I became aware of many aspects waiting to be explored. In writing this book, I touch on some of these areas. Like all ventures into the unknown, my research has had its periods of uncertainty and its share of pleasant surprises. My abiding memory, though, is of working on a fascinating dimension to the politics of modern Ireland. This book, with all its strengths and weaknesses, is my contribution to the study of women and politics in Ireland.

I am deeply indebted to the many people who assisted me as I struggled to make sense of the jigsaw puzzle of modern Irish feminist politics. I owe a debt of gratitude to the politicians, civil servants and interest group representatives who agreed to speak to me about their activities. Each one received me with unfailing courtesy and gave generously of his or her valuable time. Their views and interpretations of events enriched my academic efforts to analyse patterns of feminist political engagement.

Special thanks go to Michael Gallagher, who gave me guidance at critical moments in the earlier stages of this work. Thanks are also due to Michael Laver, Elizabeth Meehan, Norah O'Neill, Sylvia Meehan, Richard Humphreys, Roisin McDermott and Olive Braiden, all of whom read and commented on drafts of one or more chapters of this book.

Thanks are due to the librarians in Trinity College, Dublin, the National Library of Ireland and the Institute of Public Administration. Their assistance in the course of my search for dusty documentation is a tribute to their professional skills. I would especially like to thank my family and friends who have lived with this book for a long time. Patrick and Patricia Galligan gave me special encouragement. Particular thanks must go to John Coakely for his invaluable intellectual and practical support which helped me to bring this project to a successful conclusion. Cian and Eimear Fitzsimons bore my preoccupation with understanding and patience. Nicola Vinnikka from Pinter first showed interest in this book while Petra Recter guided the manuscript to its present form. I alone am responsible for any shortcomings it contains.

Yvonne Galligan
February 1997

LIST OF ABBREVIATIONS

AA	Alcoholics Anonymous
AIM	Action Information Motivation
CAP	Contraception Action Programme
CPSU	Civil and Public Service Union
DAG	Divorce Action Group
EEA	Employment Equality Agency
EU	European Union
FLAC	Free Legal Aid Centres
FUE	Federated Union of Employers
ICA	Irish Countrywomen's Association
ICCL	Irish Council for Civil Liberties
ICTU	Irish Congress of Trade Unions
IFL	Irish Family League
IFPA	Irish Family Planning Association
IHA	Irish Housewives Association
ILO	International Labour Organization
ISPCC	Irish Society for the Prevention of Cruelty to Children
IU	Irishwomen United
JCWR	Joint Committee on Women's Rights
LWNC	Labour Women's National Council
MEP	Member of the European Parliament
NWCI	National Women's Council of Ireland
OECD	Organization for Economic Co-operation and Development
PCW	Programme for Competitiveness and Work
PESP	Programme for Economic and Social Progress
RCC	Rape Crisis Centre
WAC	Women's Action Committee
WRC	Women's Representative Committee

TO CIAN AND EIMEAR

CHAPTER 1

INTRODUCTION

In Ireland today, the story of the relationship between women and public policy is told through the media. The 1997 presidential election contest among five candidates, four of whom were women, suggests that women's political involvement is vibrant and extensive. The election of Mary McAleese as presidential successor to Mary Robinson is interpreted as a triumph for women's participation in political life. In other news stories, women are portrayed as victims of the failure of politicians to tackle difficult issues. This is clearly illustrated in reports on the 1992 X case and the 1997 C case, where, in each instance, a teenage girl sought from the courts the right to travel to England for an abortion. Stories such as these highlight the failure of Irish politicians to legislate on the controversial abortion issue. In other instances, women are shown as being pro-active in their quest for answers to serious wrongs visited upon them by careless public officials and insensitive politicians. The efforts of Positive Action to reveal the truth behind a sequence of public policy decisions on the handling of infected blood products typifies this pro-active, questioning strand of feminist activity. Whether the story is one of success or of personal tragedy, the overall impression is of an active female citizenry prepared to challenge inadequate and unjust public policies and ready to play a full role in electoral politics. Yet, twenty-five years ago, few newspapers reported on women's civic involvement. Indeed, there was little to say on the matter. What has brought about this transformation in Irish women's perception of their citizenship? Why are political decision-makers today aware of women's issues in a way they were not a generation ago? How have representatives of women's interests and policy-makers regarded one another over the course of the last quarter-century? In this book, some answers are offered to these questions based on an analysis of feminist activity over a twenty-five-year period.

The potentially large scale of the subject matter meant that it was necessary to be selective about what material to include. As this was a modest venture into unknown territory in terms of Irish political research, it was decided to play safe and draw on the demands of the Irish women's liberation movement which had led to a revitalization of feminist political activity. Equal pay, reform of family law, removing the ban on the sale of contraceptives and protection from male violence were identified as the key issues which mobilized Irish women during the course of the 1970s and 1980s. These issues are traced through the political system until they emerge as laws. As the dynamics of this process unfolded, it revealed a fascinating picture of how woman-focused policies were shaped, and it brought into relief the disputes, the compromises and the agreements between women's interest representatives and politicians. It also threw further light on the workings of the Irish policy-making machinery.

There was a resurgence of women's political activism in the Republic of Ireland in the 1970s. This contemporary mobilization of women to political action appeared to be related to the emergence of the new feminist movement in the early 1970s. As my knowledge of women's political engagement expanded, this hypothesis was modified. A realization emerged that the basis for the growth in women's political consciousness in the 1970s was laid in the 1960s through the politicization of women's issues by trade union women, business and professional women's groups and women's social organizations. Indeed, the leading members of these groups were clearly conscious of the second-order citizenship of women some time before the women's liberation movement came about. Their commitment to bringing about change in society for the benefit of all women led them to become advocates of women's rights within the political system. Not surprisingly, I came to the view that the term 'women's movement' should be used in a more all-embracing manner than is normally the case. By giving an inclusive meaning to the term 'women's movement', an acknowledgement and exploration of the contribution of 'pre-liberation' women's groups to the feminist agenda became possible.

Political lobbying, by its very nature, is not a visible feature of the political process. Given that Irish women are also considerably under-represented in Irish parliamentary institutions, the 'invisibility' of their interest representation is reinforced. As a consequence, the study of women's interest group activity in Ireland is largely confined to their mobilization around the contentious policy issue of abortion.[1] Many of the other issue areas in which women have campaigned to secure their rights have been overlooked. Alternatively, women are seen as 'consumers' in studies of women and public policy.[2] While accounts of the mobilization of Irish women in the 1970s describe the organic development of the new feminist movement,[3] there are no studies of the interest groups which emerged from this period of social protest. The aim of this book is to fill that gap by focusing on women's political activity around issues which, while less socially divisive than abortion, were none the less significant in shaping the political and social context of modern Ireland.

In focusing on women's political activity around specific issues, I hope to make a contribution to the understanding of the relationship between women and the policy process in Ireland.

There is a growing body of evidence from studies of feminist activity in other countries which indicates that there is a causal connection between women's demands and changes in public policies, and qualitative research in this area is well established and widely recognized.[4] Quantitative analysis of the impact of women's associations on public policy outcomes is beginning to emerge, with findings that support the argument that women's interest groups do have an appreciable influence on policy.[5] The literature further notes that certain public policies, are viewed as having a particular significance for contemporary feminism. The issues of abortion, equal rights, rape, domestic violence and equal opportunities comprise the common agenda of feminists in every liberal democratic country in which a women's movement has emerged.[6] This book seeks to add an Irish dimension to that corpus of knowledge.

THE IRISH POLITICAL SYSTEM

A highly centralized bureaucracy, executive monopoly of legislation and a tightly controlled party system shape the general parameters of political decision-making in the context of a highly personalist political culture.[7] These basic features of the Irish political system make a study of this kind something other than a replica of the research on women and politics in Britain. Certainly, electoral politics, conducted in a system of proportional representation in multi-member constituencies, puts pressure on political representatives to listen to the views of organized groups, be it at local or national level, making access to decision-makers relatively easy for representative organizations. Further, the personalist political environment has nurtured a culture of direct contact between government ministers, senior administrators and group elites. This pattern of face-to-face negotiations is reinforced by the centralization of political power.

There is really only one significant locus of political power in Ireland, and that is in the office of each government minister: precious little political power is devolved to regional or local authorities. Decisions are made at the top and interest-group representation is accordingly directed at central government. However, as no government has been returned for a second term since 1969, leaders of representative organizations do not confine their activities to government alone, but devote considerable attention to the parties in opposition, again concentrating on those at elite level in these parties. Over time, decision-makers and leaders of non-governmental organizations come to know one another quite well, and access to government ministers can often be facilitated by friendship and past association.

The long history of British rule in Ireland has left a significant legacy in terms of public policies. The process of changing those policies offers interesting insights into how a relatively new country shapes a national identity, especially for its female citizens. One recurring pattern in the course of policy formulation is the extent to which Irish policy-makers refer to policy developments in the United Kingdom and, to a lesser extent, other English-speaking nations. For instance, when the Irish legislation on employment equality was being considered, similar policies in Britain were closely examined by government officials. A similar search for comparative policy experience characterized the formulation of Irish policy-makers' thoughts on violence against women. While Ireland may be an independent nation, the bond of a common language and the ties of a shared Westminister tradition of government and administration encourage Irish policy-makers, then, to look to the British experience in specific policy areas. This offers researchers in both countries material for comparative policy studies.

THE RESEARCH

This book seeks to determine the extent of the influence exercised by women's groups in bringing a range of demands to the attention of policy-makers and in shaping the policy outcomes. As already noted, employment equality, fertility control, equal rights, rape and domestic violence are issues of importance to the new women's movement in Ireland as elsewhere. The case studies were chosen on the basis that they represented different examples of women's movement demands. Equal pay and employment equality issues were standard women's movement demands which held particular appeal for trade union women. Family law reform, again a feminist issue, was taken up by a liberal offshoot of the women's movement. Contraception was a key demand of the women's movement, and indeed was an issue common to all politicized women's groups in Ireland. The identity-centred politics of the radical movement brought gender-specific issues to the fore. In Ireland, sexual violence and wife-beating became mobilizing issues which found expression both outside and inside the political structures. Together, these case studies provide an illustration of the range of women's issues raised and the manner in which they were handled by women's representatives, public officials and politicians during the course of the policy process. As a legislative outcome resulted in all cases, this outcome could be measured against the original policy position.

The methodological approach to this book consisted of an exhaustive documentary study, drawing information from a wide range of sources. This is the first time material of this kind has been compiled in the case of women in Irish politics. The documents consulted consisted of newspaper reports, parliamentary debates and research publications, along with leaflets, pamphlets and newsletters produced by the issue groups in question and by related organizations. Much of the detail for the activities of women trade unionists came from the reports of the Irish Congress of Trade Unions' (ICTU) annual congress dating from 1959 to 1979. The newsletters of the Action Information Motivation (AIM) group spanning twelve years from 1972 to 1984 were an invaluable source of information. AIM also provided access to unpublished submissions to government. Information on the activities of both the Rape Crisis Centre (RCC) and Women's Aid was gleaned through interviews and unpublished material made available by the groups. The contraception debate was charted through feminist magazines, parliamentary debates and personal interviews.

The documentary study was supported by a series of formal interviews lasting approximately one hour each with spokespersons from feminist groups, former government ministers and public officials responsible for the formulation of the legislation discussed in this study. Access to the latter group was facilitated by personal networks among policy-makers. The formal interviews were supplemented by a range of informal discussions with group activists and parliamentarians. At this point, it is only proper and fitting to acknowledge the gracious response accorded my ongoing requests for information. Politicians, administrators and spokeswomen from the organizations studied were very willing to be interviewed and gave generously of their time and knowledge. This highlighted the accessibility to researchers of political elites in Ireland – a truly invaluable resource for students of politics.

THE POLITICS OF GROUP ACTIVITY

This introductory chapter looks at what the literature has to say about groups and the policy process. The relevance of this literature to the present research is assessed. A number of analytical points are drawn from it which will aid an understanding of the relationship between women's political mobilization and public policy outcomes in Ireland.

Group involvement in public policy-making is the subject of two major sets of literatures: the sociological study of social movements, and political science research on interest groups. Both recognize the importance of group behaviour and seek to assess the degree of access and the extent of the influence wielded by politically-oriented groups. Social movement literature looks at the relationship between institutional political participants and the mobilization of mass groups. The interest group literature places a focus on groups active within the established political structures. A clearly defined subset of both literatures is the study of women's political behaviour in the form of social movement and interest group activity.

The following section examines the main strands of the social movement literature and assesses their significance for the study of feminist mobilization. The interest group literature is analysed with a view to uncovering some pointers which appear to offer fruitful possibilities for understanding the relationship between women's groups and the State. In the final section, the factors which appear to be most likely to influence the impact of feminist demands are identified. These will provide a framework for analysing the succeeding chapter case studies.

SOCIAL MOVEMENTS

The literature on social movements, dominated by sociological research, has consistently focused on the nature of pre-existing social conditions enabling the mobilization of a sizeable segment of people in support of a particular value, belief or concern. Mobilizing issues highlight social and political matters which are not being addressed by the institutional processes in a political system. As such, they have been found to pose a challenge to the dominant political paradigm in the societies in which they occur, confirming Smelser's view that social movements consist of a 'mobilization on the basis of a belief which redefines social action'.[8] The new movements such as the civil rights protests in the 1960s, the environmental and feminist agitation of the 1970s and the resurgence of the peace movement in the 1980s have posed radical questions about the nature of the prevailing social and political order. This type of mobilization is not revolutionary in intent. As Offe puts it, new social movements offer a selective radicalization of existing values:

> new social movements are, in their basic normative orientation neither *post-modern*, emphasising values not yet shared by society, nor premodern, adhering to the remnants of a romanticised pre-rational past.

They are rather the contemporaries of the societies in which they live and whose institutional embodiments of economic and political rationality they oppose.[9]

Taking this analysis further, Clemens suggests that when viewed from the perspective of organizational theory, 'social movements appear as not only vehicles of pre-existing interests and causes of specific political outcomes, but as critical sources of institutional change'.[10] In a succinct description of the nature of the challenge presented by social movements, Dalton *et al.* suggest that it is multi-layered:

> It is claimed that new social movements challenge the contemporary political order on several fronts. On the ideological level, these movements advocate a new social paradigm which contrasts with the dominant goal structure of Western industrial societies. . . . New social movements also illustrate a style of unconventional political action – based on direct action – that contrasts with the traditional neo-corporatist pattern of interest intermediation in many contemporary democracies. Even the organizational structures of these movements are supposedly unique, stressing participatory decision-making, a decentralized structure and opposition to bureaucratic procedures. Thus, it is claimed that new social movements challenge the basic goals, structure and organizational style of Western industrial democracies.[11]

A further feature of new social movements is the essentially middle-class nature of the phenomenon. This has held true across all social movements and in all countries. Making this point, Rootes, for instance, notes that in Britain, as elsewhere in Western Europe,

> support for new social movements is concentrated among the highly educated members of the new middle classes, with a particular concentration of support among those employed in the teaching, caring and welfare professions in the non-market sector of the economy.[12]

With the rise in social movements from the late 1960s on, scholars of group theory sought to explain the renewal of popular interest in this form of political activity. The quest for a better understanding of this type of collective political behaviour led to the creation of a number of different analytical approaches. Some, such as collective behaviour and relative deprivation, have been found over time to have a rather limited explanatory value when applied to the dynamic cycle of social movement evolution. Other conceptual formulations such as the resource mobilization approach and the political opportunity structure thesis have been shown to offer more fruitful explanatory perspectives. These two models underpin a considerable amount of the literature on new social movements and therefore merit some attention.

RESOURCE MOBILIZATION THEORY

Resource mobilization theory is based on the proposition that political dissatisfaction is ever-present in society. In order for this dissatisfaction to be mobilized, it is necessary for existing social groups to work together to organize this potential challenge around a specific grievance. This view was taken by Oberschall among others, who observed that

> the central problem in creating an enduring movement is not in the development of novel beliefs and of opposition ideas, but the cementing together of an organizational network, which is always easier when some group networks already exist. Ideas and beliefs that have revolutionary potential are usually present and are available for use by a protest leadership.[13]

A second requirement for the mobilization of a potential social movement is a catalyst, a grievance-producing event, often (but not necessarily) prompted by the decisions of public officials or the government that leads to like-minded groups and individuals uniting in an expression of protest. Rudig, for instance, traces the origins of the environmental movement in Western Europe to the mobilization of large segments of the population to demonstrate against nuclear issues:

> The key conflict which contributed to a transformation of a sizeable number of groups from single issue pressure groups to broader-based ecological movement was the protest against nuclear energy.[14]

In the case of Ireland, for example, the declared intention of the Electricity Supply Board to build a nuclear-powered electricity generating station resulted in the development of a significant anti-nuclear lobby which successfully mobilized a considerable degree of popular protest.[15] The catalyst for the civil rights movement in the United States was the arrest of Rosa Parks for refusing to give up her seat to a white man on a bus in Montgomery, Alabama,[16] while the emergence of the feminist movement in Britain has been attributed to the commemoration by women's peace groups of the fiftieth anniversary of women's suffrage in 1968.[17]

Resource mobilization studies point to the dual aspect of social movements which makes them distinct from conventional interest groups. The decentralized, unstructured aspect of social movements has been found to play a significant role in changing personal orientations and attitudes. The centralized organizational element is seen as appropriate for achieving short-term goals involving institutional change. Rucht has classified the strategy followed by the organized components of social movements as being power-oriented, while the radical branch pursues identity-oriented strategies. These are manifest in cultural alternatives and challenges which 'primarily seek to change personal behaviour by espousing and adhering to deviant cultural practices'.[18] Both aspects of a social movement are interdependent. The complexity of their interaction, first emphasized by Ash and Zald, is referred to extensively in the literature on the women's movement. Freeman[19] suggests that the more viable movements contain both power- and identity-oriented groups, each playing different roles and pursuing different strategic options at any given time. This duality has been observed for the women's movement,[20] but is not exclusive to feminism. A similar pattern is evident in the ecology movement,[21] the Irish anti-nuclear movement,[22] and many other social movements.

The main focus of resource mobilization theory is on social movement organizations, their use of the resources at their disposal and the limitations of these resources. In one study, Freeman contrasts the resources and strategies of the civil rights and women's movements in the USA and concludes that they followed different patterns because

the women's movement did not use court action as readily as the civil rights movement did – even though many of the same laws proscribed sex discrimination – because it had never organised legal resources adequately.[23]

McCarthy and Zald[24] discuss some of the more strategic tasks of social movement organizations and the role they play in maintaining and directing the movement from which they emerge. These include 'mobilizing supporters, neutralizing and/or transforming mass and elite publics into sympathizers, achieving change in targets'. Social movement organizations are also referred to as 'incipient interest groups' and 'nascent groups'. In representing the aims of the social movement from which they have grown, they are, as Knoke has noted, 'subject to many of the constraints that shape the viability of other organizations'.[25] Thus, it may be difficult to distinguish a social movement organization from an interest group. Boneparth, writing on the women's movement in the United States, emphasizes this point in the following terms:

In the past fifteen years, the women's movement has evolved from a diffuse social movement to an increasingly organized political interest.

New women's groups such as the National Organization for Women (NOW), the National Women's Political Caucus (NWPC) and the Women's Equity Action League (WEAL) have established themselves as general lobbying organizations. Many other lobbies have been established in specialized issue areas such as employment, health, education, reproductive rights and violence against women.

In focusing on social movement organizations, resource mobilization scholars provide a connecting link between the socio-political phenomenon of social movement and institutional politics. The theory is particularly suited to the political conditions of the United States, given the extent to which interest-group activity is integrated into the political process. While the resource mobilization approach has influenced many social movement studies in Europe, its value as a conceptual tool has been limited. Challenging groups in European politics experience different kinds of obstacles and opportunities for influencing public policies. This has much to do with the nature of European political systems, dominated by the institutions of parliamentary government, a focus on national politics and generally tightly disciplined party systems.[27] Thus, the resource mobilization perspective, concentrating as it does on the internal factors facilitating or hindering movement activity, cannot of itself provide a comprehensive framework for studying the impact of social movement groups on policy in European liberal democracies.

POLITICAL OPPORTUNITY STRUCTURE

In order to address this lacuna, Herbert Kitschelt devised the concept of 'political opportunity structure'.[28] This approach shifts the focus away from the internal dynamics of a social movement organization and towards the relationship between the social movement and the political environment to which it belongs. This permits consideration of the 'configuration of resources, institutional arrangements and historical precedents for social mobilization'[29] which facilitate or hinder the development of a social movement. This, in turn, has a bearing on the extent and influence a movement can have on policy and politics. Political systems are classed as being either open or closed to the demands of social movements on the basis of a combination of the above characteristics. Sweden, for instance, is perceived as having an open system, resulting in state co-option of movement goals with the minimum of conflict. The United States also falls into this category. France and Germany have closed political systems, which encourages radicalism among social movement activists and places an emphasis on direct action and civil disobedience strategies.[30]

The political opportunity thesis has provided a valuable conceptual framework for explaining why movements adopt confrontational or assimilative strategies.[31] Gelb uses this concept to underpin her comparative study of the feminist movement in the United States, Britain and Sweden. She argues that 'differences in the political opportunity structures or institutions, alignments and ideology of each nation structure the development, goals and values of feminist activists'.[32] Thus, she argues, the nature of the feminist challenge is conditioned by the political environment of each country. Along with other social movement analysts, Gelb found that the degree of corporatism, extent of political centralization and the level of pluralism are all crucial variables in affecting movement activity.[33] She classifies the type of feminist activity in the three country cases according to the dominant response of the women's movement to the nature of the political system. In the United States, interest group feminism is dominant. This strategy places a focus on equal rights and legal equality, the development of lobbying groups and the dominance of assimilative strategies on the part of movement activists. In contrast, British feminism is described as ideological. The closed British political system has provided few opportunities for the movement to organize along interest group lines. Instead, the women's movement is decentralized, locally based, with a strong emphasis on the ideological component. State feminism characterizes the Swedish system. In this case, the anticipation of feminist demands by successive governments and their incorporation into the repertoire of action by the State has led to the integration of gender issues into public policy with little pressure from feminist organizations.

The political opportunity structure is not without its drawbacks. The determinism of the concept has been questioned. In particular, the underlying assumption that open political systems lead to the adoption of assimilative strategies by social movements while confrontational tactics are employed in the context of closed systems has been challenged. Geier,[34] in a study of the peace movements in the United States and West Germany, found that although the German peace movement functioned in a closed political system, the majority of the actions engaged in by the movement could be classed as assimilative rather than confrontational. In the case of the British women's movement, Lovenduski and Randall, while not explicitly referring to Gelb's discussion of feminism in Britain, point to an increasing professionalization and involvement with government and other public institutions throughout the 1980s.[35] They also suggest, in a challenge to Gelb's analysis, that by the early 1980s the political opportunity structure for feminism in Britain had become more open, with two significant political groups, the Labour Party and the trade unions, becoming more receptive to women's issues.

ISSUE DEFINITIONS

While scholars of feminist politics utilize the concepts of resource mobilization and political opportunity structure to assess the impact of the women's movement on public policy, this sub-field of the social movement literature has developed a set of key concepts of its own to explain the specific nature of women's demands. One is the concept of role equity and role change, which has been used to identify the nature of the demands of women's organizations in conjunction with an assessment of the responses of policy-makers. Gelb and Palley, for instance, study the demands of American feminist organizations in five policy areas and the political response to these representations in the light of this model. They distinguish between role equity and role change policies as follows:

> Role equity issues are those policies which extend rights now enjoyed by other groups (men, other minorities) to women and which appear to be relatively delineated or narrow in their implications, permitting policy makers to seek advantage with feminist groups and voters with little cost or controversy. In contrast, role change issues appear to produce change in the dependent female role of wife, mother and homemaker, holding out the potential of greater sexual freedom and independence in a variety of contexts. The latter issues are fraught with greater political pitfalls, including perceived threats to existing values in turn creating visible and often powerful opposition.[36]

As ideal types, this bipolar classification of demands and policy outcomes is useful in highlighting the underlying ideological and perceptual differences between feminist representatives and public policy-makers. As the corpus of studies on women's mobilization shows, there is a consistent mismatch between what women want and what public officials are prepared to give. Not surprisingly, the point is repeatedly made that public policies continue to be framed in a manner that holds particular implications for women's social roles.[37] The role equity and role change model offers a framework for discussing these implications and for measuring the extent to which feminist demands are met in policy outcomes.

The concept of issue definition is utilized by scholars of European feminist political activity to highlight the nature of women's demands. This concept is a feature of conventional interest group politics and as such is not unique to the study of women's interest representation. The difference is that women's movement researchers highlight the term in order to analyse the nature and extent of women's engagement with the policy-making process. It is therefore not surprising to find that many of the accounts of women's movement representations are concerned with the manner in which opposing constructions of policy issues are reconciled. McBride Stetson analyses changes in public policy on women's rights in France using this perspective, observing that

the crucial conflict in policy making revolves around how to frame the problem that will be treated by policy. Winning control of the way the issue is perceived and defined by the government means determining the content of statutes and administrative regulations. Feminists have battled to control their issues and persuade the government to adopt their logic.[38]

If, as McBride Stetson concludes, women were ultimately successful in having a feminist agenda adopted by the French government and officials, this level of success is not always replicated in other countries. In Italy, Pisciotta[39] describes how the conflict between the feminist understanding of the abortion issue and the definition of the problem by parliament eventually led to feminist withdrawal from political engagement on the issue. This resulted in the parliamentary view, which perceived the issue in legal and moral terms rather than as an issue of personal choice, dominating the legislative outcome. As a result,

it felt defeated by the political system that had stripped the abortion issue of its feminist content and had converted it into a law. Although the abortion law is by no means the worst law possible, many women of the feminist movement withdrew from the public sphere and refused to fight for the application of the law. Renouncing this possibility, the movement weakened its impact in the field of public awareness.[40]

Indeed, the Italian experience on the abortion issue has close parallels with the outcome of feminist mobilization and political activity in Britain. Discussing the deradicalization of the women's liberation movement in Britain, Lovenduski and Randall observe that

Success in getting important issues on to the political agenda meant that feminists lost control over them. A good example of this is the way in which the work of the rape crisis collectives has led to the adoption of feminist rhetoric in police rape work with the loss of much of its accompanying empowering strategy. Another example is the way in which NCC [National Co-ordinating Committee of the women's liberation movement] demands were redefined as its issues were taken up by new campaigning organizations.[41]

The concept of issue definition allows for an assessment of policy outcomes in relation to the definition of the issues offered by the feminist movement and the extent to which women succeeded in having their perspectives included in policy solutions. Interchangeable with the role equity and role change model, it is a useful benchmark for assessing the extent to which demands remain true to their original feminist construction as they are absorbed into the routine of policy-making.

The new social movements of the 1960s, 1970s and even 1980s have evolved beyond the protest stage to develop more permanent links with the political systems in which they occur. The ecology movement, for instance, has given rise to 'green' parties in some countries. There have been attempts (mostly unsuccessful) by women's movement activists to establish women's parties. A more typical interaction with conventional political structures is the participation of non-governmental and social organizations in the formal arena of interest representation. In order to ascertain the location of social movement organizations and feminist groups in particular in the interest group–state network, I turn now to the interest group literature.

INTEREST GROUPS

Knoke makes the point that theories of collective action 'largely talk past one another rather than directly confronting the same aspects from opposing angles'.[42] The conventional study of interest groups assumes that the organizations under scrutiny are part of the institutional political system. Normally, this excludes the nascent interest groups of a social movement. However, when a social movement has evolved to the stage where it has groups working within the parameters of institutional politics, these groups can also be considered to be acting as normal interest groups. One of the observations that can be made following a reading of the resource mobilization literature is that the social movement organizations incorporated into the structured interest representation process appear to share many common features with conventional interest groups. Although there may be differences in the resources at their disposal, the nature of their goals, the composition of their support base and their degree of access to policy-makers, they none the less behave in a similar fashion to standard pressure groups. The power-oriented strategies pursued by social movement organizations are broadly similar to the representational activities of interest groups. Social movement organizations and interest groups may encounter similar obstacles in the pursuit of their objectives, and they may, when strategically appropriate, choose to engage in direct action and acts of civil disobedience. In terms of women's political activity, Gelb notices that feminists in all three nations lobby, petition and engage in electoral campaigning to gain support for their demands; they rely on protest in order to demonstrate their ability to mobilize mass constituencies and seek to coerce elites to make concessions and bargain accordingly, especially when previous efforts have not produced change.[43]

These activities are not very different from the strategies used by conventional interest groups who also lobby public officials, seek access to policy-makers and negotiate with decision-makers on policy issues affecting the interests of their members. While social protest is an intrinsic part of the tactical repertoire of social movements, interest groups also claim the strategies of protest and direct action as a legitimate form of political activity. Conventional interest groups may turn to mobilizing mass constituencies when the politics of negotiation have failed to deliver the required result. Trade unions, for instance, have a long tradition of engaging in protest activities. Lindblom offers a definition of an interest group which is sufficiently broad to encompass both social movement representatives and the more conventional interest groups:

> We mean by interest group activities all interactions through which individuals and private groups not holding government authority seek to influence public policy together with those policy-influencing inter-actions of government officials that go well beyond the direct use of their authority.[44]

The observation made in the previous section regarding the opportunities for social movements to articulate their demands within the political system also holds true for interest groups. Thus, all groups with a representational function have their influence mediated by the power structures in which they operate. The literature on interest groups offers two distinct paradigms in which non-party representational activity is analysed. These paradigms are the theories of pluralism and corporatism. They relate closely to the concept of closed and open political systems discussed in the social movement literature. What both theories have to say about the structuring of interest representation is examined in the next section.

PLURALISM

Pluralist theory is based on the understanding that political power is fragmented and dispersed among a multiplicity of organized interests. These groups are engaged in a complex process of negotiation and bargaining with government in order to achieve their goals. Pluralist theorists recognize that groups are not equal: differences exist among groups in respect to their resources, degree of access to government and extent of influence on political decisions. However, classical pluralists such as Dahl hold that all groups have some resources which they can use to achieve some level of political effectiveness:

> few groups in the United States who are determined to influence the government – certainly few if any groups of citizens who are organised, active and persistent – lack the capacity and opportunity to influence some officials somewhere in the political system in order to obtain at least some of their goals.[45]

Classical pluralist theory sees the diffusion or dispersal of power as preventing the emergence of a single dominant group from monopolizing political outcomes. Interest representation is akin to free market activity, where groups compete for power and the State acts as an arbitrator between competing demands.[46] There was, however, no real unanimity among early pluralist scholars on the role of the State. Truman and Lindblom, for instance, disagreed with the idea of ascribing too much influence to pressure groups and instead saw the State as an important participant rather than a neutral arbiter in the decision-making process.[47] Pluralist theorists now argue that state institutions have as a minimum an agenda of self-perpetuation. This observation leads Smith to recognize that states have interests of their own, more resources than most interest groups and powerful mechanisms for reducing the influence of other groups.[48]Although the literature on interest representation in Ireland is very limited, there is general agreement with Chubb's view of the role of the State as being a very pro-active one:

> over most areas of public policy and a wide range of policy issues, the government has a virtual monopoly in proposing policy and legislation and an almost complete control of the activities and output of the Oireachtas. . . . It is still Irish ministers and their professional advisers, mostly senior civil servants in the departments, who are the initiators and formulators of policy and administrative action. It is on them, therefore, that pressure groups tend to concentrate their main efforts, if they have access to them.[49]

A third main theme in the pluralist literature is the focus on accommodation and consensus among groups and the State as a way of resolving policy problems. This suggests that there is a shared set of values underpinning the setting of political priorities which comes to dominate decision-making on any one occasion.

There is some evidence to show, particularly in the literature on women's interests, that groups which share in the ideological bias of a government are more readily admitted into the policy-making process. Interest groups which do not conform to the dominant set of values in a policy sector are likely to be excluded from the policy process. Thus, the dominance of a liberal ideology in Western democracies in the 1970s excluded groups with a conservative point of view from an influential role in policy-making. Similarly, the dominance of new right thinking in the 1980s excluded the participation of groups advocating interventionist policies.[50] Critics of pluralist theory point out that pluralist explanations of power relationships between groups and the State are based on the admittance of safe political issues into the political arena to the exclusion of conflict-laden issues.[51] Schattschneider observes this to be a systematic mobilization of bias.[52]

In spite of the criticisms directed against the theory, studies of the relationship between interest groups and the State are still informed by the pluralist perspective, albeit a modified one.[53] Pluralists accept that politics is not a competitive market place open to all interests. Instead, the concept of open access is refined to suggest that access is limited to certain groups and that their relationship with administrators is an ongoing one. For instance, educational policy is determined by negotiation between officials in the government department of education, teacher union representatives, parent representatives and other major interests. In Ireland, this group of interest representatives would extend to include spokespersons for the Roman Catholic Church.[54] In any given policy area, group interest representatives, public officials and executive decision-makers form a closed, semi-autonomous unit with an influence on the decision-making process. This style of policy-making is labelled 'segmented pluralism'.

The perceived differences between groups has also become more central in the literature. Groups are classed according to their area of interest, with the terms 'sectional' and 'cause-centred' being commonly used to distinguish between economic-oriented and social-oriented groups respectively. The status and degree of access by groups to policy-makers is a further significant elaboration of the original pluralist approach. This is commonly denoted by the attribution of the self-explanatory terms 'insider' and 'outsider'. In this context, business, agricultural and labour interests would be seen as sectional groups with the status of insiders. McCann[55] confirms this general proposition in an Irish context. He finds that Irish business interests have regular access to policy-makers and that they enjoy a relationship with government similar to that of major business representative associations in other European states.

Groups which are formed to promote a cause are generally classed as outsiders, with little access to policy-makers and a minimal influence on public policy. In reality, though, not all cause groups are condemned to remaining on the outside of the policy process. In Britain, Jordan and Richardson[56] cite the instance of the Howard League for Penal Reform as a cause group with 'insider' status. Baker's[57] study of the policy of developing lignite deposits in Northern Ireland highlights the disparity in the resources, status and access to decision-makers between the private sector and the local pressure group. Yet the local group, which opposed the plan to develop this industry, finally gained access to the policy-making process and, by the end of the campaign, had 'consolidated their right to be consulted'.

CORPORATISM

Corporatism is a concept developed in the 1970s to explain the growing intervention of the State in economic activity and the consequent group–state pattern of relations. Unlike pluralism, which as a theory has proved difficult to define, corporatism is a clearly delineated concept. In the words of one of its originators, Schmitter:

> Corporatism can be defined as a system of interest representation in which the constituent units are organized into a limited number of singular, compulsory, non-competitive, hierarchically ordered and functionally differentiated categories, recognized or licensed (if not created) by the state and granted a deliberate representational monopoly within their respective categories in exchange for observing certain controls on their selection of leaders and articulation of demands and supports.[58]

Corporatist theory holds that the State has a considerable interest in controlling the outcome of the bargaining process between groups and between economic interests in particular. Dowse and Hughes illustrate the distinction between the pattern of interest group–state relations in conditions of ideal-type pluralism and ideal-type corporatism as follows:

> Unlike liberal capitalism with its individualistic ethic and the strict separation of the economic and political spheres, allowing the state effectively only an arbitrator role between the demands made by competing groups, the corporatist state actively seeks to organize and dominate labour by forging a unity between state, capital and labour.[59]

Corporatist theory also holds that the 'peak' economic organizations representing business and labour interests join with the State in negotiating on economic policy matters and in the implementation of the agreed policy outcomes. Thus, the State seeks to make a contract with 'social partners' on economic matters.

A second difference between this form of interest representation and that considered by the pluralist school is the role given to the interest organizations in ensuring that their members implement the agreement. This form of monopolistic interest representation is seen to operate in varying degrees in Europe, with Austria cited as the prototype corporatist state and Britain as the political system having the least manifestation of corporatist arrangements. Ireland is, in comparative studies, grouped in the middle of this spectrum along with Belgium, Germany, Denmark, Switzerland and Finland.[60]

However, the assessment of other scholars concerning Ireland's level of corporatism is not as definitive as would appear from this classification. Chubb,[61] for instance, emphasizes the strong relationship between the State and economic interest groups and appears to support the contention that Ireland displays a distinctly corporatist pattern. Yet Regan and Wilson[62] find little evidence to support the view that interest-group activity is organized around a set of corporatist relations. O'Halpin[63] points to the continuing debate among political scientists as to whether the tripartite arrangement which exists in Irish economic policy decision-making constitutes corporatism or not. None the less, there is considerable factual evidence of a trend towards corporatist policy relations in Ireland, particularly in the economic arena.

The corporatist model is heavily criticized by pluralists for ignoring the role of non-economic interests. In countering this criticism, some corporatist theorists have developed a 'dual-state' thesis, which recognizes interest groups other than producer associations. A similar recognition is given in the term 'societal' corporatism, in which the State plays a role similar to that identified by the pluralist model.

Pluralist and corporatist theory are used by interest group scholars to explain the pattern of group–state relations in a given society. Both theories contribute to the identification of the structural nature of power arrangements in a given polity. The pluralist concept is a flexible one, which Jordan describes as 'a multiplicity of ideas about interest groups loosely tied together by a pluralist tag'.[64] Pluralist theory analyses all interests, categorizing them according to their representational function and status. Corporatist theory is more applicable to economic interests and allocates a more interventionist role to the State than is conceived in the pluralist model. Corporatism also allocates to the economic interest groups a role in overseeing the implementation of agreements arrived at between producer interests and the State. Both forms of interest representation can be found in most liberal democratic states. Their relative presence to one another is an important factor which, as Gelb has pointed out, structures the opportunities for feminist activity and interest representation.

The political challenge of new social movements is generally located in the non-economic policy sphere, although this is not to ignore the fact that many of the policy changes advocated by social movements contain significant implications for the economic as well as the social order. However, in studying the activities of social movement organizations, a pluralist paradigm has been found to be most appropriate. None the less, groups which seek to directly influence economic arrangements may have their choice of strategies and activities influenced by corporatist patterns of interest representation. Indeed, the closed, hierarchical structure of a corporatist pattern of interest group–state relations inevitably contains implications for the realization of women's economic demands. As noted above in the discussion on social movements, both patterns of power shape the political opportunity structure for groups to emerge and to influence the policy process. Our concern is with feminist groups, so we must also take a third dimension into account – the manner in which women's issues are defined and the degree to which they are incorporated into the policy process under any of the above models of group–state arrangements. The next section indicates the questions on women's interests posed by the literature review. An analytical model is suggested to explain the political dynamics of feminist interest representation in Ireland.

ANALYSING WOMEN AND THE STATE

The aim of this book is to understand the specific relationship between women's interests and politics in the Republic of Ireland. The literature reviewed above offers some pointers towards developing an analytical framework which can be usefully applied to the cases to be studied. It appears that the following features of the political process are significant in a policy context: the structure of power in a policy area, the existing policy position, political attitudes towards new demands and the lobbying skills of group representatives. To these can be added another factor which is implied but not explicitly stated in the literature: the capacity of the State to advocate and support policies which reflect women's demands. These factors, I suggest, can, in various combinations, substantially account for the differing interactions between women's interest groups and policy-makers. They offer, in my view, a fairly comprehensive analytical framework for a process which often takes place behind the closed doors of government offices, far removed from the public gaze.

In this book five different policy areas are looked at which have been the subject of women's rights activity: employment equality, family law, contraception, rape and domestic violence. An examination is made of the extent to which women's interest group activity in each of these policy areas has had an impact on legislative outcomes. A modification of a question framed by Robert Salisbury is posed: 'What do Irish women's groups do in order to influence public policy decisions?'[65] This question implies that, in Ireland, women's interests are represented through organized associations. In line with some recent research findings,[66] it is suggested that the more visible part of the women's movement in Ireland has been assimilated into the political system to a significant degree. This has led women in politics to emphasize rights and legal change and to operate within the decision-making processes. In response, I believe that the mainstreaming of feminist priorities has made a significant contribution to the increased output of public policies with a woman-centred focus in modern times.

Chapter 2 examines the role of women in Irish society over time. The socio-economic and political context is considered in some detail, as this environment has shaped the opportunities for women's political engagement. The political mobilization of Irish women in the 1970s and the subsequent development of the feminist movement is the subject of Chapter 3. In the following chapters, attention is focused on women's political agitation on specific issues: employment equality (Chapter 4), family law reform (Chapter 5), sexual assault and domestic violence (Chapter 6) and contraception (Chapter 7). In each case I assess the impact of the chosen groups in the light of the analytical framework. This enables some general conclusions to be drawn in Chapter 8 about women's interest groups and politics in Ireland. It also furthers an understanding of the manner in which policy is made in an Irish context and suggests a direction for future research on the influence of groups in public policy-making.

NOTES

1. Tom Hesketh, *The Second Partitioning of Ireland: The Abortion Referendum of 1983* (Dun Laoghaire: Brandsma Books, 1990); Pauline Conroy Jackson, 'Women's movement and abortion: the criminalization of Irish women', in Drude Dahlerup (ed.), *The New Women's Movement: Feminism and Political Power in Europe and the USA* (London: Sage, 1986), pp. 48–63; Cornelius

O'Leary and Tom Hesketh, 'The Irish abortion and divorce referendum campaigns', *Irish Political Studies*, **3** (1988), 43–62; Ailbhe Smyth (ed.), *The Abortion Papers: Ireland* (Dublin: Attic Press, 1992); Yael Yishai, 'Public ideas and public policy: abortion politics in four democracies', *Comparative Politics*, **25**(2) (January 1993), 207–28.

2. Ursula Barry and Pauline Jackson, 'Women on the edge of time: part-time work in Ireland, North and South', in Mary Buckley and Malcolm Anderson (eds), *Women, Equality and Europe* (Basingstoke: Macmillan, 1988), pp. 78–94; Catherine Hoskyns, 'Give us equal pay and we'll open our own doors – a study of the impact in the Federal Republic of Germany and the Republic of Ireland of the European Community's Policy on women's rights', in Buckley and Anderson (eds), *Women, Equality and Europe*, pp. 33–55; Jenny Beale, *Women in Ireland: Voices of Change* (London: Macmillan Education, 1988); Alpha Connelly (ed.), *Gender and the Law in Ireland* (Dublin: Oak Tree Press, 1993).

3. Ailbhe Smyth, 'The women's movement in the Republic of Ireland 1970–1990', in Ailbhe Smyth (ed.), *Irish Women's Studies Reader* (Dublin: Attic Press, 1993), pp. 245–69.

4. Some of the standard works in this area include Dorothy McBride Stetson, *Women's Rights in France* (New York: Greenwood Press, 1986); Joyce Gelb and Marian Lief Palley, *Women and Public Policies* (Princeton, NJ: Princeton University Press, 1987); Joyce Gelb, *Feminism and Politics: A Comparative Perspective* (Berkeley: University of California Press, 1989); Elizabeth Meehan and Selma Sevenhuijsen, *Equality Politics and Gender* (London: Sage, 1991); Joni Lovenduski and Vicky Randall, *Contemporary Feminist Politics: Women and Power in Britain* (Oxford: Oxford University Press, 1993).

5. See, for instance, the path-breaking research of Theda Skocpol, Marjorie Abend-Wein, Christopher Howard and Susan Goodrich Lehmann, 'Women's associations and the enactment of mothers' pensions in the United States', *American Political Science Review*, **87**(3) (September 1993), 686–97.

6. Barbara J. Nelson and Najma Chowdhury (eds), *Women and Politics Worldwide* (New Haven: Yale University Press, 1994).

7. A comprehensive study of the Irish political system can be found in John Coakley and Michael Gallagher (eds), *Politics in the Republic of Ireland*, 2nd edition (Dublin and Limerick: Folens and PSAI Press, 1993).

8. Neil Smelser, *Theory of Collective Behaviour* (London: Routledge & Kegan Paul, 1962), p. 8.

9. Claus Offe, 'Challenging the boundaries of institutional politics: social movements since the 1960s', in C. S. Maier (ed.), *Changing Boundaries of the Political* (Cambridge: Cambridge University Press, 1987), p. 88.

10. Elizabeth S. Clemens, 'Organizational repertoires and institutional change: women's groups and the transformation of US politics, 1890–1920', *American Journal of Sociology*, **98**(4) (1993), 771.

11. Russell J. Dalton, Manfred Kuechler and Wilhelm Burklin, 'The challenge of new movements', in Russell J. Dalton and Manfred Kuechler (eds), *Challenging the Political Order: New Social and Political Movements in Western Democracies* (Cambridge: Polity Press, 1990), p. 5.

12. C. A. Rootes, 'The new politics and the new social movements in Britain.' Paper presented to Political Studies Association Conference, Lancaster, 15–17 April 1991, p. 21.

13. Anthony Oberschall, *Social Conflict and Social Movements* (Englewood Cliffs, NJ: Prentice-Hall, 1973), p. 194, quoted in R. Turner, 'Collective behaviour and resource mobilization as approaches to social movements: issues and continuities', in L. Kriesberg (ed.), *Research in Social Movements, Conflict and Change*, vol. 4 (Greenwich, CN: JAI Press, 1984), p. 16.

14. Wolfgang Rudig, 'Peace and ecology movements in Western Europe', *West European Politics*, **11**(1) (1988), 28.

15. Susan Baker, 'The nuclear power issue in Ireland: the role of the Irish anti-nuclear movement', *Irish Political Studies*, 3 (1988), 5–6.

16. Jo Freeman, 'On the origins of social movements', in Jo Freeman (ed.), *Social Movements of the Sixties and Seventies* (New York: Longman, 1983), p. 10.

17. Elizabeth Meehan, 'British feminism from the 1960s to the 1980s', in Harold L. Smith (ed.), *British Feminism in the Twentieth Century* (Aldershot: Edward Elgar, 1990), p. 193.

18. Dieter Rucht, 'The strategies and action repertoires of new movements', in Dalton *et al.*, *Challenging the Political Order*, pp. 162–3.

19. Jo Freeman, 'A model for analyzing the strategic options of social movement organizations', in Freeman (ed.), *Social Movements of the Sixties and Seventies*, p. 204.

20. Joyce Gelb, 'Feminism and political action', in Dalton *et al.*, *Challenging the Political Order*, p. 141.

21. Rudig, 'Peace and ecology movements in Western Europe', pp. 29–30.

22. Baker, 'The nuclear power issue in Ireland', pp. 3–17.

23. Freeman, 'A model for analyzing the strategic options of social movement organizations', p. 198.

24. John D. McCarthy and Mayer N. Zald, 'Resource mobilization and social movements: a partial theory', *American Journal of Sociology*, **82** (1977), 1217, quoted in D. Knoke, *Organizing for Collective Action – The Political Economies of Associations* (New York: Aldine de Gruyter), p. 19.

25. Knoke, *Organizing for Collective Action*, p. 19.

26. Ellen Boneparth, 'A framework for policy analysis', in Ellen Boneparth (ed.), *Women, Power and Policy* (New York: Pergamon Press, 1982), p. 7.

27. Michael Gallagher, Michael Laver and Peter Mair, *Representative Government in Western Europe* (New York: McGraw-Hill, 1992), pp. 14–33.

28. Herbert P. Kitschelt, 'Political opportunity structures and political protest: anti nuclear movements in four democracies', *British Journal of Political Science*, **16**(1) (January 1986), 57–85.

29. Kitschelt, 'Political opportunity structures', p. 58.

30. Kitschelt, 'Political opportunity structures', pp. 64–6.

31. L. Martin Overby, 'West European peace movements: an application of Kitschelt's political opportunity structures thesis', *West European Politics*, **13**(1) (January 1990), 1–11.

32. Gelb, 'Feminism and political action', p. 137.

33. Gelb, *Feminism and Politics*, p. 6.

34. Karsten D. Geier, 'Peace movements and the struggle within: a reply to L. Martin Overby', *West European Politics*, **13**(1) (January 1990), 275–9.

35. Lovenduski and Randall, *Contemporary Feminist Politics*, p. 15.

36. Gelb and Palley, *Women and Public Policies*, p. 10.

37. Virginia Sapiro, 'The women's movement, policy and politics in the Reagan era', in Dahlerup (ed.), *The New Women's Movement*, p. 125; Vicky Randall, *Women and Politics: An International Perspective*, 2nd edition (Basingstoke: Macmillan Education, 1987), pp. 157–67; Jo Freeman, 'Women and public policy: an overview', in Boneparth (ed.), *Women, Power and Policy*, p. 47.

38. McBride Stetson, *Women's Rights in France*, p. 196.

39. Elenore Eckmann Pisciotta, 'Challenging the establishment: the case of abortion', in Dahlerup (ed.), *The New Women's Movement*, pp. 38, 40.

40. Pisciotta, 'Challenging the establishment', p. 46.

41. Lovenduski and Randall, *Contemporary Feminist Politics*, p. 361.

42. Knoke, *Organizing for Collective Action*, p. 21.

43. Gelb, 'Feminism and political action', p. 151.

44. Charles Lindblom, *The Policymaking Process* (Englewood Cliffs, NJ: Prentice-Hall, 1980), p. 85, quoted in A. G. Jordan and J. J. Richardson, *Government and Pressure Groups in Britain* (Oxford: Clarendon Press, 1987), p. 15.

45. R. A. Dahl, *Who Governs?* (New Haven: Yale University Press, 1961), p. 386, quoted in P. J. Williamson, *Corporatism in Perspective: An Introductory Guide to Corporatist Theory* (London: Sage, 1989), p. 52.

46. William Kelso, *American Democratic Theory – Pluralism and Its Critics* (London: Greenwood Press, 1978), pp. 13–19.

47. David B. Truman, *The Governmental Process* (New York: Alfred Knopf, 1971), quoted in Jordan and Richardson, *Government and Pressure Groups in Britain*, p. 291; Charles E. Lindblom, *The Intelligence of Democracy* (New York: Free Press, 1965), quoted in Jordan and Richardson, *Government and Pressure Groups in Britain*, p. 292.

48. Martin J. Smith, *Pressure Power and Policy: State Autonomy and Policy Networks in Britain and the United States* (London: Harvester Wheatsheaf, 1993), p. 5.

49. Basil Chubb, *The Government and Politics of Ireland*, 3rd edition (London: Longman, 1992), p. 121.

50. Sapiro, 'The women's movement, policy and politics in the Reagan era', pp. 122–139.

51. P. Bachrach and M. Baratz, 'The two faces of power', *American Political Science Review*, **56** (1962), 948.

52. E. E. Schattschneider, *The Semi-Sovereign People – A Realist's View of Democracy in America* (Hinsdale, IL: Dryden Press, 1975), p. 1.

53. Martin J. Smith, 'Pluralism, reformed pluralism and neopluralism: the role of pressure groups in policy-making', *Political Studies*, **38** (1990), 302–22.

54. David Barry, 'The involvement and impact of a professional interest group', in D. G. Mulcahy and Denis O'Sullivan (eds), *Irish Educational Policy – Process and Substance* (Dublin: Institute of Public Administration, 1989), pp. 153–6.

55. Dermot McCann, 'Business power and collective action: the state and the Confederation of Irish Industry 1970–1990', *Irish Political Studies*, **8** (1993), 37–54.

56. Jordan and Richardson, *Government and Pressure Groups in Britain*, pp. 32–33.

57. Susan Baker, 'Public policy agenda setting: the use of Northern Ireland's lignite deposits', *Administration*, **39**(2) (1991), 147–66.

58. P. C. Schmitter, 'Still the century of corporatism?', in P. C. Schmitter and G. Lembruch (eds), *Trends Towards Corporatist Intermediation* (London: Sage, 1979), p. 22.

59. Robert E. Dowse and John A. Hughes, *Political Sociology*, 2nd edition (New York: John Wiley and Sons, 1986), p. 357.

60. Gallagher *et al.*, *Representative Government in Western Europe*, p. 252.

61. Chubb, *The Government and Politics of Ireland*, pp. 126–8.

62. Marguerite C. Regan and Frank L. Wilson, 'Interest group politics in France and Ireland: comparative perspectives on neo-corporatism', *West European Politics*, **9**(3) (1986), 393–411.

63. Eunan O'Halpin, 'Policymaking', in Coakley and Gallagher (eds), *Politics in the Republic of Ireland*, p. 191.

64. A. G. Jordan, 'The pluralism of pluralism: an anti-theory?' *Political Studies*, **38** (1990), 301.

65. Robert H. Salisbury, 'Interest groups', in Fred I. Greenstein and Nelson W. Polsby (eds), *Handbook of Political Science*, vol. 4 (Reading, MA: Addison-Wesley, 1975), p. 206, quoted in Knoke, *Organizing for Collective Action*, p. 20.

66. Yael Yishai, 'Public ideas and public policy', p. 224.

CHAPTER 2

WOMEN IN IRISH SOCIETY AND POLITICS

This chapter focuses on the participation of Irish women in civic society since the 1970s. The first section takes a comparative look at trends in general social conditions shaping the extent of women's public involvement. These include family patterns and public perceptions of the role and status of women. The following sections examine women's situation in significant civic arenas: the law, the labour force and in politics and administration. The chapter concludes with an assessment of how general political and social conditions have influenced the development of a feminist consciousness among Irish women.

There are a number of factors which are generally accepted as being important in assisting the emergence and articulation of new feminist demands. Among these are the existing status of women in society and the presence or absence of a generalized dissatisfaction with this position. Changing family patterns, too, have been identified as assisting the formation of a political consciousness among women, leading to a questioning of the boundaries of their lives. Labour force participation is seen as an important step towards the liberation of women, providing opportunities for economic independence. Further, the extent to which women are represented in decision-making arenas offers a measure of the openness of a political system to women's demands. The degree to which these factors are important is influenced by the dominant values of a society, which fundamentally shape women's opportunities for political activity. Each of these factors will now be treated in turn and their relative significance for the politicization of women in Ireland assessed.

FAMILY STRUCTURE

Traditionally, Irish families were large and marriage was a significant social and religious ceremony. A strict adherence to the rules of the Roman Catholic Church, which forbade family planning, along with a public policy which made the provision of contraceptives illegal, resulted in families having six or more children. However, a perceptible drop in the fertility rate from 1970 onwards suggests that public policy and Church teachings were less relevant to the lives of a new generation. As we can see from Table 2.1, the fertility rate, which stood at about 6.0 children per woman of childbearing years in 1951, was reduced to 1.85 in 1994, below the level for population replacement. The decline in fertility is generally seen as an indication of a growing secularization in Irish society, accompanied by a more assertive attitude among women on family planning issues. From the mid-1960s, as the discussion on the contraception debate will show, more and more Irish couples, and Irish women in particular, were making decisions on family size with little reference to existing religious and legal restrictions.

Table 2.1 Marriage, birth and fertility rates per 1000 population

	1951	1971	1991	1994
Marriage rate	5.4	7.4	4.8	4.6
Fertility rate	6.0	3.5	2.1	1.8
Birth rate	21.2	22.7	15.0	13.4
Births outside marriage as percentage of total births	2.5	2.7	15.0	19.7

Source: Central Statistics Office, *Department of Health Vital Statistics* (1951, p. vi; 1971, p. vii; 1991, pp. 7–8; 1995, p. 99).

Although Irish women still bear more children than women in other EU countries,[1] they have significantly fewer children than did their mothers or grandmothers. In line with European trends, the numbers of children born out of wedlock account for an increasingly significant percentage of all births. As Table 2.1 shows, this increased over seven-fold between 1971 and 1994, bringing the incidence of births in Ireland outside marriage close to the 1992 EU average of 20 per cent.[2] Marriage as a social institution fell out of favour during the course of the 1970s, and it comes as no surprise to find that patterns of marriage in Ireland from 1971 to 1995 reflect trends in other European countries. Indeed, the tendency among Irish couples to forgo a marriage ceremony resulted in Ireland having one of the lowest rates of marriage in the EU as early as 1977. The unpopularity of marriage continued into the 1990s. In 1994, Ireland, with a marriage rate of 4.6 per thousand, shared with France (4.4 per thousand) the lowest marriage rate in the EU, which averaged at 5.3 per thousand.[3]

Thus between 1951 and 1994, family patterns in Ireland underwent considerable change, marking a growing distance between people's public religious observances and their personal decisions. Marriage declined in popularity, women had significantly fewer children and the numbers of children born outside of marriage grew to reflect the general pattern elsewhere in Europe. These trends contained implications for public policy on women, particularly in the area of family law and women's participation in employment. Over time, these trends also had a bearing on public attitudes towards women's social role.

ATTITUDES TOWARDS WOMEN

Surveys which seek to measure public perceptions of women's citizenship indicate that there are conflicting ideas on women's participation in the polity. A survey on attitudes towards the role and status of women in Ireland carried out by Fine Davis[4] for the parliamentary Joint Committee on Women's Rights found that in 1975 a majority of the population espoused traditional attitudes towards the role and status of women. These findings were confirmed by King.[5] In a study of the attitudes of workers in Irish industry towards married women returning to employment, she found that a substantial number of married men, single men and single women held negative views about married women working. Towards the end of the 1980s, there were some indications of a growing espousal of egalitarian beliefs among the Irish population. This was illustrated by a liberalization of public views on the participation of mothers in the workforce. It was modified, however, by the general expectation that women would carry the burden of home duties as well. A poll conducted in 1987 highlighted the continued perception of women's unequal status, with only 29 per cent of the total sample agreeing with the statement that 'Irishwomen are treated equally with men', while 57 per cent expressed their disagreement.[6]

When placed in a comparative context, attitudes in Ireland towards gender equality and women's participation in public activities appear to be more conservative than those espoused in other EU countries. A study of attitudes towards social issues in EU member states by Wilcox[7] indicated that the attitudes of Irish men and women in relation to equality within the family were the most conservative, while women in Italy and France were the most supportive of equality in the home. In Denmark and the Netherlands, both men and women consistently espoused egalitarian attitudes towards all types of gender roles. EU attitudinal surveys reinforced these findings, indicating the co-existence of stated liberal positions on women's workforce participation and conservative views on the traditional role of women.[8] The research suggests that by the 1980s, although Irish attitudes towards equality issues had changed to reflect a modest liberal position, there was little evidence of a shift in the traditional thinking on women's role within the family.

Various reasons have been advanced for the perpetuation of traditional views on women's role in society. O'Dowd identifies the basis for these views:

> The social conservatism of both unionist and nationalist states in Ireland, the social ideologies of the Churches and the pre-eminence of laissez-faire ideology in the North and in the Free State (until 1932) were all inimical to the extensions of women's political role.[9]

Beale supports this perspective, emphasizing the dual oppression of women by the combined conservative ideologies of Church and State.[10] This pattern, however, is one which has been identified as being part and parcel of the political culture of Ireland: conservative economic policies, the influence of clericalism on social policy and in shaping people's values underpinned by a nationalist, inward-looking political ideology.[11]

Thus, the recurring theme in successive studies on women's civic role in Ireland is one of women's public participation being clearly predicated on traditional social attitudes reinforced by the ideology, institutions and structures of an authoritarian Roman Catholic Church and a conservative, nationalist State. Although there is a greater acceptance of women's right to be involved in civic affairs today, the presumption that women will shoulder the major responsibility for home-making remains strong. In this respect, the position of women in Irish society appears similar to that of women in other European countries with agricultural economies, an institutionalized church with close connections to political elites, and with social customs which restrict women's roles, namely Portugal, Spain, Italy and Greece. Women in these countries traditionally had little status, were treated as dependants of the male head of household for the purposes of public policy, had few opportunities for employment outside the home and minimal legal rights.[12]

The fact that women's lives in Ireland were largely constructed around the home and family leads us to a consideration of the extent to which public policy reflected social perceptions of women's role. One obvious way of examining this is to look at the formal legal position of women in Ireland.

WOMEN AND THE LAW

John Whyte, in a seminal study of Church and State relations in Ireland, noted that family policy in Ireland consisted of

> a series of constitutional and legislative provisions [which] ignored by and large the viewpoints of minority religions and meticulously

implemented the values of conservative Catholic social thinking, within which the family is the basic unit of society.[13]

It is not surprising that Scannell, in a study of the position of women subsequent to the enactment of the 1937 Constitution, found that

> For almost thirty years after the constitution was adopted, the position of women in Irish society hardly changed at all. The common law relegation of women to domesticity and powerlessness continued. Laws based on the premise that women's rights were inferior to those of men survived in and indeed even appeared on the statute books.[14]

Three broad and interrelated areas of discrimination can be identified: employment, the family and women's relationship to the State. These areas encompass many aspects of public policy in which the dependent status of women and the general acceptance of female inferiority were reinforced. Scannell provides a long list of the differential treatment of women with men in law and public policy from the 1930s to the 1960s. This catalogue includes discrimination in employment, unemployment allowances, the tax code, family laws, prohibitions on information on and access to birth control, uncertainty regarding women's claims to family property on the death of her spouse, denial of access to free legal aid and little or no state aid to unmarried women with dependent children. Adding to this tale of discrimination, O'Dowd remarks on the considerable inequalities applying to married women in terms of property ownership, the inability to make a valid contract and discrimination in respect of the family home and the limited scope for women to initiate legal action.[15]

Legislators began to show some awareness of the extent of formal gender-based inequalities in the late 1950s. In 1957 parliament passed the Married Women's Status Act, the first family law reform measure to be enacted since Victorian times. The legislation gave married women the right to sue and be sued, to enter into contracts and to hold property in their own name – rights already enjoyed by all men and by women without husbands. This statute, which followed similar reforms in Britain, gave a legal basis to the less restrictive interpretation of the rights of married women in family law which had been in practice for some time. In 1957 also, the ban on the employment of married women teachers was removed by order of the Minister for Education, Jack Lynch. None the less, the more extensive prohibition on married women taking up employment in the Civil Service, health and local authorities – known as the 'marriage bar' – remained in force until 1973.

In 1964, the Guardianship of Infants Act gave mothers an equal say in all decisions relating to the upbringing and welfare of their children. Prior to the passage of this legislation, only a father, recognized as head of a household, had legal authority over the children in a family. The Succession Act of 1965 was another attempt to redress some of the gender inequalities in law. This act gave a widow a legal entitlement to a share in her husband's estate on his death. Before this law was introduced, a wife could be completely disinherited by her husband in his will. Although the 1972 report of the government's Commission on the Status of Women recognized the contribution which the above legislation made to giving women some measure of equal rights in a family context, it also drew attention to many other major public policy inequalities. The report contained forty-nine specific recommendations and a further seventeen suggestions on the removal of identified discriminations against women.[16]

The Commission on the Status of Women was not working in a political vacuum when calling for the redress of formal and substantive inequalities. The need to redress specific discriminations in public policy became apparent in the late 1960s and early 1970s. This was largely prompted by two factors – pressure to ratify international labour agreements, and the need to respond to the acute legal and financial problems of deserted wives and their children. This resulted in preparations being made to grant women equal pay on the one hand and the introduction of an allowance for deserted wives on the other. However, the road to reform was neither steady nor smooth. Yet, in tackling specific policy discriminations such as equal pay and social supports for mothers in financial need, the political agenda opened sufficiently to allow the inclusion of further equality issues as determined by the women's movement. Before discussing the growth in women's political consciousness, however, we need to complete our picture of women's position in Irish society. An important facet of this is women's involvement in paid work.

WOMEN IN THE LABOUR FORCE

Women's right to paid employment was limited by the Irish government as far back as 1925, with the enactment of the Civil Service (Amendment) Act. This legislation gave a government the right to limit employment opportunities in the bureaucracy of the new state on the grounds of sex alone.[17] Ostensibly justified by the need for efficiency in the administrative system, the real reason for limiting women's employment was the crisis in male employment in the 1920s. In 1932, women's job opportunities were further circumscribed when married women were formally excluded from employment in the public service and the administrative system.

This order remained in force until 1973. Furthermore, the Conditions of Employment Act of 1935 gave the Minister for Labour the power to ban women from certain areas of the industrial labour force in order to ensure the employment of men.[18] Indeed, it was the view of Eamonn De Valera, one of the most influential leaders of the Irish nationalist movement and later President of Ireland, that women should forgo paid employment to give priority to their duties as wives and mothers:

> In regard to labour and in regard to work, our aim ought to be that the breadwinner, who is normally and naturally in these cases, when alive, the father of the family, should be able by his work to bring in enough to maintain the whole household and that women ought not to be forced by economic necessity to go out and either supplement his wages or become breadwinners themselves.[19]

In 1973, after political agitation by the women's movement and following the recommendation of the Commission on the Status of Women, the 'marriage bar' was removed. From that point, married women began to enter the workforce in increasing numbers. Factors such as the decline in fertility rates, increases in women's wages and higher levels of education among women also contributed to the growth in married women's employment in Ireland as in the EU.[20] In a study of women's labour force participation rates in Ireland, Callan and Farrell observed that 'although the overall level of female participation in the Irish labour market has been relatively stable over the past three decades, there have been substantial changes in the nature of that participation'.[21] Thus, as Table 2.2 shows, while the proportion of women in the labour force grew at a modest rate between 1951 and 1991, there was a seven-fold increase in the numbers of married women at work. More recent statistics indicate that in 1993 almost half of women in regular employment were married[22] and by 1996 there were more married women than single women in paid employment.

Table 2.2 Women's participation in the labour force in Ireland (thousands except where percentage)

	1951	1971	1991
Numbers employed			
Total	1298.3	1049.5	1125.0
Women	314.6	289.3	429.1
Percentage of women	24.2	26.3	33.5
Married women as percentage of women in labour force	6.8	13.6	44.5

Sources: Central Statistics Office, *Statistical Abstracts* (1952, pp. 38–9); Blackwell (1989, p. 11); *Labour Force Survey* (1991, pp. 11, 16, 22).

In a comparative European context, Ireland shares the lowest overall levels of women's labour force participation in the EU with the southern European states of Spain, Italy and Greece. However, the removal of the structural obstacle of the prohibition on married women working has given Ireland a unique profile in terms of married women's employment. Yet, when we examine the type of work engaged in by women in the Irish labour force, we see that it reflects trends in other European states.

OCCUPATIONAL ACTIVITY

In the transition to a modern economy, married women were provided with greater opportunities for participating in the labour market. In the meantime, the nature of that work changed. In 1985, a government study of women's status noted that 'the last twenty years have seen a substantial shift of female employment away from agriculture and into certain areas of the services sector'.[23] As we can see from Table 2.3, the proportion of women employed in agriculture decreased significantly, reflecting the general shift away from farm-related occupations. On the other hand, the services sector provided employment for almost four-fifths of the total number of women in work, reflecting the overall occupational pattern for women in the EU.[24]

Table 2.3 Sectoral distribution of women at work

	1951		1971		1991	
	000	%	000	%	000	%
Agriculture	67.5	21.5	25.5	9.2	12.3	3.3
Industry	61.8	19.6	68.1	24.4	68.9	18.2
Services	185.6	58.9	184.7	66.4	295.8	78.5
Total	314.9	100.0	278.3	100.0	377.0	100.0

Source: Working Party on Women's Affairs (1985, p. 53); Central Statistics Office, *Labour Force Survey* (1991, p.11).

In 1992, the proportion of women engaged in agriculture in Ireland (3.4 per cent) resembled that in other countries with similar patterns of land-holding: Denmark (2.6 per cent), the Netherlands (2.3 per cent) and Luxembourg (3.4 per cent). In the industrial sector, the participation rate of Irish women fell midway between that of countries with a high proportion of their female labour force employed in this sector (Germany, 24.9 per cent; Portugal, 25.4 per cent; and Italy, 23.2 per cent) and countries at the lower end of the scale (Greece, 17.3 per cent; France, 17.4 per cent; and Spain, 17.0 per cent). In terms of the tertiary sector, the level of employment for Irish women in this grouping closely mirrored that in France (76.9 per cent), and was well above the total EU average rate of 70.7 per cent.

Within the services sector, the main locus of women's employment in Ireland, the pattern of women's occupational activity has been much more restricted than that of men. Four occupational groups (commerce and finance, professional and technical, services, clerical) account for the employment of two-thirds (64.8 per cent) of women at work in 1991. We can see a similar pattern of horizontal segregation of women's occupational activities in other EU states, with women predominating in the service, commerce, banking and distributive trades.[25]

The persistence of a horizontal segregation of the labour market has implications for women's pay. In general, it has been found that in the advanced industrialized and industrializing countries, women receive on average 70 per cent of the wage of men. Between 1955 and 1971, the average weekly earnings of women in Ireland stood at 53 per cent of the average male earnings.[26] Between 1971 and 1991, the ratio of female to male weekly industrial earnings increased to 60 per cent.[27] Studies on wage structures in Ireland have consistently shown that low pay is most prevalent in occupations traditionally associated with women. In the Civil Service, for instance, the majority of the 12,000 low-paid workers are women.[28]

There is also evidence of vertical segregation of the labour market, illustrated by the low numbers of women in senior positions in companies and as employers. In manufacturing, women are involved in only one of every five small manufacturing businesses grant-aided by the State.[29] Self-employed women are more likely to be found in the services sector, particularly in the financial and business services area. In 1993,[30] only 3.2 per cent of all proprietors and managers were women, compared with 4.9 per cent of men, differing little from the figures in 1987 when women comprised 3 per cent of all proprietors and managers as against 5.3 per cent of men in these positions. In 1993 also, 2.4 per cent of the female workforce were in senior management and executive positions, contrasting with 5.9 per cent of employed men. This represents a worsening over time of women's holding of senior jobs: in 1987, 2 per cent of women were executives as compared with 4.6 per cent of men. By contrast, in 1993, 52 per cent of women were employed as clerical, professional and technical workers, while 17.7 per cent of men in employment held positions in these two categories.[31] The absence of flexible working hours, the virtual non-existence of childcare facilities and lack of appropriate training due largely to the negative attitudes of employers towards women's work are consistently cited as being the main barriers to women's career advancement.[32]

In summary, then, there have been considerable changes in the pattern of women's employment since 1951. The growth in the services sector of the economy has provided employment opportunities for the majority and has balanced the decline in the numbers employed in the agricultural sector. However, the segregation of women into a small number of occupational groupings has been a persistent feature of the labour force since 1951. This reflects a similar trend in women's employment in other EU states, where the feminization rates of occupations such as education, healthcare, shop assistants and domestic service are particularly high.[33] One result of this occupational segregation is the concentration of women in low-paid, low-skilled, often part-time occupations.

The disparity between the numbers of women involved in the work-force and their under-representation at senior levels in all occupations carries over into policy-making arenas. The following section will look more closely at the pattern of women's representation in the decision-making centres of Irish political, social and economic life.

WOMEN IN PUBLIC LIFE

The six parties with representation in parliament have, on average, a female membership of 40 per cent.[34] This mirrors closely the participation rate of women in the workforce. This respectable membership level, however, is not reflected in the numbers of women holding decision-making positions in Irish political parties. Indeed, if we first take the presence of women on the national executives of the parties (Table 2.4), we find a considerable degree of fluctuation in their representation at this level. Women are most likely to hold national executive office in the relatively new and small Progressive Democrat Party and least likely to be represented at executive level in the largest party, Fianna Fáil. There has been a continuous, though modest growth in the numerical representation of women on the executive of the Labour Party. In contrast, the pattern of women's representation on the national executive of Fine Gael and Fianna Fáil in the last decade has been less consistent. Although most parties (Fianna Fáil and the Progressive Democrats being the exceptions) have formally adopted positive action strategies designed to promote women into decision-making ranks, the result has been mixed. Only the Progressive Democrats and the tiny Green Party have a significant balance of both genders at senior party level.

Table 2.4 Women's representation on national executives of political parties, 1983–93 (%)

	Fianna Fáil	Fine Gael	Progressive Democrats	Labour
1982	8.3	21.4	-	7.3
1984	8.3	13.0	-	17.0
1986	9.2	8.8	21.5	13.3
1991	7.9	27.0	27.5	17.0
1993	12.6	23.7	28.0	21.0
1995	16.8	28.0	32.0	22.0
1997	17.9	23.5	38.8	26.0

Source: For 1983–89, Farrell (1992, p. 444); other data supplied by the political parties.

Women's poor representation among party elites is also reflected in the low numbers selected to contest general elections (Table 2.5). In the seven elections held between 1977 and 1992, women have comprised on average 11.3 per cent of the total number of candidates. Although party executives have become more involved in candidate selection since the 1970s, this has not significantly redressed the gender imbalance in candidate tickets. The low numbers of women contesting elections to parliament has, of course, an impact on their representation in that institution. Until 1977, women were almost invisible in parliamentary politics. In recent years there has been some increase: on average, twelve women were elected to each Dáil from 1977 to 1992. The 1992 election results saw the figure rise to twenty (12 per cent), the highest number of women ever returned to parliament. This has increased to twenty-three (13.8 per cent) women parliamentarians with the successful election of women in a number of by-elections held since 1992.

Table 2.5 Women candidates and TDs at elections, 1977–92

	Candidates			Deputies		
Election	Total	Women	%	Total	Women	%
1977	376	25	6.6	148	6	4.1
1981	404	41	10.1	166	11	6.6
1982 (Feb)	365	35	9.6	166	8	4.8
1982 (Nov)	364	31	8.8	166	14	8.4
1987	466	48	10.3	166	14	8.4
1989	370	51	13.8	166	13	7.8
1992	482	89	18.5	166	20	12.0
1997	484	96	19.8	166	20	12.0

Source: Calculated from *Nealon's Guides*, various editions 1977–87; Walker (1992, pp. 228–76); Department of the Environment election returns.

The pattern of women's representation in the Seanad, the upper house, is not very different. This is hardly surprising, given that the composition of the Seanad is largely determined by indirect election – that is, by local councillors and parliamentarians from both houses.[35] Over the forty-year period from 1937 to 1977, there were only nineteen female senators in total in the second chamber. There was a perceptible increase in the number of women senators from 1977 onwards, when the Prime Minister included three women among his eleven appointees. In the following decade, membership of the Seanad was utilized by women politicians, in the same way as by many of their male colleagues, as a base from which to develop a parliamentary career. After the 1992 election, the eight women senators accounted for 13.3 per cent of the membership of the Seanad, which in 1996 was less than the proportion of women in the Dáil.

When we come to assess the level of Irish women's representation in the European Parliament we encounter a more positive story, albeit containing a reflection of national trends. Ireland has fifteen seats in the European Parliament. The four direct elections have seen the return of a total of seven individual women, only one of whom has been successfully re-elected. The successful women in the elections prior to 1994 were from well-known political families. For instance, in 1979, Síle De Valera, granddaughter of the leader of Fianna Fáil and later president of Ireland, Eamonn De Valera, was elected to the European Parliament. The 1994 elections broke this pattern with the return of four (26.6 per cent) women MEPs, three without connections to the nationalist past – one from the Labour Party and two Green Party representatives. Indeed, these women represent the total number of MEPs elected by both parties on this occasion. The fourth woman MEP elected is a long-serving Fine Gael representative in European politics. The number of women elected to the European Parliament from Ireland in 1994 doubled the figures for previous elections. Despite being the largest party in the State, Fianna Fáil failed to have any of its high-profile women candidates elected, partly due to internal dissent and partly due to an electoral swing away from the party.

With only one exception, no women held a cabinet post until 1979 when Máire Geoghegan-Quinn was promoted from a junior ministry to become Minister for the Gaeltacht (Gaelic-speaking areas of the Republic). In the ten administrations formed between 1979 and 1994, twelve women politicians in total have held ministerial positions or junior ministries. It is only since 1993 that women's presence in cabinet has increased from one to two. In 1996, women occupied four of the seventeen junior ministries. Thus, at government level, the representation of women in all ministerial positions has increased modestly from one out of twenty-five

(4 per cent) in December 1979 to six out of thirty-two (19 per cent) in December 1996.

In general, the portfolios held by women in government are not overly gender-biased. Although the allocation of senior ministries can be viewed as having some degree of gender bias, there are counterbalancing portfolios held by other government ministers or in the junior ministerial ranks. Thus, although Education has been held by three women ministers, two women have held the difficult Justice ministry. A male cabinet member was assigned the gender-sensitive portfolio on Equality and Law Reform – a new ministry established in 1993. In the last number of administrations, women have held the portfolios of Social Welfare, Health and Tourism, Transport and Communications. Women have been allocated junior ministerial duties in ministries such as Finance, Foreign Affairs, Environment and Enterprise and Employment. In government, women are perceived as being as successful as their male colleagues in handling their portfolios, in obtaining funding for their ministries and in carrying through their legislative agendas. Furthermore, there appears to be a trend in favouring women for elevation to ministerial positions since the general election of 1992, when women parliamentarians won a higher proportion of ministries (17 per cent in total) than seats in parliament.[36] Further analysis points to the greater chances of a woman deputy being a member of government, with 26 per cent of all women in parliament gaining government office in the administration formed in 1994 compared with 18 per cent of men. At this point in time, a core of women politicians from all parties has built up ministerial experience at junior and senior level which should encourage the continued and possibly increased representation of women in government positions.

The point of debate is not whether women are assigned 'women and family-oriented' ministries. Nor is it about why there are so few women in cabinet positions. As the figures show, women parliamentarians have a better chance than their male colleagues of being given a cabinet portfolio. We find that the most significant hurdle faced by women hoping to hold government office is their difficulty in being elected to parliament. And, given that local government service has been identified as a stepping stone to national political representation, the dearth of women elected to local authorities (11.4 per cent in 1991) is one factor in women's under-representation in public life.

Other factors identified as militating against women's political involvement in Ireland centre around aspects of socio-political culture such as the negative attitudes held towards women's participation in politics. In a study of obstacles to women's political participation in Ireland, Randall and Smyth noted that:

Irish women have until the very recent past been subject to a particularly intense, if complex, process of socialisation, through the agency of family, school and the church, into an acceptance of an extremely traditional division of labour, with implications for women's political role.[37]

For these authors, the socialization process which transmits traditional assumptions about women's role in society (a feature, to varying degrees, of all societies in the liberal democratic world) has been reinforced in Ireland through the Roman Catholic Church, which continues to prioritize a home- and family-based role for women. This, argues Inglehart,[38] leads to women in predominantly Roman Catholic countries having less interest in politics than men, and so being less inclined to participate in the political process and its institutions. Taken along with other research on the status of women, it is obvious that social attitudes which place women in the home exert a powerful influence on women's own attitudes towards political involvement.

However, the socially determined constraints on women wishing to engage in a political career are not as all-encompassing in the 1990s as they were twenty or more years ago. The greater acceptance of a broader role for women, the availability of contraception enabling women to limit family size, the higher level of education now enjoyed by women and the more extensive occupational opportunities available to them should suggest that women and men will have similar access to political careers. None the less, certain obstacles remain more salient for women than for men.

If, as research has repeatedly shown, both education and occupation are relevant factors in the development of a political career for both women and men, then one must ask, in what way are they significant? This can be answered in one word: networks. Given the significance of localism in Irish politics, the building of a personal support base, or 'bailiwick' in a constituency is a matter of considerable importance for both aspiring candidates and incumbents.[39] One of the most effective methods of building a personal following is through local government service. However, as we have seen, there are relatively few women in local government. One way of overcoming this disadvantage is through the development of local networks based on occupation. However, while professions such as teaching, law and business may appear to offer opportunities for building local support bases, it seems that the utility of these occupations lies in the economic independence and relative flexibility of time they offer rather than being the foundation for personal bailiwick-building. However, the influence of localism is one which many aspiring women politicians find difficult to counteract if they have not had the opportunity to break into a brokerage network through local authority service. Significantly, women political hopefuls are increasingly looking to party elites for 'sponsorship' at the candidate selection stage in order to compensate for a lower degree of access to local networks.

Furthermore, while the relationship between political involvement, electoral success and family connections with politics has been an important feature in determining women's routes to political power, in the context of Irish politics it has been a more significant factor for women than for men. In particular the 'widow's inheritance' has provided women with the main route of entry to political life. In contrast, the traditional routes of entry for men have been less restrictive, encompassing an involvement in nationalist politics, prowess in national sports and local government service. Although the significance of the family connection has declined for both women and men in the last decade, it was still twice as important on average for women as for men. However, there are indications from the 1992 election that the significance of the family is declining for women and remaining stable for men. Comparing the 1989 and 1992 elections, we find that in 1989, 46 per cent of women parliamentarians were related in varying ways to former members of the Dáil; in 1992 this figure dropped to 35 per cent. In other words, while in 1989 just over half of the women elected to parliament had no connections with earlier parliamentary representatives, in 1992 almost two-thirds had no such family political history. The proportion of men with family connections to politics did not change as dramatically as that of women over the same period: in both elections, just over three-quarters of male politicians (76 per cent in 1989 and 78 per cent in 1992) were unrelated to a previous incumbent. These factors, along with the institutional obstacles of party selectorates, militate in combination to prevent women from seeking public office.

The electoral process itself may not be immune to the charge of gender bias. A study of a number of general elections between 1948 and 1982 found that non-incumbent female candidates of Fianna Fáil, Fine Gael and Labour received on average 595 fewer votes than male candidates with the same credentials.[40] There is also evidence of a gender differential in the chances of incumbents being returned to parliament. Darcy noted that in the 1987 general election, 'women incumbents were almost 20 per cent less likely to return than men'.[41] Both conditions were borne out in the 1992 general election. Male candidates attracted 1,200 more votes than female candidates and had a better chance of being elected than women. This general trend carried through for the individual parties and for incumbency, with men faring better than women on both counts. When we focus on the mechanics of the electoral process, however, there is growing evidence that multi-member constituencies increase the opportunities for women's candidacy.[42] These findings point to the need for a more thorough study of the relationship between women and electoral politics than has been undertaken to date before a definitive picture can be presented. However, while women on the whole fare less well than men in electoral terms, the influence of party selectorates on the numbers of women candidates and overall levels of party support appears to have a significant bearing on women's political representation in Ireland.

ADMINISTRATION

The dearth of women in positions of power in parties and political life is, of course, only part of the wider pattern of women's absence from decision-making centres generally. In a survey of the numbers of women serving on state boards in 1970, the Commission on the Status of Women noted that there was only one woman among the board members of the ten leading state-sponsored bodies. This figure had increased to 12 per cent by 1985.[43] In the 1988 government report on the development of equal opportunities,[44] 298 (12.6 per cent) of 2,336 members of the boards of fifty state-sponsored bodies were women. In 1993 the Fianna Fáil–Labour government stated its intention to increase gender representation on state boards to 40 per cent within five years. By July 1996, women comprised 34.2 per cent of government nominees on state boards. However, the record of other nominating bodies is less satisfactory, drawing the following warning from the minister for Equality and Law Reform:

> I am determined to tackle this problem, by legislation if necessary. I am giving a final warning to all those bodies which nominate members to State boards to put their house in order and comply with the 40 per cent gender balance requirement, which is a reasonable and balanced measure to promote appointment on merit, by ensuring that meritorious candidates of both genders are represented.[45]

This record, which is largely positive, stands in contrast to the representation of women on the boards of the main private companies in Ireland. In 1993, women's representation on the boards of the top ten companies amounted to two (1.6 per cent) out of the 128 board directors.[46] This is much worse than the position in Britain, where women make up 4.2 per cent of the directors of the top one hundred private companies.[47] Further highlighting the absence of women in the corporate sector, in 1994 there was no female chief executive among the country's top one hundred companies. While there may be a move towards gender equality in the public decision-making sphere, the major private companies appear resistant to appointing women as chief executives and board members in any significant numbers.

BUREAUCRACY

The poor record of women's representation in the senior levels of the Civil Service was highlighted with the publication of research which found that there were no women among the senior positions of secretary and deputy secretary, that only 2 per cent of the assistant secretaries and 3 per cent of the principal officers were female, and that the majority of women employed in the Civil Service filled the lower clerical and typing grades.[48] This study reflected the conclusion of the parliamentary Joint Committee on Women's Rights report on equal opportunity in the Civil Service, which found that, despite the existence of an equal opportunity policy since 1986,

> [while] women make up 63 per cent of the total general service grades in the Civil Service, they are concentrated in the Clerical Officer and Clerical Assistant grades, with declining representation in the ascending grades to a total absence of women in the two top echelons. This preponderance of women in two of the lowest grades helps to retain and reinforce the idea of male superiority.[49]

In 1994, a woman was appointed to the position of Assistant Secretary – a senior management position – the first woman to hold this office in over twenty years. The situation has been improving slowly and by 1996 one woman held the top post of Secretary in a government department, 6 per cent of assistant secretaries were women, and just under 13 per cent of principal officer posts were held by women.[50] Yet, women remain the majority in the lowest-paid grades in the administrative system, with women holding over 80 per cent of clerical assistant posts and 79 per cent of clerical officer posts in 1996. In other areas of the administration, women are equally absent. Among the state-sponsored bodies, only 2 per cent of women are in senior management positions. In local authorities, this drops to 1 per cent, with no woman holding any of the top positions of county manager. The pattern of women's representation in the eight regional health boards is similar to that in the rest of the public service. Although 76 per cent of health board employees are women, there are no women at senior management levels in the health administrative structure.[51]

JUDICIARY

This pattern is repeated in the judicial arena. As Connelly and Hilliard observed in their study of the legal profession:

In December 1992, Ms Justice Denham was appointed to the Supreme Court, the first woman ever to be appointed to this position. At the end of 1992, there was one woman on the High Court, four women at District Court level and none at Circuit level.[52]

Table 2.6 shows the relative levels of gender representation among the judiciary. Although the proportion of Irish justices who are women compares favourably with the situation in Britain (3.4 per cent in 1989), the number of women working as justices at the level of the District Court has actually decreased since 1985, even though about half of solicitors and one-quarter of barristers are women.[53] In France and The Netherlands, over one-third of the judiciary are women.[54]

Table 2.6 Women in the judiciary, 1993

Court	Total number of justices	Number of women	%
Supreme Court	5	1	20.0
High Court	16	1	6.2
Circuit Court	17	0	0.0
District Courts	46	4	8.7
Total	84	6	7.1

Source: Connelly and Hilliard (1993, p. 216).

MAIN INTEREST GROUPS

The numbers of women in decision-making positions in the organizations of the 'social partners' – the trade union, employer and agricultural interests influential in shaping government economic policy – are also low. Women have consistently formed over one-third of trade union membership since the 1980s. In 1993 the total female membership of the fifty-one trade unions affiliated to the Irish Congress of Trade Unions was 37 per cent.[55] However, women held only 27 per cent of the places on the executive committees of the twenty unions that represented 97 per cent of the female membership.[56] Between 1982 and 1991, three women filled reserved seats on the Irish Congress of Trade Unions executive. In 1992, only five (17.2 per cent) of the twenty-nine executive council members were women, with four of these holding reserved positions, even though, according to the Irish Congress of Trade Unions women's committee, there should be ten women on the executive to effect a gender balance in representation on that body. None of the senior official positions in the Irish Business and Employers Confederation (IBEC), or the Irish Farmers' Association is held by women.

DISCUSSION

This chapter has set out to describe the position of women in Irish society both prior to and during a period of economic modernization from the 1970s onwards. From this discussion it is clear that the role and status of women in Ireland have undergone considerable change in one generation. Women are having fewer children, married women are participating in the workforce in growing numbers and there are some tentative signs that women's involvement in political decision-making arenas is on the increase. Irish women's lives are gradually changing to become more like that of their European sisters.

We have seen that the changing role of women in society can be attributed to the complex interplay of a number of factors. Alongside a modest egalitarianism in social attitudes towards women's public role, a traditional attitude towards women's family duties remains. Specific court judgments have led to the removal of discrimination in public policy. The influence of EU legislation has assisted in breaking down the barriers to women's participation in employment. Changes in family patterns have given women more freedom to pursue activities outside the home. While women's foothold in the major decision-making arenas is still tentative, there are signs that political parties are becoming increasingly sensitive to the need for equality in gender representation.[57] The economic context of the 1970s laid the foundations for the development of a feminist agenda based on a demand for equality with men. The lessons from feminist movements elsewhere heightened awareness of gender-based discrimination. The changing social patterns of the 1970s encouraged the articulation of that agenda. However, the almost complete absence of women from decision-making levels in the political, corporate and administrative spheres suggests that the only route available to women to express their demands was through the women's movement and organized women's groups. Given the basically conservative nature of Irish politics and society, and given the significance accorded to adherence to moral values as interpreted by the Catholic Church, Irish feminism was unlikely to develop a radical political perspective. Chapter 3 looks at the nature of feminist mobilization in Ireland during the 1970s and shows how a reformist movement provided the catalyst for the formation of a range of issue-specific groups which carried the feminist agenda into the political sphere.

NOTES

1. Eurostat, *Women and Men in the European Union: A Statistical Portrait* (Luxembourg: Office for Official Publications of the European Communities, 1995), p. 61.

2. Eurostat, *Women and Men in the European Union*, p. 63.

3. Eurostat, *Women and Men in the European Union*, p. 51.

4. Joint Committee on Women's Rights, *Changing Attitudes to the Role of Women in Ireland: Attitudes Towards the Role and Status of Women 1975–1986* (Dublin: Stationery Office, May 1988) [Pl. 5609].

5. Deborah King, *Women at Work* (Dublin: AnCO, September 1976), p. 127.

6. The poll was conducted by the Market Research Bureau of Ireland and is cited in Frances Gardiner, 'Political interest and participation of Irish women 1922–1992: the unfinished revolution', in Ailbhe Smyth (ed.), *Irish Women's Studies Reader* (Dublin: Attic Press, 1993), p. 71.

7. Clyde Wilcox, 'Support for gender equality in west Europe – a longitudinal analysis', *European Journal of Political Research*, **20**(2) (1991), 127–47.

8. See, for example, Commission of the EC, *Men and Women of Europe in 1987* (Brussels: Commission of the European Community, 1987), p. 49.

9. Liam O'Dowd, 'Church, State and women: the aftermath of partition', in Chris Curtin, Pauline Jackson and Bernadette O'Connor (eds), *Gender in Irish Society* (Galway: Galway University Press, 1987), pp. 32–3.

10. Jenny Beale, *Women in Ireland, Voices of Change* (Dublin: Gill & Macmillan, 1986), p. 9.

11. John Coakley, 'Society and political culture', in John Coakley and Michael Gallagher (eds), *Politics in the Republic of Ireland* (Dublin and Limerick: Folens and PSAI Press, 1993), pp. 40–1.

12. Gisela Kaplan, *Contemporary Western European Feminism* (London: Allen & Unwin, 1992), p. 180.

13. Richard Breen, Damian F. Hannan, David B. Rottman and Christopher T. Whelan, *Understanding Contemporary Ireland: State, Class and Development in the Republic of Ireland* (Basingstoke: Macmillan, 1990), p. 101.

14. Yvonne Scannell, 'The constitution and the role of women', in Brian Farrell (ed.), *De Valera's Constitution and Ours* (Dublin: Gill and Macmillan, 1988), p. 127.

15. O'Dowd, 'Church, State and women', pp. 24–5.

16. Commission on the Status of Women, *Report to the Minister for Finance* (Dublin: Stationery Office, December 1972), pp. 173, 227–45 [Prl. 2760].

17. Mary E. Daly, 'Women in the Irish Free State, 1922–1939: the interaction between economics and ideology', *Journal of Women's History*, **6**(4)/**7**(1) (winter/spring 1995), 109–10.

18. Margaret Ward, *Unmanageable Revolutionaries: Women and Irish Nationalism* (Dingle: Brandon Press, 1983), p. 254.

19. Eugene McLaughlin, 'Ireland: Catholic corporatism', in Allan Cochrane and John Clarke (eds), *Comparing Welfare States: Britain in International Context* (Milton Keynes: Open University Press, 1993), p. 211.

20. The influence of these factors on the participation of married women in the labour force is discussed in detail in Tim Callan and Brian Farrell, *Women's Participation in the Irish Labour Market* (Dublin: National Economic and Social Council, 1991) [Pl. 8449]; Brendan M. Walsh, 'Labour force participation and the growth of women's employment, Ireland', *Economic and Social Review*, 24(4) (July 1993), 369–400; Daniele Meulders, Robert Plasman and Valerie Vander Stricht, *Position of Women on the Labour Market in the European Community* (Aldershot: Dartmouth, 1993).

21. Callan and Farrell, *Women's Participation in the Irish Labour Market*, p. 104.

22. Employment Equality Agency, *Women in the Labour Force* (Dublin: EEA, 1995), pp. 7, 13.

23. Working Party on Women's Affairs and Family Law Reform, *Irish Women: Agenda for Practical Action* (Dublin: Stationery Office, February, 1985), p. 37 [Pl. 3126].

24. Eurostat, *Women and Men in the European Union*, pp. 138–9.

25. Meulders *et al.*, *Position of Women on the Labour Market in the European Community*, pp. 68–9.

26. Working Party on Women's Affairs, *Agenda for Practical Action*, p. 55.

27. In 1992, women's average weekly earnings were 60.5 per cent of the male industrial wage. This is computed from information in the Central Statistics Office, *Economic Series* (Dublin: Stationery Office, December 1993), p. 21.

28. Joint Committee on Women's Rights, *Motherhood, Work and Equal Opportunity – A Case Study of Irish Civil Servants* (Dublin: Stationery Office, July 1991) [Pl. 8249].

29. Second Commission on the Status of Women, *Report to Government* (Dublin: Stationery Office, January 1993), p. 125 [Pl. 9557].

30. Employment Equality Agency, *Women in the Labour Force*, p. 17.

31. Employment Equality Agency, *Women in the Labour Force*, p. 17; John Blackwell, *Women in the Labour Force* (Dublin: Employment Equality Agency & Environmental Policy Centre, UCD, 1989), p. 33.

32. Joint Committee on Women's Rights, *Changing Attitudes to the Role of Women in Ireland*, pp. 37–40; Commission on the Status of Women, *Report*, p. 99.

33. Eurostat, *Women and Men in the European Union*, pp. 140–5.

34. Yvonne Galligan, 'Ireland', in Beate Hoecker (ed.), *Handbuch Politische Partizipation von Frauen in Europa* (Leverkusen: Leske & Budrich, 1997).

35. John Coakley, 'The Seanad elections', in Michael Gallagher and Michael Laver (eds), *How Ireland Voted 1992* (Dublin and Limerick: Folens and PSAI Press, 1993), p. 135.

36. Frances Gardiner, 'Women in the election', in Gallagher and Laver (eds), *How Ireland Voted 1992*, pp. 91–2.

37. Vicky Randall and Ailbhe Smyth, 'Bishops and bailiwicks: obstacles to women's political participation in Ireland', *Economic and Social Review*, 18(3), 200.

38. Margaret Inglehart, 'Political interest in west European women: an historical and empirical comparative analysis', *Comparative Political Studies*, **14**(3), 299–326.

39. Randall and Smyth, 'Bishops and bailiwicks', pp. 204–5.

40. Michael Marsh, 'Electoral evaluations of candidates in Irish elections', *Irish Political Studies*, **2** (1987), 70.

41. R. Darcy, 'The election of women to Dáil Eireann: a formal analysis', *Irish Political Studies*, **3** (1988), 73.

42. Michael Gallagher, Michael Laver and Peter Mair, *Representative Government in Western Europe* (New York: McGraw Hill, 1992).

43. Randall and Smyth, 'Bishops and bailiwicks', p. 194.

44. Ireland, *The Development of Equal Opportunities, March 1987-September 1988: Coordinated Report* (Dublin: Stationery Office, 1988), p. 61 [Pl. 6056].

45. *Irish Times*, 14 October 1996.

46. This information was extracted from data in the 1994 Institute of Public Administration *Yearbook* (Dublin: IPA, 1994).

47. *Sunday Tribune*, 2 February 1997.

48. Clare Eager, 'Splitting images – women and the Irish civil service', *Seirbhis Phoibli*, **12**(1) (1991), 19.

49. Joint Committee on Women's Rights, *Motherhood, Work and Equal Opportunity*, pp. xii–iv.

50. *Irish Times*, 1 November 1995 and 4 March 1996.

51. Institute of Public Administration, *Yearbook* (1994).

52. Alpha Connelly and Betty Hilliard, 'The legal system', in Alpha Connelly, *Gender and the Law in Ireland* (Dublin: Oak Tree Press, 1993), p. 216.

53. Hansard Society Commission, *Women at the Top* (London: Hansard Society for Parliamentary Government, January 1990), pp. 44–5; Connelly and Hilliard, 'The legal system', p. 232.

54. Hansard Society Commission, *Women at the Top*, p. 7.

55. Employment Equality Agency, *Women in the Labour Force*, p. 43.

56. Irish Congress of Trade Unions, *Implementation of Equality Report 'Programme for Progress'* (Dublin: ICTU, 1992), pp. 2, 7.

57. Yvonne Galligan, 'Party politics and gender in the Republic of Ireland', in Joni Lovenduski and Pippa Norris (eds), *Gender and Party Politics* (London: Sage, 1993), pp. 147–67.

CHAPTER 3

WOMEN'S POLITICAL MOBILIZATION

As discussed so far, a range of socio-economic factors in Ireland are generally accepted as being significant in facilitating the emergence of women's demands. The under-representation of women in civic society has resulted in limited opportunities for the formal articulation of a woman-centred perspective on decision-making. This chapter deals with the resurgence of the women's movement in Ireland from the 1970s onwards. I believe, with Randall, that 'any account of the relationship between women and politics, in contemporary Western societies at least, must assign a central place to the women's movement'.[1] As the form and shape of feminism is largely dictated by the socio-economic and political environment in which it occurs, attention is drawn to the similarities and differences between the Irish phenomenon and women's political mobilization in other countries.

The origins and early days of the women's liberation movement in Ireland are considered first. Then the appearance of second-wave feminism is linked with the activities of existing women's groups which, while following a feminist agenda, did not identify themselves as a contemporary feminist social movement. Both aspects of feminism, it is suggested, pursued a similar agenda – equality with men – albeit using different tactical methods to achieve their aim. This theme can be seen as a continuation of the agenda set by politicized women in a previous generation.

I then turn to the second phase of the movement and argue that the equality agenda was replaced by the 'difference' agenda. Mobilization around this norm was less widespread than around equal rights, given the conservative nature of Irish social attitudes. Both themes stem from the dominant feminist ideology within the movement at the time. The third phase of feminist political engagement is described as 'integrationist', although given the appropriate issue, there is scope for a radical mobilization of women. At this point, it is important to note that these three categories of feminist activity are not mutually exclusive. In reality, the feminist political agendas formed during these phases continually overlapped with one another, eliciting a range of political responses. These political agendas were integral to the 'institutionalist' wing of the movement and to 'radical' feminists alike. The impact that the women's movement has had on social and institutional developments is described. The final part of the chapter summarizes the reasons why Irish feminists by and large adopted an 'interest group' rather than a mass mobilization format in pursuit of their demands.

THE WOMEN'S MOVEMENT IN IRELAND

The emergence of the second wave of feminism in Europe is often viewed, either explicitly or implicitly, as a 'virgin birth' – a social and political phenomenon with no links with past campaigns for women's rights. This approach does not take account of the complexities of the women's movement in Ireland. Instead, I see the Irish women's liberation movement as having its roots in the political activities of a small number of women's groups which articulated a feminist agenda long before the advent of second-wave feminism. The demand for equal pay and proper working conditions for women was central to the campaigns of the Women Workers Union from the early 1900s.[2] The role assigned to women in the Constitution was strongly opposed by a feminist coalition in 1937. Food shortages and family poverty in Ireland during the Second World War (a period known in Irish history as the 'Emergency') provided a catalyst for the political mobilization of a group of women who formed the Irish Housewives Association (IHA).[3] This organization 'absorbed a network of long-time, highly committed feminists', became involved with the international women's movement and 'forged a direct international link and continuity between the first-wave suffrage movement which peaked in the early 1900s, and retreated after 1922, and the contemporary women's movement which mobilized globally in the late 1960s'.[4]

The international links of the IHA were to play a significant role in the re-emergence of modern Irish feminism. Through the International Alliance for Women to which the IHA was affiliated, IHA leaders learned of the directive issued to women's non-governmental organizations by the United Nations (UN) Commission on the Status of Women in 1967. This directive sought two things: it looked for an examination of the status of women in UN countries, and it encouraged women's organizations to lobby their respective governments for the setting up of an official National Commission on the Status of Women. The Irish section of the Association of Business and Professional Women's clubs had also become aware of this directive through its own international links. In 1968, members of both groups called a meeting of all women's organizations in the Republic of Ireland to discuss the UN directive. In all, twenty groups sent representatives. They came from traditional women's organizations and associations of graduate and professional women.[5] This meeting led to the formation of an *ad hoc* committee consisting of representatives from eleven women's groups; they were charged with the task of investigating the status of women in Ireland. Equality issues covered by this research included taxation, education, women in public life, social welfare and health. The committee members utilized the existing network of women's organizations to gather information and to receive submissions. It was the first assessment of women's position in Irish society. The resulting report was presented to the Taoiseach (Prime Minister) Jack Lynch, who, after some concentrated lobbying by the *ad hoc* committee, agreed to establish a national Commission on the Status of Women.

The Commission came into being on 31 March 1970 with a brief:

> to examine and report on the status of women in Irish society, to make recommendations on the steps necessary to ensure the participation of women on equal terms and conditions with men in the political, social, cultural and economic life of the country and to indicate the implications generally – including the estimated cost – of such recommendations.[6]

The Commission was chaired by Dr Thekla Beere, the only woman to obtain the position of Secretary of a government department until 1996, when a second woman was appointed to this top civil service job.

Of the forty-four organizations making submissions (written and oral) to the Commission on the Status of Women in 1970–71, just over half (twenty-three) were from women's groups. Of these, only four could be identified with the new phase of feminist politics.[7] The report of the Commission recommended action on forty-nine specific areas of direct discrimination against women in employment, taxation, social welfare, the law and public life. Furthermore, it suggested the radical measure of including women's associations in the political processes leading to the abolition of inequality.[8] Critically, too, it recommended that state funding be given to an organization recognized by the government as representing women's interests.[9] The *ad hoc* group seized the initiative and formed an umbrella association, the Council for the Status of Women, to represent women's interests to government. In 1995, the name of the Council was changed to the National Women's Council of Ireland (NWCI). Group affiliations to the NWCI have grown steadily since its inception, from twenty organizations in 1973 to 115 in 1993.[10] Indeed, the success of the organization over the years in representing women's interests and views to government led one observer to conclude that Ireland has 'the best organised institutional movement of women in Europe'.[11] It is important to note that on the eve of the resurgence of the women's liberation movement in Ireland, organized representation on women's rights was a part of institutional politics.

THE WOMEN'S LIBERATION MOVEMENT

The origins of the Irish women's liberation movement can be traced to early 1970 when eleven Dublin-based women began to meet regularly for informal consciousness-raising discussions on the situation of women in Ireland.[12] In a short time, the group had expanded to twenty women who formed the leadership of the nascent grass-roots feminist movement.

The initiative for holding discussions on the public and private situation of Irish women stemmed from personal contacts between a small number of Irish women active in nationalist politics and feminists from the United States who had come to Ireland to study the resurgence of republicanism. Furthermore, some of the early members of the women's movement had been politicized through their involvement in campaigns for social and political reform. Some of these feminists were active in a radical housing action campaign in Dublin which utilized political protest as a strategy for drawing attention to the crisis in the government's urban housing policy. Others were politicized through participation in the Northern Ireland civil rights movement and through their connections with republican politics.[13] These two features illustrate the 'demonstration effect' that the mobilization of an existing movement may have on an incipient movement.[14]

Although tensions existed between the institutional feminists and their radical sisters, Connolly notes that there was little difference in their political agenda. Instead,

> The primary difference between the two derived from preferred strategy – persistently lobby the state for moderate, gradual legislative change on the one hand, and engaging in controversial, direct action tactics (pickets, protests, expressive action) on the other. However, even though these methods were more concentrated in each sector, each drew on the same repertoire of tactics (and symbols, ideologies, and resources) in a strategic fashion when the need arose. For example the fight for change through the courts was utilized both by mainstream and autonomous feminists, as were petitioning, mass meetings and demonstrations.[15]

Indeed, there is ample evidence in the remaining chapters of this book of the overlap of political agendas and strategic actions between the two aspects of the women's movement in Ireland.

In terms of social profile, these modern Irish feminists fitted readily into the category of social movement proponents. They were mainly drawn from the middle class and had received a high level of education. Some were in full-time paid professional employment, others worked from home, a number held positions in the media as newspaper journalists or had backgrounds in left-wing and republican politics. Thus, the small group had a considerable reservoir of resources to draw on when seeking to disseminate feminist ideas and information in a country still quite insular in its social perspectives. In this dissemination process, the openness of the media to feminist concerns was striking and, without doubt, advantageous for the movement.

Towards the end of 1970, the energies of a core group of about twenty feminists began to focus on formulating a series of gender-specific demands around which they intended to mobilize public support. The result was the identification of six demands highlighting the social and economic discriminations against women in Ireland. These were published in a feminist manifesto entitled 'Chains or change: the civil wrongs of Irish women'. This process of identifying and highlighting major areas of gender-related discriminations in existing legislation and public policy practices paralleled similar developments in feminist movements in other countries. Indeed, the issues themselves – equality in pay, education, social welfare and the law, the demand for legal contraception and adequate housing for families – bore a modest resemblance to the agenda of the Spanish women's movement, whose demands included 'the decriminalization of birth control, divorce and abortion; equal wages for equal work; and the provision of social services, mainly child care'.[16] They also closely reflected the campaigns of their feminist sisters in the NWCI.

The public launch on 6 March 1971 of the women's liberation movement and its manifesto sparked a lively public debate on women's rights. The discussion was assisted by the fact that the Roman Catholic Church was campaigning at the time against a parliamentary bill introduced in the Seanad (upper house) by three non-party senators which sought to legalize the sale of contraceptives. The ensuing political conflict provided the new movement with an immediate issue around which to mobilize.[17] In this, it was not unique. Other feminist movements also quickly found a mobilizing issue in the early stages. What marks out the Irish women's liberation movement from that in other countries is the kind of issue around which feminist activity was concentrated. For Irish women, the legalization of contraception was the politicizing issue. For feminists in Britain, France, Italy and West Germany, abortion was one of the key campaigns engaged in by feminists. In Ireland, abortion was not on the agenda of the women's movement, and not placed there to any significant degree until the emergence of a strong interest group in the mid-1980s which sought to secure the ban on abortion through a constitutional amendment.[18] In response to the public interest shown in the movement, the first major public meeting of the women's liberation movement was held in the Mansion House on 14 April 1971. Accounts of this period estimate that almost 1,000 people, the vast majority of whom were women, attended this meeting. Many personal instances of discrimination were aired. There was unanimous support for the demand for legalizing the sale of contraceptives. From this gathering, the movement began to proliferate. In all, twenty-eight semi-autonomous groupings, located mainly in Dublin, were established subsequent to this meeting.[19]

A period of direct action followed. Walk-outs occurred when a priest decried the women's liberation movement from the pulpit during Mass in a city-centre Roman Catholic church. Picket protests took place in and around the parliament building, Leinster House and the General Post Office. Feminists took a train from Dublin to Belfast in order to buy contraceptives and import them into the Republic in defiance of laws prohibiting the importation of contraceptives. These and other media-catching activities engaged the energies of the early second-wave feminists in Ireland.

All was not well within the movement. Strain began to appear on two fronts. First, the organizational demands of directing a disparate social movement and retaining some degree of cohesion around the original political agenda resulted in tensions between the core group and participants in other groups. Second, conflict surfaced within the founding group based on political differences. Some of the core members identified with left-wing and republican politics and sought to shape the movement to reflect these priorities. Others wished to give primacy to a reformist feminist agenda. These and other differences within the founder group led to the resignation of a leading activist, Nuala Fennell, and other moderate feminists who sought to achieve change from within the political system and regarded protest from outside the institutional political processes as being futile.[20] The resignation of Fennell, the further polarization of the group between socialist and feminist ideologies and a general disillusionment with the lack of direction of the movement led to the disintegration of the movement by September 1971.

The fragmentation of the women's liberation movement in Ireland was not an unusual phenomenon in the pattern of women's mobilization. Such an event was a common occurrence, as feminists failed to reconcile their differing ideological and strategic approaches to women's politics. The situation in France, for instance, was typical of that generally experienced by feminist movement activists: for instance, Randall observes that 'the women who came to identify with this movement were from tremendously varied ideological and social backgrounds and, beyond their shared recognition of women's continuing oppression, inevitably disagreed over tactics'.[21] Indeed, similar forces led to the alienation of liberal feminists in Ireland from radical tactics which were not deemed appropriate by the majority of women in a conservative society.

The fragmentation of the women's movement led to the emergence of the radical feminist Fownes Street group which concentrated on exploring the identity and culture of feminist ideology rather than in developing an engagement with the political system. It continued in existence for some time, but remained a small grouping. The energies of other activists in the women's movement diverged into the formation of a range of single-issue organizations delivering information and social services to women on areas of public policy, legislation and political practice. Groups such as AIM (Action, Information, Motivation) and Cherish (a single mothers' organization) became important lobbying agencies for changes in family law and the status of women. The newly founded Women's Political Association began to work for the election of more women to political positions, and the NWCI, representing established women's organizations, sought to influence government policy in a wide range of areas affecting women.

The feminist agenda at this time was one of equal rights. This reflected the tone of the political demands contained in the women's movement manifesto. Based on arguments of justice and equality, the feminist agenda did not present an overly radical challenge to prevailing social and political values when compared with the demands of feminists in other countries. However, given the conservative nature of Irish society, this liberal agenda was viewed by the public and politicians as a radical challenge to established public policy customs and practices.

The dominance of a liberal, equal rights perspective among feminists in Ireland was in contrast to the outcome of feminist splits in other countries. In Spain, the advent of democratic politics led to the affiliation of feminists with left-wing political parties. It also integrated feminist demands into the programmes of the emerging parties, while the new constitution provided for equality between men and women in marriage and employment. In Italy, the politics of radical separatism dominated, although it is interesting to note the extent to which left-wing parties and institutions accommodated radical feminist demands. This relationship is not, however, viewed uncritically by Italian feminists.[22] The pattern of feminist engagement with the Irish political system is similar to that of the women's movement in Greece,[23] where women's political activity centred around winning incremental changes in public policies on the family, and in the United States, where women's interest group activity has been dominant.[24]

RADICAL FEMINISM

The feminist movement in Ireland underwent a resurgence some years later. On this occasion the demands were more specific, the politics clearly left wing, the movement leaders younger and more militant and the base of the movement much more narrowly defined. In January 1975 (International Women's Year), women trade unionists adopted a 'Working Women's Charter' modelled on that drawn up the previous March by the Women's Sub-Committee of the London Trades Council and designed as a minimum programme of feminist demands to be put to trade unions.[25] In April 1975, a group of feminist activists gathered to discuss the possibility of organizing a conference to discuss and adopt a charter of demands for women's rights based on that drawn up by the trade union women. This conference was held on 8 June and subsequently Irish-women United (IU) was founded.[26] This new manifestation of the feminist movement mainly comprised women with an involvement in trade union activity and radical political fringe groups such as the People's Demo-cracy, Movement for a Socialist Republic, the Revolutionary Marxist Group, the Irish Republican Socialist Party and the International Lesbian Caucus.[27] Many of the core activists had attended meetings of the Fownes Street group, but had little connection with the founders or the activities of the women's liberation movement.

The new set of feminist demands sought the 'removal of all legal and bureaucratic obstacles to equality', free legal contraception and abortion, State provision for adequate housing and twenty-four-hour nurseries, community-controlled secular education with an end to sex stereotyping, equal pay to be based on a national minimum wage, positive measures to ensure the welfare of pregnant female workers, state provision of women's centres and 'the right of all women to a self-determined sexuality'.[28] This agenda closely resembled the demands of the Spanish and British movements.

Again, there followed a period of direct action, although this time the activities were organized by a small cadre group rather than occurring as dispersed expressions of protest. Activities included swimming at traditionally male-only bathing places, protesting against the exclusion of women from membership of private tennis clubs, demands for changes in the law on contraception and pressure on politicians for the implementation of equal pay.

Although IU claimed to be a feminist movement, it was unable to touch the lives of ordinary women in the way the women's liberation group had done some years previously. This alienation of IU activists from other feminists and ordinary women was illustrated in the protests centred around equal pay. Although the daring IU venture of occupying the headquarters of the employers' organization brought attention to the demand, one sympathetic observer noted that IU as a feminist grouping did not appeal to Irish women:

> The Federated Union of Employers occupation was important because until then pressure for Equal Pay had been centred on government rather than the employers. However, it also showed how isolated IU was from the mainstream of the Irish women's movement. When IU organised a further meeting – envisaged as an open workshop – where women could ask questions about the pending legislation and how to place equal pay claims, fewer than a hundred people turned up.[29]

The resolution of the equal pay issue took place within the context of institutional politics, where feminists with access to the conventional levers of power played an important role. None the less, the equal pay campaign engaged in by IU members resulted in a significant mobilization of public interest, placed pressure on the government and unions to treat the issue with serious intent and provided a support network for women in trade unions who were actively campaigning from within the political structures for the introduction of equal pay.[30]

The demand for legal contraception, which had not been resolved from the time of the women's liberation movement, was a second mobilizing issue for members of IU. On 22 June 1976, the group initiated a pressure campaign for changes in the legislation on contraception. The initial steering committee was composed of a representative from each of the two family planning organizations, IU, the Labour Women's National Council (LWNC), the remnants of the women's liberation movement, Women's Aid, the Women's Political Association and the North Dublin Social Workers Association.[31] It later grew to become a coalition of a wide range of groups in Irish society, and became known as the Contraception Action Programme (CAP). This committee adopted conventional forms of pressure activity such as petitions, lobbying of politicians and taking legal action. Although the campaign lost some of its momentum after the initial mobilization period it remained a functioning organization, and in time was to become associated in the public mind with demands for reform on this issue.[32]

IU remained a Dublin-based group, although radical feminists were meeting in other urban centres, in particular in Cork and Limerick. These non-Dublin groups became instrumental in setting up rape crisis centres and the Cork group established a women's resource centre. However, Irishwomen United was never a cohesive grouping with a coherent ideological outlook, and as such it was prone to internal conflicts. The disagreements among this feminist group were of a more radical nature than the internal tensions which had beset the earlier women's liberation movement. Brennan argues:

> This time there was a three way split: the radical lesbians who argued for separatist policies and sometimes suggested that heterosexuality was another form of dependence on men; the socialists whose first allegiance was to a political party (i.e. the ultra left minority groups) and the radical feminists who found themselves somewhere in the middle.[33]

However, out of the ashes of Irishwomen United there grew a number of feminist-oriented self-help and service organizations which began to address problems arising from the unequal power relationship between women and men in terms of sex and sexuality. The feminist agenda now concentrated on issues of difference, problems which were specific to women. Violence against women was the major feminist theme and mobilizing issue of the late 1970s. A refuge for battered women had been opened in Dublin in 1974 and by 1977 similar refuges were operating or in the process of being established in Limerick, Cork and Galway. The country's first rape crisis centre opened in Dublin in 1979. Others followed in the main urban centres outside Dublin. Feminists began to campaign for changes in the law on rape and sexual violence.

The Irish experience of feminism in the late 1970s was not exceptional. In Britain, radical feminists set the movement agenda, with a mushrooming of rape crisis and women's aid centres.[34] In Greece, the radical feminist movement formulated and promoted demands for reform of public policies on abortion and rape, and for legalizing the distribution of contraceptives.[35] Spanish feminists also sought the decriminalization of the sale of contraceptives along with reform of abortion laws before fragmenting into two camps, one composed of political feminists, the other of radical feminists.[36]

By the end of the 1970s, feminist energies in Ireland had been diverted into grass-roots activity and single-issue politics or were absorbed by a range of radical political groupings. As with the Spanish movement, Irish feminist groups adopted a different style of political organization subsequent to the demise of Irishwomen United. From this time on, they would work together only on specific issues such as countering the campaign to introduce a prohibition on abortion into the constitution in 1983 and opposing the signing of the Maastricht Treaty in 1992. As Smyth notes:

> The various feminist groupings which coalesced during the abortion amendment campaign in 1982/83 conferred a sense of strength and cohesion on the movement which was to prove somewhat illusory when measured in terms of success in the public arena. It proved difficult for women to come together – and to maintain momentum – to campaign on major issues, as the experience of the June 1986 divorce referendum, the failure of the government to implement the EC social security directive within the deadline, and the 'defend the clinics' campaign demonstrated.[37]

Again, the experience of the Irish feminist movement in this regard is not unique. In France, internal conflict within the feminist movement in the late 1970s led to a loss of movement energy in the 1980s.[38] In Spain, feminist unity around a broad political agenda had disappeared by 1979 and subsequent attempts to revive it failed.[39] In Britain, where feminist activity was strong, the mass-based movement suffered a decline.[40] However, if feminism as a social movement has – as is often the case with social movements – retreated from directly challenging the political system,[41] it has left its mark on Irish politics and society.

FEMINISM AND WOMEN IN SOCIETY

Although the days of mobilization in support of a broad feminist agenda were largely over by the late 1970s, this aspect of the women's movement left a legacy which became apparent over time. It became most visible at the level of national political structures, but could be deemed to be most potent in the less visible arenas of community and local activities. The nature, quantity and outcomes of women's public activities at grass-roots level have yet to be analysed in any form. For Connolly,

> The rapid growth of locally based women's groups is a most exciting development. New forms of structure and organization are emerging in the 1990s. These groups tend to be non-hierarchical, autonomous, participatory and empowering. They are mainly based in working-class urban areas and their impact tends to be localized. However, there are also some groups recently formed in rural, peripheral areas. In terms of structure and methods of organization, such organizations resemble the

small-group, consciousness-raising, radical women's sector which emerged in the 1970s.[42]

This trend reflects the pattern of women's civic and political participation in other European countries (Spain and The Netherlands, for instance) once the women's movement diversified. Irish women in the 1990s have become actively involved at local level, often with the needs of their children as a catalyst for action (for instance, the provision of playgroups for pre-school children and summer activities for older children). Women have also assessed their own needs and have developed a range of support groups and services at local level. The mushrooming of adult education activities and community writing workshops attest to this desire for self-improvement. Women are contributing to their communities through initiatives to solve local unemployment, in campaigning for improved maternity and general health services and, most recently, in tackling the serious drug problem that has ravaged working-class families living in inner-city Dublin. The pattern of women's activity is specific and issue-driven. It is seen as an end in itself, not necessarily the start of a broader level of political involvement, as the dearth of women in local politics does not reflect the extent of women's participation in local political activities.

In a discussion on the development of community-based women's organizations in Ireland, Coulter provides an example which reinforces the impression of the vibrancy and number of these groups:

> The mushrooming of locally-based women's groups over the past few years has been the result of a marriage between the influence of modern feminism and tradition. No-one knows precisely how many there are, but one indication of their growth is given by the fact that a meeting of western women's groups with President Robinson was called in Headford, Co. Galway in 1992. A hall was hired for two hundred and fifty people. Over one thousand people representing forty-two women's groups turned up.[43]

The traditional women's organization, the Irish Countrywomen's Association (ICA), is still strong in rural Ireland, with over 1,000 locally based guilds. These guilds have been complemented by numerous women's educational, community and self-help groups which began to form after the advent of the women's movement. In the 1970s, women's groups were formed within the major trade unions and feminists established a more radical presence in the Irish Congress of Trade Unions (ICTU). Most of the political parties have established women's units, the exceptions being the Progressive Democrats and the Green Party.[44]

One reason why many women's groups have been able to flourish is because of government subsidies. In 1979, only the NWCI and the Employment Equality Agency (EEA) received state funding. In 1993, three years after a government initiative to provide a modest level of financial support for women's groups, over 600 women's organizations were being funded by the Department of Social Welfare. The Department of Health provides significant subsidies through the regional health boards to rape crisis centres and women's refuges. It is ironic that, in a society where adherence to traditional beliefs and values is deeply ingrained, women's empowerment has been facilitated through public funding. These developments suggest that, over time, decision-makers responded to the politics of the women's movement.

FEMINISM AND POLITICAL INSTITUTIONS

As we have seen, there was little recognition prior to 1970 of the differing impact of legislation on gender by either politicians or the public. However, the focus placed by the women's movement on discriminations against women and the demand for a recognition and redress of unjust and unfair treatment in public policy was part of a growing worldwide recognition of the gender bias in legislative formulation and practice. In Ireland, government attention was increasingly being drawn to its non-ratification of Convention 100 of the International Labour Organization, which provided for the implementation of equal pay for men and women. Furthermore, the negotiations in relation to Ireland's accession to the EU clarified that the State would be required to implement EU legislation in respect to equal pay.[45] Thus, removing pay-related discriminations between men and women became part of the government agenda. This single-issue equality agenda was to be challenged simultaneously by the women's liberation movement from outside the formal institutions and by feminists within the political system. Their views were given weight and legitimacy when the Commission on the Status of Women supported the immediate introduction of equal pay.

If the establishment of the Commission on the Status of Women was the first response by government to women's demands for equality, the second instance of the political incorporation of a women's rights agenda came with the establishment of the Women's Representative Committee (WRC) in 1974 by the Minister for Labour, Michael O'Leary. The task of the WRC was to monitor the implementation of the recommendations of the Commission on the Status of Women. This committee found that the single-issue equal pay agenda continued to dominate policy-making on women's rights and criticized the government to that effect in its final report:

> While satisfactory progress continues to be made in eliminating discrimination in many of the areas referred to in the Report, particularly in employment and working conditions, the Committee is concerned about the extent and level of discrimination which still remain in other areas. This applies particularly to the taxation of married working women, educational opportunities for girls, family law, social welfare benefits and pensions and the absence of maternity protection legislation.[46]

The role of the WRC in monitoring the implementation of employment equality policies was superseded in 1977 with the creation of the Employment Equality Agency (EEA). In 1978, the government and the NWCI agreed that the NWCI would monitor progress on women's rights in areas other than employment with the assistance of state funding. Although the organization had received small government grants for specific projects from 1975, this decision made the funding of the organization more secure. Since 1979, the NWCI has received an annual grant from government and is recognized as the official representative of women's interests, with formal consultative status on women's rights policies.

By the end of the 1970s, feminist politics had found a niche in the political institutional framework. The NWCI and individual women's groups lobbied independently of one another, dealing directly with government departments for legislative changes. These activities were to influence the shape of the political system. The high profile given to equality issues by the women's movement sensitized political parties to the need to appeal to the growing politicization of women. From 1977 onwards, party campaign programmes began to incorporate policies with specific appeal to women.[47] In 1983, the equality agenda articulated by feminists in the early 1970s was incorporated into the institutional framework of government and parliament. Two initiatives attest to this development. A ministry for women's affairs and a parliamentary committee on women's rights were created. This signified a move by government from conceptualizing equality purely in employment terms to opening executive decision-making to a broader equal rights agenda. However, political commitment to equality was characterized by symbolism in the allocation of a marginal status to these institutional initiatives.

The Joint Committee on Women's Rights (JCWR), which has been reinstated after each election since 1983, commissions and publishes research on the status of women in social and political life. Although suffering from the same restrictions as other parliamentary committees in the Irish system,[48] the Women's Rights Committee has become an important parliamentary voice for the articulation of gender inequalities in public policies through its published reports. It has, however, no power to initiate legislation.

The Ministry for Women's Affairs established in 1982 had few resources, was a junior position spread across two departments – that of the Taoiseach and Justice – and did not have cabinet status. Within these constraints, the issue of women's affairs was at least given political legitimacy and the Minister, Nuala Fennell, succeeded in steering a number of pieces of equal rights legislation through parliament. To the disappointment of many women's groups, the Minister failed to carry through her promise to draft legislation providing for women's equal access with men to consumer services, finance, sport and recreational facilities. Equal access to cultural, financial and recreational facilities remained an unresolved political issue at the end of 1996.

The institutionalization of equal rights within the government ministries has had an uneven history. The Department of Women's Affairs was abolished in 1987 and its functions assigned to a junior minister in the Taoiseach's department. Progress on implementation of an equal rights agenda during the period of this government (which lasted from 1987 until 1989) came from the Minister for Justice rather than the Minister of State for Women's Affairs. A renewed political interest in women's issues was displayed in late 1990 when, as a result of pressure from the NCWI, the Taoiseach established a second Commission to provide an updated report to government on the position of women in Irish society. This renewed political interest in women sprang in part from developments within political parties, assisted by a new assertiveness on the part of women's units for inclusion in internal decision-making structures. Parties of the left, and the Labour Party in particular, underwent a period of modernization after 1987. However, possibly the strongest argument for including women in political decision-making came with the election of Mary Robinson, a candidate with liberal and feminist credentials, to the office of President of Ireland.[49] Her argument for a reappraisal of the concept of value to include a 're-evaluation of the role, the worth and the contribution of all women in society'[50] highlighted the feminist demand for the inclusion of women and women's issues in the world of politics. The desire to reassess the contribution of women to the creation of a more balanced society underpinned the report of the Second Commission on the Status of Women, which made 210 recommendations for public policy reform. In doing so, the Commission sought to encourage the permeation of society by women's values to complement men's values, the adoption of the creative methods of problem solving used by women with correspondingly less reliance on hierarchical and patriarchal methods and the evolution of a 'norm' in society from a male-only stereotype to a composite one which takes account of the entire population, both women and men.[51]

These recommendations include the assessment of the impact which legislative proposals would have on women ('gender-proofing') before being submitted to government, the adoption of 40 per cent gender quotas by parties to facilitate women's political representation, the application of the 40 per cent quota to appointments to state boards, and a proposal that the present system in operation for Seanad elections should be modified to facilitate the election of women to the second chamber.[52]

By the time the Second Commission had completed its investigations and published its report in January 1993, the political climate had once again swung in favour of incorporating an equality agenda into the institutional structures. A joint programme for government agreed between Fianna Fáil and the Labour Party contained significant commitments to the pursuit of equality between men and women, this time in the context of equality for all marginal groups.[53] A Department of Equality and Law Reform was established as a full ministry, although without a significant budget. To date, two progress reports on the implementation of the recommendations of the Second Commission on the Status of Women have been published by a monitoring committee drawn from the ranks of administrators in the government departments and representatives of the main sectional interest groups – employers, trade unions and farmers – along with representatives from the NWCI.[54]

DISCUSSION

The women's movement in Ireland needs to be seen as a diverse social phenomenon, consisting of an institutional, liberal element and a radical component. Although both forms of feminism co-existed uneasily on occasion, we can identify a considerable degree of consensus between both wings based on an issue-specific feminist agenda. Many activists participated in both sections of the movement. Differences between feminists, based as they were on tactical approaches and ideological orientation, did not lead to segregation within the women's movement. Their combined efforts to improve the status of women in Ireland has left its mark. Feminists and feminist demands became part of the mainstream political structure and agenda, with a significant presence in the 1990s.

Although the women's movement in Ireland has never attained the strength and continuity of the British feminist movement, the intellectual vibrancy of French feminism nor the passion of the Spanish movement, it remains, in an Irish context, an important agency for the politicization of women and the sensitization of political elites to women's rights. New forms of feminist activism and organization have emerged in the 1990s, co-existing with the more established patterns of feminist political and social engagement.

Prior to the emergence of Irish feminism, the public arena was dominated by patriarchal values and perspectives which viewed women's place as being in the home. The feminist movement began the process of carving out a space for women in the midst of this male dominant culture. In doing so, it encountered difficulties common to all feminist movements. It had its share of internal ideological conflicts and disagreements on strategies for engaging in the political process. Inevitably, the hegemony of conservative cultural, social, political and religious values which Irish feminism encountered influenced its manifestation. Attempts to form a radical autonomous movement similar to the British model failed. Given the limited cultural space available for the expression of feminist politics, the activities of mainstream women's groups and reform-minded feminists converged. They promoted a liberal-oriented campaign of women's rights in the 1970s followed by an institutionally focused agenda of difference in the 1980s.

The political agenda fashioned by feminists, first of equal rights and second of difference, led to a slow change in the attitudes of political parties towards women. It also led to a fundamental politicization and mobilization of women around various national and local issues. Due to the restricted political space afforded to women's groups and the centralization of political decision-making (both factors similar to the experience of women in Greek politics), the most effective strategy for the achievement of change was to organize around specific and clearly defined issues. This involved engagement with the established political system through a new set of power-focused interest groups.

In terms of the political institutionalization of a feminist agenda, the Irish experience parallels (inevitably to a lesser degree) that of France. In France, the success of a women's rights agenda within the political system remains tied to the fortunes of left-wing politics. In Ireland, the periods of greatest acceptance of women's agendas within the political structures are linked with the dominance of a centre–left coalition government. As we shall see, it is generally during the period of office of a cautiously reforming government that most gains in women's rights have been made. We will observe that in the process of lobbying for change, women's groups have become both more professionalized and institutionalized. We will also see that the extent to which feminist groups can influence change in specific policy areas is dependent on a complex interaction of a number of crucial factors. Let us now take the story of women's engagement with the Irish State a step further by examining the politics of employment equality.

NOTES

1. Vicky Randall, *Women and Politics: An International Perspective* (Basingstoke: Macmillan Education, 1987), p. 207.
2. Mary Jones, *These Obstreperous Lassies: A History of the Irish Women Workers Union* (Dublin: Gill & Macmillan, 1988).
3. Hilda Tweedy, *A Link in the Chain: The Story of the Irish Housewives Association, 1942–1992* (Dublin: Attic Press, 1992).
4. Linda Connolly, 'The women's movement in Ireland, 1970–1995: a social movement analysis', *Irish Journal of Feminist Studies*, 1(1), 51.
5. Council for the Status of Women, *Who Makes the Decisions?* (Dublin: CSW, 1985), p. 36.
6. Commission on the Status of Women, *Report to the Minister for Finance* (Dublin: Stationery Office, December 1972), p. 7 [Prl. 2760].
7. Commission on the Status of Women, pp. 253–4.
8. Commission on the Status of Women, p. 196.
9. Commission on the Status of Women, p. 197.
10. For a discussion of the origins and development of the National Women's Council, see Yvonne Fitzsimons, 'Women's interest representation in the Republic of Ireland: the Council for the Status of Women', *Irish Political Studies*, 6 (1991), 37–51.
11. Pauline Conroy Jackson, quoted in Ailbhe Smyth, 'A sadistic farce', in Ailbhe Smyth (ed.), *The Abortion Papers: Ireland* (Dublin: Attic Press, 1992), p. 23.
12. Pat Brennan, 'Women in revolt', *Magill*, 2(7) (1979), 34.
13. Ailbhe Smyth, 'The women's movement in the Republic of Ireland', in Ailbhe Smyth (ed.), *Irish Women's Studies Reader* (Dublin: Attic Press, 1993), pp. 245–69.
14. Herbert P. Kitschelt, 'Political opportunity structures and political protest: anti nuclear movements in four democracies', *British Journal of Political Science*, 16(1) (January 1986), 62.
15. Connolly, 'The women's movement in Ireland, 1970–1995', p. 55.
16. Maria Teresa Gallego Mendez, 'Women's political engagement in Spain', in Barbara Nelson and Najma Chowdhury (eds), *Women and Politics Worldwide* (New Haven: Yale University Press, 1994), p. 665.
17. *Irish Times*, 12–29 March and 1 April 1971.
18. Tom Hesketh, *The Second Partitioning of Ireland: The Abortion Referendum of 1983* (Dun Laoghaire: Brandsma Books, 1990); Pauline Conroy Jackson,

'Women's movement and abortion: the criminalization of Irish women', in Drude Dahlerup (ed.), *The New Women's Movement: Feminism and Political Power in Europe and the USA* (London: Sage, 1987), pp. 51–5; Yael Yishai, 'Public ideas and public policy: abortion politics in four democracies', *Comparative Politics*, **25**(2) (January 1993), 207–28.

19. Brennan, 'Women in revolt', p. 37

20. Smyth, 'The women's movement', p. 255.

21. Randall, *Women and Politics*, p. 235.

22. Elenore Eckmann Pisciotta, 'The strength and powerlessness of the new Italian women's movement: the case of abortion', in Dahlerup (ed.), *The New Women's Movement*, pp. 26–47.

23. Ann R. Cacoullos, 'Women confronting party politics in Greece', in Nelson and Chowdhury (eds), *Women and Politics Worldwide*, pp. 317–8.

24. Joyce Gelb and Marian Lief Palley, *Women and Public Policies* (Princeton, NJ: Princeton University Press, 1987); Elizabeth S. Clemens discusses the emergence of interest group feminism in the USA in the early 1900s in 'Organizational repertoires and institutional change: women's groups and the transformation of US politics, 1890–1920', *American Journal of Sociology*, **98**(4) (1993), 755–98.

25. *Irishwomen United*, 3 June 1976, p. 5.

26. *Banshee*, **1** (March 1976), p. 2.

27. Brennan, 'Women in revolt', p. 44.

28. *Banshee*, **1** (March 1976), p. 12.

29. Brennan, 'Women in revolt', p. 44.

30. Smyth, 'The women's movement', p. 262.

31. *Banshee*, **4** (August 1976), p. 12.

32. *WICCA*, **1** (April/August 1978), p. 6.

33. Brennan, 'Women in revolt', pp. 45–6.

34. Randall, *Women and Politics*, p. 233.

35. Cacoullos, 'Women confronting party politics in Greece', in Nelson and Chowdhury (eds), *Women and Politics Worldwide*, pp. 318–19.

36. Mendez, 'Women's political engagement in Spain', in Nelson and Chowdhury (eds), *Women and Politics Worldwide*, pp. 666–7.

37. Smyth, 'The women's movement', p. 265.

38. Jane Jensen and Mariette Sineau, 'The same or different? an unending dilemma for French women', in Nelson and Chowdhury (eds), *Women and Politics Worldwide*, p. 250.

39. Mendez, 'Women's political engagement in Spain', in Nelson and Chowdhury (eds), *Women and Politics Worldwide*, p. 669.

40. Joni Lovenduski and Vicky Randall, *Contemporary Feminist Politics: Women and Power in Britain* (Oxford: Oxford University Press, 1993), p. 94.

41. Dieter Rucht, 'The strategies and action repertoires of new movements', in Russell J. Dalton and Manfred Kuechler (eds), *Challenging the Political Order: New Social and Political Movements in Western Democracies* (Cambridge: Polity Press, 1990), p. 163.

42. Connolly, 'The women's movement in Ireland, 1970–1995', p. 69.

43. Carol Coulter, *The Hidden Tradition: Feminism, Women and Nationalism in Ireland* (Cork: Cork University Press, 1993), p. 48.

44. Yvonne Galligan, 'Party politics and gender in the Republic of Ireland', in Joni Lovenduski and Pippa Norris (eds), *Gender and Party Politics* (London: Sage, 1993), pp. 160–5.

45. Catherine Hoskyns, 'Give us equal pay and we'll open our own doors – a study of the impact in the Federal Republic of Germany and the Republic of Ireland of the European Community's policy on women's rights', in Mary Buckley and Malcolm Anderson (eds), *Women, Equality and Europe* (Basingstoke: Macmillan, 1988), pp. 33–55.

46. Women's Representative Committee, *Second Progress Report on the Implementation of the Recommendations in the Report of the Commission on the Status of Women* (Dublin: Stationery Office, December 1978), p. 2.

47. Galligan, 'Party politics and gender in the Republic of Ireland', pp. 157–60.

48. Audrey Arkins, 'Giving real power to the Oireachtas committee system', *Irish Times*, 26 June 1989, p. 2.

49. Alice Brown and Yvonne Galligan, 'Views from the periphery: changing the political agenda for women in the Republic of Ireland and Scotland', *West European Politics*, 16(2) (April 1993), 172–4.

50. President Mary Robinson, The Allen Lane Foundation Lecture, Trinity College, Dublin, 25 February 1992, quoted in Second Commission on the Status of Women, *Report to Government* (Dublin: Stationery Office, January 1993), p. 9 [Pl. 9557].

51. Second Commission on the Status of Women, *Report to Government*, p. 9.

52. Second Commission on the Status of Women, pp. 209–30.

53. Fianna Fáil and Labour, *Programme for a Partnership Government 1993–1997* (Dublin: Fianna Fáil and Labour, January 1993), pp. 34–8.

54. Ireland, *First Progress Report of the Monitoring Committee on the Implementation of the Recommendations of the Second Commission on the Status of Women* (Dublin: Stationery Office, May 1994) [Pn. 0798]; *Second Progress Report of the Monitoring Committee on the Implementation of the Recommendations of the Second Commission on the Status of Women* (Dublin: Stationery Office, March 1996) [Pn. 2489].

CHAPTER 4

EMPLOYMENT EQUALITY

The concept of equality for women in employment is not exclusive to the modern phase of women's mobilization. The demand for equal pay dates from the end of the nineteenth century in many countries, including Ireland. There was little progress in this area until the 1960s, when equal pay for both women's and men's work was gradually introduced in liberal democratic states. By then, the issue had become part of a broader employment-based equal rights agenda which included training, recruitment and promotion opportunities for women along with sexual harassment and childcare.

The obligation on national governments to comply with international labour agreements and EU directives is often seen as the catalyst for the successful passage of various forms of employment equality legislation. This is not the whole story. Davies, in a discussion on the introduction of equality legislation in Britain, argues that to attribute employment equality to EU imperatives alone 'would seem to involve an under-valuation of the indigenous pressures for legislation that had been building up'.[1] In Britain, equal pay and equal opportunities campaigns united feminists and trade unionists in a number of broad coalitions during the 1970s.[2] In Canada, a similarly close relationship between feminists and women in trade union organizations led to demands for a fundamental change in employment policies.[3] Kaplan captures the relationship between the external forces of the EU and the internal pressure from women quite neatly when she observes:

> That the broader European aims [to standardize labour market and employment practices and to avoid competition distortion caused by a lower-paid female labour force], debated at almost exclusively male summit meetings, happen to work in favour of women's interests in at least the one definable area of employment may be seen either as a predictable outcome or as a fortunate accident of history. The timing, however, was useful because the women's movements were able to inject new energy into these programmes and promote from below what most individual countries were not willing to tackle from above at state level.[4]

Thus, parallel to the European directives and the rule-making of the International Labour Organization (ILO), women's mobilization played a significant part in placing employment equality issues on national political agendas.

A second critical factor in the enactment of employment equality provisions is the existence of socialist or reformist parties in government. In the literature on women's rights, there are repeated references to the support given by socialist governments to issues such as equality at work. In Portugal, Spain and Italy, for instance, full constitutional and legislative provisions for women's equality were enacted by democratically elected socialist governments.[5] In France, significant equal opportunity legislation was enacted by a socialist government after extensive consultations with union and employer interests, women's associations and feminists.[6] Although Ireland has not had a single-party socialist government, the major legislative initiatives on employment equality were taken during the period of a reformist coalition Fine Gael–Labour government.

This chapter looks at the process leading to the enactment of equal pay and employment opportunity legislation in an Irish context. In doing so, the role of women's groups in this policy-making process is evaluated. As in Britain, the setting for the politics of employment equality lay within the established political structures; the participants were the traditional political actors of parties, unions and employers' organizations. A description of the manner in which organized women succeeded in gaining support and eventual acceptance for their demands in this policy area follows. In the course of seeking to influence decision-makers, organized women were working within a structured policy process with long-established relationships between the main interests. The value of a study of the politics of employment equality lies in what it reveals about the nature of the relationship between women and the established policy participants, between trade union women and the women's movement and between organized women and the European Union. In the conclusion, it is suggested that a convergence of pressure from the EU Commission and feminist activity from within the Irish political system breached the dominance of conservative thinking among the main interests – labour, employers and the State – on employment equality matters. Once the relevant legislation was passed, the return to corporatist relations in economic policy matters operated to exclude a feminist agenda. In other words, the political opportunity for developing a woman-centred agenda in employment matters became restricted once more as traditional relationships among the main interests were reasserted.

In looking at this policy area, the contribution of women to the political process which led to the enactment of two specific pieces of legislation is stressed. The first is the issue of equal pay and the passing of the Anti-

Discrimination (Pay) Act, 1974. The second is the development of an equal opportunities policy and the enactment of the Employment Equality Act, 1977. The chapter is divided into two main sections, the first of which deals with the politics of equal pay. Treatment of the issue is covered in two subsections: the first deals with the mobilization of women around equal pay, the second considers the policy debate on equal pay. In the second part of the chapter, an analysis is made of the politics of employment opportunity policies and the role of women in bringing it to the centre of the decision-making process. Finally, I summarize my views on the decision-making process in the employment arena and assess the opportunities for the development of a feminist agenda within a set of tightly knit corporatist economic relationships.

EQUAL PAY

Equal pay had its roots in the first wave of feminism in Ireland at the end of the nineteenth century, particularly among trade union women.[7] This development was not surprising, given the close connections between the British and Irish labour organizations at the time. But Irish feminists failed to have equal pay introduced. The issue continued to be raised at intervals by representatives of women workers and was subsequently sought by non-working women's groups such as the ICA and the IHA.[8] However, entrenched attitudes among politicians and trade unionists, who feared that equal pay would draw down male wages, prevented equal pay from becoming a political issue. The passage of anti-woman employment legislation in 1925 and 1935 did not go unnoticed in the circle of international labour. In fact, Ireland was placed on a blacklist in 1937 because of the enactment of these discriminatory laws.[9]

It was not until the 1960s that women workers began to press for equal pay in a sustained way. The initiative came from within the trade union movement. In 1959, the newly formed ICTU set up a women's ancillary group known as the Women's Advisory Committee (WAC) 'for the purpose of furthering trade union organisation among women workers generally, and of acting as an advisory committee to the Executive Council on economic, industrial and social matters of special concern to women workers'.[10] In time, the members of WAC were to play an important role in arguing for the implementation of equal pay. Their influence extended to contributing to shape the equal pay legislation, the Anti-Discrimination (Pay) Act, 1974. At the beginning of the 1960s, however, equal pay was an exotic demand to which a trade union movement, with a membership supportive of traditional attitudes towards women's roles, was largely opposed. The Women's Advisory Committee was not treated with any degree of seriousness by trade union leaders.[11] In its report to Congress in 1961, the Women's Advisory Committee[12] expressed frustration at the resistance of union members to the adoption of the equal pay issue. Two years later, the lack of interest shown by union representatives and government in implementing equal pay was again the subject of comment by the women's committee:

> The Committee is very anxious that in future negotiations the principle of equal pay for equal work will be borne in mind by all trade union representatives. It is noted that while the government has recognised the principle of equal pay for equal work, no real effort has been made to put it into practice in State or Semi-State concerns.[13]

Times were changing, however, and three separate influences came to bear on equal pay politics: an EU directive, trade union activity and feminist agitation. These factors intertwined to bring about the enactment of equal pay legislation. However, the path leading to this outcome was a long and arduous one. First, the preliminary negotiations between the Irish government and the European Commission from 1961 to 1963 on Ireland's entry to the European Union served to draw the attention of the national government to equal pay. Under Article 119 of the Treaty of Rome, all member states were obliged to introduce equal pay on joining the Community. The breakdown in these negotiations in 1963 meant that the issue of equal pay was also removed from the national political agenda. However, indigenous pressures within the Irish political system were to lead to equal pay becoming the focus of political attention. These factors initially involved activism on the part of women in the trade union movement. At a later stage, the activism of a broad coalition of women played a significant part in mounting pressure for the implementation of equal pay.

The mobilization of working women around equal pay and employment equality issues in Britain in the 1960s was closely observed by Irish women workers.[14] Irish women trade unionists were also very aware of the promise to introduce equal pay for equal work by the British Labour Party in its 1964 election manifesto. They noted, too, that a number of employees in public services were already in receipt of equal pay.[15] These developments encouraged Irish women to stand firm in their demand for equal pay. In the words of a prominent equal pay activist, Irish women trade unionists were to 'come together and say "thus far and no further, it is a matter of justice and we will hold the line on it"'.[16]

Holding the line happened sooner than most observers and participants expected. In 1963, a proposal to introduce a sex-differentiated pay scale for clerical officers in local authorities along with a wage increase emanated from the Department of the Environment (then the Department of Local Government). This was bitterly opposed by women clerical officers and women trade unionists. Ironically, the dispute centred around the removal of equal pay from a group of women workers who had hitherto enjoyed the same rate of pay as men in that administrative grade. The executive of the union concerned, the Civil and Public Services Union (CPSU), was anxious to accept the offer of increased wages even though it meant the introduction of a sex-differentiated pay scale. Women workers and trade unionists established a campaigning group, the Women in Local Authorities Group, with the sole aim of defeating the proposal. Group members lobbied all local councillors, local authority managers, trade unionists and politicians. Their campaign was high-profile, and covered the entire country. In June 1965, the local governing authority for the county of Donegal passed a resolution supporting the stand taken by the female clerical officers, and this decision was forwarded to the Minister for the Environment, Neil Blaney, for ratification, as the spending powers of local authorities in Ireland are controlled by central government. Blaney conceded the argument, allowing women clerical officers to retain equal pay with men employed in this position, but subsequently introduced a sex-differentiated scale for clerical officers recruited after 1964. The significance of this event in the history of equal pay is that it stands as the first occasion in which Irish women fought and won the right to retain equal pay.[17]

The stand taken by the women clerical officers with support from their feminist trade union representatives and the successful outcome of their campaign helped to convince the broader labour movement that equal pay was a legitimate employment issue. In 1964, the ICTU began to call in a more determined manner for legislation on the issue. This appeared to herald a considerable shift in the attitude of the labour movement. For the first time, equal pay became a point of debate at the ICTU annual conference: instead of the customary ritualistic reaffirmation of support for the principle of equal pay, the union delegates were asked to approve the establishment of an Equal Pay Committee.[18] The arguments put forward in favour of this initiative were of two kinds. One was that gender discrimination in matters of pay was in itself unjust; the other that gender-based wage differentials were a threat to male employment and promotion prospects. Both arguments were succinctly articulated by a delegate at the Congress meeting, G. Monks of the Workers Union of Ireland, in the following terms:

Women have realised for quite some time that they are being deprived of large sums of money because of their sex. It is only recently they have taken steps to rectify this injustice ... Men who argue against equal pay, on the grounds that women are inferior beings, do not seem to realise that lower wage rates for women are a threat to their own employment and also their prospects of promotion.[19]

By the following year, the argument for equal pay within the labour movement focused on the implications of gender-related wage differentials for male rates of pay.[20] The concern was to protect men's wages rather than to secure equal pay for women. Although the general principle of equal pay was supported by union representatives, there was little commitment to actively bring about its implementation. In effect, establishing the Equal Pay Committee seemed to satisfy the majority of trade unionists that progress was being made in this area. However, the real result of this initiative was a defusion of the issue. In reality, nothing was done to advance the case for the introduction of equal pay. Further-more, members of WAC were excluded from the Equal Pay Committee, a move intended to effectively silence the views of the strongest supporters of equal pay. In the event, the Equal Pay Committee did not become active until 1971, seven years after the resolution to set it up had been passed.

Between 1965 and 1966, the legitimacy of the arguments in support of equal pay suffered a number of set-backs. First, a decision of the Labour Court recommending lower rates of wage increases for women workers proved to be a major blow to the advocates of equal pay.[21] The result of this decision was to delay the introduction of equality in pay increases negotiated between employers and unions until the 1972 wage agreement.

Second, the government still held the view that 'equal pay should be brought about by the operation of free collective bargaining and not by government edicts'.[22] The government thereby ruled out ratifying Convention 100 on equal pay passed by the International Labour Organization which obligated national governments to enact equal pay legislation. The cautiously incremental approach to the introduction of equal pay by the Fianna Fáil government is neatly illustrated in an official report on Ireland prepared for the ILO:

it seems appropriate that the Government should continue to review its policy on equal pay for equal work in the public sector, where wages and salaries are controlled or can be directly influenced by Government policy. ... In reply to a question on equal pay for equal work in the Dáil on 22 July 1969, Mr Haughey, the Minister for Finance said 'The only thing I can say is that we have already started, in the recent pay agreement, applying the principle.' The official attitude in regard to the private sector is that if trade unions wish to ensure equal pay for men and women for work of equal value it is always open to them in negotiating wage agreements with employers to seek to implement this principle.[23]

There the matter rested for some time, but equal pay did not disappear quietly. By 1969, equal pay was debated in a range of forums, both at national and international level. The Federated Union of Employers (FUE) considered the implications of the introduction of equal pay, having had extensive consultations with employer interests in Britain. While accepting the principle of equal pay in the event of entry to the EU, the FUE voiced strong concerns regarding the costs of implementing equal pay to private employers.[24]

However, labour representatives were increasing their level of activity on the issue and women activists in a reinvigorated WAC were forceful in their demand for the introduction of equal pay. Individual unions, including the CPSU, began to lodge claims for equal pay. The intense debate in Britain on equality at work and the growing political support for this issue were widely referred to by union officials in the equal pay debate in Ireland. A major equal pay conference was organized by the international economic institute, the Organization for Economic Cooperation and Development (OECD), and attended by members of WAC.[25]

By 1969, informal links had been forged between women union activists and members of traditional women's organizations. Concerned with the inferior status of Irish women, these established women's organizations began to develop a more overtly political stance on women's issues. The absence of equal pay and the non-ratification by government of international conventions dealing with equality in employment was seen by them as a major obstacle to the pursuit of equality in other spheres of life.[26] Both WAC and the informal alliance of women's social organizations placed pressure on the government to set up a commission to review the status of women in Ireland. The media publicity surrounding this pressure led the authors of a government report to identify women's organizations as being the key advocates of equal pay at the time.[27]

Equal pay was once again on the government agenda with the resumption of negotiations on Ireland's entry to the EU. Furthermore, as a public service employer, the government was facing an equal pay claim brought by the CPSU on behalf of women employed in the lower clerical single-sex grades. Adding to this pressure was the recommendation of an influential government-commissioned report on the reorganization of the public services which advised that equal pay be introduced and pointed out that to continue to operate a sex-differentiated wage scale was contrary to EU law.

The matter of equal pay was thus being debated in a number of significant political and public arenas. In response to growing pressure for the introduction of equal pay, the government sought an urgent interim report on the application of equal pay in the public sector from the Commission on the Status of Women it had established in March 1970.[28] This represented a significant shift in the government's position on the issue. It accepted that the introduction of equal pay could not be the subject of negotiations between employer and labour interests alone, but also required a policy response from the State. This shift in position was confirmed when the outcome of centralized negotiations on pay became known at the end of 1970. For the first time, the need to attend to the issue of equal pay was addressed in the national agreement on wage increases between the State, employer and labour interests.[29] However, in this context, the State played the role of public service employer and did not define its role in the broader context of an institution with public policy-making duties.

The terms of reference set for the Commission on the Status of Women focused the attention of both employer and union interests on equal pay. The Equal Pay Committee of the ICTU submitted a report to the Commission which was substantially influenced by WAC. Congress sought the immediate introduction of equal pay and the adoption of the principle of equal pay for work of equal value as recommended by the ILO. The FUE, on the other hand, pressured the government to emulate the British example and sought a seven year phasing-in period for equal pay. Employer representatives also desired an application of the equal pay for equal work principle in the legislation. At this point, the main economic interest groups formally registered their agreement to the introduction of equal pay but differed on policy details and on the range of its application.

The Commission on the Status of Women, after extensive consultations with employer and labour interests and with women's groups, recommended the enactment of legislation providing for the introduction of equal pay for work of equal value. It also recommended that disputes over the application of the legislation be referred to the industrial tribunal, the Labour Court.[30] In the meantime, the newly formed women's liberation movement added its voice to that of other groups demanding equal pay.[31] The policy remained within the confines of the corporatist structures and was shaped by the negotiating relationship between the State, employers and union interests.

While the recommendation of the Commission on the Status of Women was accepted by the government, it did not result in legislation for equal pay. Instead, the government instructed the social partners – labour and employer interests – to provide for equal pay through the national wage bargaining mechanisms. The 1972 National Wage Agreement incorporated many of the recommendations on equal pay laid down in the report of the Commission on the Status of Women. Notably, the agreement provided for a phased implementation of equal pay, accepted the circumstances in which equal pay claims could be made, and finally adopted the recommendation on arbitration by the Labour Court.[32] However, the principle of equal pay for work of equal value was rejected in favour of the more restricted application of equal pay for equal work.

It took thirteen years of working within corporatist economic decision-making structures to bring the equal pay issue from the margins and into the mainstream of public policy debate. It is, of course, clear that equal pay would have been a policy matter in any event, given the need to comply with EU regulations. None the less, WAC played a key part in creating and sustaining the internal debate on equal pay within the labour movement. As the policy discussion expanded beyond internal trade union politics, other forces came into play which added to the pressure on government to introduce equal pay. Once the political decision was taken to introduce equal pay, the policy again returned to the more defined and less permeable arena of economic interests, where the collective bargaining structures determined priorities other than those of equal rights at work. It is from within these structures that organized women mounted the second phase of the equal pay campaign which had as its goal the enactment and implementation of equal pay legislation.

THE POLICY DEBATE

In practice, the 1972 National Wage Agreement provided for the full introduction of equal pay. WAC activists were not content with this measure and continued to press from within the trade union movement for legislation on equal pay. However, legislation was not a priority of the centrist Fianna Fáil government, which, as we have seen, preferred to introduce equal pay by means of a negotiated agreement rather than a binding law.[33] With the change of government in 1973 came the prospect of a very different approach to the issue of the implementation of equal pay. Instead of the incremental approach favoured by the participants of the tripartite pay talks of 1972, the new Fine Gael–Labour coalition government was committed to legislating for equal pay in fulfilment of an election promise.

This commitment was taken up by the Minister for Labour, Michael O'Leary on entering office, in spite of opposition from employer interests who sought a continuation of the process of free bargaining.[34] The policy debate now focused on draft legislation, the Anti-Discrimination (Pay) Bill of 1974 which, according to the Minister, was

> the first of a series of anti-discrimination measures which I propose to bring before the Oireachtas as soon as possible so as to give the individual citizen, whether man or woman, a fair contract of employment with statutory backing. The Bill provides that a woman will have a right to the same pay as a man who is employed by the same employer.[35]

It quickly became apparent that the proposed legislation raised a number of contentious issues. The executive of the ICTU criticized the draft bill on the grounds that it was insufficiently far-reaching.[36] Prompted by WAC, ICTU negotiators also sought the inclusion of the principle of equal pay for work of equal value. WAC members lobbied the Minister on changes which they wished to see incorporated in the legislation, chief among them being a broadening of the application of equal pay from one of 'like work' to one of 'equal value'.[37] This definition, they pointed out, was in line with the recommendation of the Commission on the Status of Women and in keeping with the guidelines of the ILO. On the other side, employer representatives sought a derogation from the implementation date of 31 December 1975. Their basic argument centred around the cost of introducing equal pay for already hard-pressed private sector companies, many of whom were undergoing difficulties in the economic recession.[38] The Minister accepted the points advanced in support of a broadening of the application of equal pay to incorporate work of equal value[39] and the measure was passed by both houses of the Oireachtas by the end of June 1974.[40] It was scheduled to come into effect on 31 December 1975, as determined by EU regulations.

The problem of meeting the deadline was again raised with the Minister by employers. Some of the craft unions, and in particular the Irish Shoe and Leather Workers' Union, displayed a marked lack of enthusiasm for the new legislation and there were fears that it would lead to a considerable loss of male jobs. Both sides had been given a loophole by the Minister. Should employer and union representatives agree to bring a joint case seeking a deferral from the equal pay legislation to the Labour Court, and should the Labour Court find in their favour, they would not be obliged to introduce equal pay. This unlikely scenario came to pass. Employer interests and representatives of the craft unions combined to make a case to the Labour Court against the implementation of equal pay on the grounds that it would entail the loss of male jobs. The Labour Court found in their favour. The finding in the test case went against the provisions of the equal pay legislation. A rethink of the implementation of equal pay was also under way within the government. There was concern in government circles that the costs of introducing equal pay in the public sector would have significant repercussions on the national finances. Given the combination of the above pressures, the government decided to postpone implementation of the equal pay legislation,[41] a decision greeted with dismay by women trade unionists, the women's movement and women political activists. It mobilized women to organize in a broad coalition under the banner of 'Save the Equal Pay Act', a coalition made up of leading trade union women, women from the single-issue pressure groups and well-known individual women.[42]

The women's campaign which mobilized as a result of the threat of derogation had a similar composition and strategy to that of the British equal pay campaign, although the catalyst for its formation was slightly different. As with the British Equal Pay campaign committee, the Irish campaign group concentrated its energies on lobbying parliamentarians and government for the introduction of equal pay. In both cases, it was a spontaneous reaction against government tardiness at introducing what was seen by organized women as a basic right. In both instances, pressure from a broad feminist coalition with support from like-minded parliamentarians added to the controversy.

Links were made between trade union women and the women's movement, IU. Although the relationship between these two was delicately balanced, they combined to mount a very public – if orthodox – campaign. Petitions, political lobbying, demonstrations, securing the public support of trade unions and extensive use of the media were the main strategies used by the activists in the equal pay campaign. A public meeting held in Dublin to protest against the delay in the introduction of equal pay attracted an attendance of over 1,000 people. The audience was addressed by prominent trade union women such as Evelyn Owens and Sylvia Meehan, women politicians such as Eileen Desmond of the Labour Party and members of the Save the Equal Pay Committee. Traditional women's organizations voiced their concerns with the delay in implementing the legislation. Strong internal party pressure was brought to bear on the five Labour government ministers to change the government decision. In addition, the government women's policy agency, the Women's Representative Committee (WRC), lobbied cabinet members to introduce equal pay without further delay.

The broadly based coalition of women's groups had another channel through which they could voice their grievance at the proposed delay – the Commission of the EU. Representatives of the NWCI went to Strasbourg to lobby the Commissioner for Social Affairs, Patrick Hillery on this issue. The Commissioner, aware of the difficulties in implementing the legislation, sent a study group to Ireland to assess the case for derogation put forward by the Irish government. The group met all interested parties including a determined and united women's lobby opposed to any further delay in the granting of equal pay. The report of the study group recommended a refusal of the derogation requested by the Irish government. The Commissioner followed this advice and directed the government to give immediate effect to the equal pay legislation.[43] While the authority of the EU finally brought about the implementation of the Anti-Discrimination (Pay) Act of 1975, the determination of campaigning women kept the issue sufficiently alive and controversial to provoke the intervention of the Commission.[44] The equal pay campaign was a significant episode in the mobilization and politicization of Irish women. To ignore this aspect of the case is to interpret the introduction of equal pay as merely a bureaucratic error on the part of the Irish govenment set right by the EU. In practice, the equal pay campaign was long and complex, lasting over a decade. It involved women in sustaining a campaign for pay reform within the trade union movement initially and later in the wider national political arena. In the end, the intervention of the EU forced the hand of the Irish government. Yet, without the sustained commitment of Irish women activists, equal pay would never have become a political issue.

EMPLOYMENT EQUALITY

Although the rumblings on equal pay were only finally put to rest in 1976, the legislative agenda on employment equality quickly gathered a momentum of its own. The obvious political impetus for the enactment of the second piece of equality legislation, the Employment Equality Act of 1977, came once again from the need for the national parliament to give effect to an EU directive. However, these issues had been on the agenda of women trade union activists for some time, and represented a broadening of the equal pay agenda to include equal opportunity in employment. In 1973, WAC defined equal opportunity as including equal access to training and education in employment and the banning of sex discrimination in advertising.[45] The Minister for Labour had signalled his intention to legislate in this area in April 1974, when he told a WAC seminar on equal pay that he intended to tackle the question of equal opportunity in employment.[46] In contrast with the earlier ambivalent position taken by the ICTU on equal pay, the leadership of the organization was firmly in favour of the proposed employment equality legislation. The introduction of the Anti-Discrimination (Employment) Bill in parliament on 17 October 1975 (later renamed the Employment Equality Bill, 1977) was welcomed by most observers. Feminists, however, accused O'Leary of political opportunism in seeking to enhance his political image with women at the close of International Women's Year.[47]

The measure sought to prohibit gender-based discrimination in a range of areas relating to work, promotion and training opportunities.[48] The Minister outlined the objectives of the Bill in the following terms:

> In the area of women's rights, the Anti Discrimination (Pay) Act, 1974 will shortly be complemented by the Anti Discrimination (Employment) Bill, 1975. The major objective of this Bill is to eliminate certain practices which impede the progress of women and tend to restrict them to the less skilled and poorly paid jobs. It will make it unlawful to discriminate on grounds of sex or marriage as regards access to employment, promotion and working conditions. It is proposed to establish an agency which will investigate practices that appear to be discriminatory. If such practices are found to be unlawful, the agency will use its enforcement powers to eliminate them. The agency will launch a comprehensive programme of information about rights under the anti-discrimination legislation and any other matters affecting the status of women.[49]

The legislation was modelled on British, Northern Ireland and American statutes and the monitoring provisions in particular were drawn from observations on the experience of monitoring bodies in these countries. In each case, an independent monitoring agency was set up with the function of enforcing and assessing the legislation. In Britain, this was the Equal Opportunities Commission; in Northern Ireland it was the Northern Ireland Equal Opportunities Commission and in the United States it was the Employment Equality Opportunities Commission.[50] Commenting on the inclusion of an equality agency, Norah O'Neill, who participated in the preparation of the legislation, observed that

> There was an agency in Britain, which was the model to go on, and there was an agency in Northern Ireland and an agency in the USA and there may have been one in Australia at the time. The Minister held out for the setting up of an independent agency.[51]

WAC members made representations to the Minister for Labour on the composition of the agency and on the resources to be allocated to the monitoring body.[52] O'Leary was responsive to their suggestions. During the course of discussion on the establishment of a monitoring agency in parliament, he praised the role of women's groups in promoting the issue of employment equality:

> My feeling about this figure of 11 people on the agency governing body is that we require representation, obviously, from trade unions, employers' interests, and women's organisations. If we look at the number of women's organisations in the country it is important that some places be set aside for them because it is their campaign over the years that has contributed largely to the fact that this house is legislating in this area today... I am anxious to encompass in the membership of the agency as wide a selection of the principal women's organizations as possible.[53]

In effect, the traditional tripartite economic policy-making structure was expanded to include representatives of women's interests. In this way, advocacy of a feminist perspective on employment matters was integrated into a section of the employment policy structures.

There was resistance from within the bureaucracy to the setting up of an independent monitoring agency, with fears that the work of the civil service would be usurped by a feminist organization. Sylvia Meehan, former chief executive of the EEA, recalled the sources of opposition to the agency at the time of the passage of the legislation:

> It had been set up with strong resistance from the public service, that is from the Departments of Finance and Public Service, and it's significant that the meeting of the cabinet to endorse the setting up of the agency took place after the defeat of the coalition government, but before it went out of office. I'm also told that it came before the cabinet in the absence of the Minister for Finance, Ritchie Ryan, who at that time was attending a meeting of the World Bank in New York. Michael O'Leary had always pressed very much for the setting up of the agency and so did the Irish Transport and General Workers' Union at that time, and that view prevailed.[54]

The bill had passed through all parliamentary stages by 18 May 1977, the evening before the Fine Gael–Labour government went out of office. The speed of its passage was facilitated by the chairperson of the Seanad, Evelyn Owens, who had a long history of involvement in the equal pay campaign. The political priority given to this legislation was remarked upon by the opposition parliamentarian, Máire Geoghegan-Quinn, who also credited women's organizations with effective lobbying on employment equality.[55]

In contrast to the politics of equal pay, the passage of this legislation was not marked by a significant level of controversy, either in the public arena or within the economic policy network. Members of WAC worked within the established political structures, this time with little resistance to the case being presented for equal opportunity. A more militant feminist grouping within the labour movement, the Trade Union Women's Forum (established in 1975), also strongly advocated the establishment of an equality monitoring body.

This policy initiative did not require a broad feminist mobilization to secure the enactment of equal opportunity provisions, since women lobbying from within the existing interest structures found their demands included in the legislative framework. This suggests that once the equal pay issue had been resolved, the policy arena was sensitive to the inclusion of the employment equality agenda. Thus one can say that the enactment of the equal pay policy cleared the way for the 1977 Employment Equality Act. This is a pattern which, as Lovenduski has noted, is common to many liberal democratic states:

> An important objective in most states, therefore, has been equal opportunity in employment, at first most often found in the simply expressed goal of equal pay. As experience of the difficulties of achieving equal pay for men and women has been gained, more complex anti-discrimination measures have been introduced. These have been conceptualized in a number of ways, ranging from legislation designed to remove barriers to particular kinds of employment, to more controversial policies, including affirmative action.[56]

It must be remembered, though, that the employment equality measures did not pose the same concerns for employers as equal pay. The financial costs implicit in the equal pay legislation were not a factor in the employment equality issue. Furthermore, European law required national governments to put employment equality statutes in place. The 1977 Employment Equality Act was designed to comply with this directive.

Reforming these core statutes gained political attention in the 1990s. In 1990, the leader of the small Labour Party, Dick Spring, moved an Equal Status Bill while in opposition to the Fianna Fáil–Progressive Democrat coalition government. The aim of this bill was 'to create a climate of understanding and mutual respect in which all are recognised as equal in dignity and in rights'.[57] Although this measure was intended to apply to a range of groups discriminated against in public policy, there was a strong focus on the unequal status of women in the course of the debate.[58] This Bill, although defeated by the government's parliamentary majority, became part of the Labour Party's election manifesto in the subsequent general election. Equality and women's rights became part of the agreement for government negotiated between Fianna Fáil and the Labour Party after the 1992 general election.[59]

Political attention to the issue of gender equality was also reflected in a national agreement between the government, employer and union interests on social and economic issues (the Programme for Economic and Social Progress (PESP)) in 1991. This agreement included a commitment to pursue equal opportunity initiatives in the public and private sectors.[60] The relevant clauses referred to the initiatives taken in this area with the assistance of the EEA. The intention to reform equality legislation was part of the negotiated agreement succeeding PESP, the Programme for Competitiveness and Work (PCW). Thus, for the social partners, the issue of equality at work was once again a matter for inclusion in national agreements. The Report of the Second Commission on the Status of Women added to the growing pressure for change in this area. The Report recommended a series of amendments to the equality legislation, a more systematic and integrated implementation of equal opportunities initiatives, and a stronger role for the EEA in supporting, encouraging and monitoring equal opportunities policies.[61]

The political commitment to equality survived the collapse of the Fianna Fáil–Labour coalition and the installation of a new three-party coalition government in January 1995. In July 1996, the Minister for Equality and Law Reform, Mervyn Taylor, published the long-promised Employment Equality Bill which focused on updating and extending the existing law on equality at work. The 1996 Bill made provision for nine discriminatory grounds in employment: gender, marital status, family status, sexual orientation, religious belief, age, disability, race and membership of the travelling community. The scope of the previous employment equality code was enlarged to include sexual harassment and to provide for positive action measures to promote equal opportunities for women in employment, promotion and vocational training. The new measures entailed a reorganization of the EEA and an extension of its remit. While the content of the Bill was influenced by EU judgements and practices over a twenty-year period, the Minister recognized the input of the social partners, the EEA and the Commission on the Status of Women, in his statement on the publication of the Bill.[62] The measure has proved to be a controversial one, redefining the scope for religious control in schools, hospitals and other institutions where church authorities act as employers. It was referred to the Supreme Court in April 1997 by President Mary Robinson prior to being signed into law. In May 1997 the Supreme Court found the Bill to be unconstitutional and the measure then fell. Work on a revised Bill is ongoing at the time of writing.

DISCUSSION

The elimination of workplace discrimination against women has had a long history of active involvement on the part of women within the economic interest structures. The demand for equal pay mobilized women in trade unions and in the broader feminist movement to engage in a period of intensive lobbying and campaigning during the 1970s. The establishment of a formal independent structure, the EEA, which included representatives of women's interests, was an acknowledgement by political decision-makers of the part played by organized women in bringing discrimination in employment to the forefront of the political agenda. The EEA has since become the voice of working women, lobbying for the removal of discrimination and promoting positive action programmes within individual employments, while monitoring and enforcing the equality legislation.

The development of a gender-sensitive employment equality policy from exotic demand at the 1960 Annual Conference of the ICTU to legislative enactment was not easy. It took some considerable time and a sustained level of campaigning on the part of women before the major economic interests were willing to accept legislation for equal pay. At critical points in the campaign for equal rights at work, the onus on government to implement EU directives on employment equality provided a significant political impetus to indigenous pressures. Thus the enactment of equality legislation in 1974 and 1977 served to meet women's demands, satisfy EU rules and legitimize the concept of equality at work. For a short period of time, political forces combined to open the tightly controlled corporatist economic interest structure, dominated by traditional and patriarchal values, to the more liberal demands for equal rights. This slight move in the policy agenda was assisted by the mildly reformist ideology of the government in power between 1973 and 1977.

It is clear, though, that while organized women might have moved from the margins to the mainstream of economic policy-making, it was not to the centre of the employer, union and government relationship. Rather, it was to the periphery of the economic interest group arena. The low priority accorded by policy-makers to reforming the equality laws subsequent to 1980 suggests that once the issue had been dealt with in the legislation of 1974 and 1977, the problem was, in political terms, solved. All that remained to be done was to oversee the implementation of the legislation while the social partners considered male unemployment and other issues of political urgency.

Demands for equal rights do not have an end, and, not surprisingly, the employment equality agenda did not remain static. If the 1970s is considered to be a peak period for the articulation and politicization of employment equality demands, the 1980s can be seen as a valley period for such issues. The 1990s ushered in a second phase in the employment equality agenda, when the newly invigorated Labour Party rediscovered the liberal agenda and championed the cause of women's rights. Employer, union and government interests became more creative in their development of national agreements, with the issue of equal opportunities again a part of the negotiated plans between the corporate partners. Socio-political forces raised the question of the status of women and successive reforming governments indicated a commitment to developing work-based equality policies. Since 1993, governments have sustained the reform process, culminating in the framing of the Employment Equality Bill of 1996, suggesting once again a window of opportunity for the equality agenda. But, if the lessons of the past are to be learned, the openings for change in the corporatist-style economic interest structure seldom last for long.

We can identify two factors as being critical in shaping the politics of employment equality. The first is the structure of interest representation in the policy sector; the second is the willingness or unwillingness of government to support new initiatives. As we have seen, the politics of employment equality have taken place within the arena of established political actors with a highly structured relationship. The closed system of interest intermediation, closely resembling corporatist relations, began in the 1950s with negotiations between employer, union and government on price and wage fixing, and more generally on economic and social planning.[63] The social contracts negotiated between these groups did not include provision for equal pay, as it did not form part of the wage bargaining process in the 1950s. When trade union women began to agitate for equal pay in the 1960s, they faced a pre-structured policy agenda and an established interest structure. Not surprisingly, the tripartite economic interest relations were slow to respond to the equal pay demand.

Members of WAC used the trade union network as a channel of access to the policy sector. However, whole-hearted commitment to the demand from labour representatives was difficult to win. The ambivalent attitude of the trade union movement to equal pay was displayed in two ways, the first being the rationale used for supporting the equal pay demand. It was not fashioned as a matter of equal rights for women workers or as a principle of justice but was instead given a negative construction in the context of male wages. The continuance of gender-based wage differentials was seen as threatening the wages and the employment prospects of men. Not all unions accepted even this negative rationale for supporting equal pay: some argued the opposite, seeing the introduction of equal pay as causing increased male unemployment. This argument was presented by unions to the Minister for Labour as a reason for deferring the introduction of equal pay, and further evidence of trade union reservations about the introduction of equal pay can be found in the low priority given to the Equal Pay Committee. Only when equal pay was part of the negotiating agenda between government and social partners did the Equal Pay Committee begin to function.

Trade union women faced considerable obstacles to their equal pay demand within the trade union movement, yet the labour movement representatives offered the most likely route of access to the economic policy-making arena. Employer interests, as we have seen, were strongly opposed to the introduction of equal pay and the government chose to allow the matter to be bargained between the employer and union interests, although it was aware that EU rules would eventually require some action on its part. The politics of equal pay demonstrates the power of national economic interests to exclude equality issues from their agenda.

A second factor, that of government support for new policies and its capacity to implement them, can also be seen as playing a critical role in the case of economic equality. The history of the equal pay debate illustrates a government with little commitment to policy development on this issue. The buildup of indigenous pressure for the implementation of equal pay was resisted by the government as it sought to accommodate the wishes of the social partners. It required an intervention by the EU Social Affairs Commissioner to bring about the implementation of the equal pay legislation. This pattern is also evident in subsequent development of the employment equality agenda. It is clear that a government will not take any initiatives in this area without first reaching a general consensus on the principle of policy reform within the tripartite economic interest structure. In sum this case study shows us how the combined factors of a closed policy sector and an ambivalent or uninterested government can combine to exclude feminist demands. For a complete contrast in the political management of women's rights, I now turn to a study of family law reform.

NOTES

1. P. L. Davies, 'European Community legislation, UK legislative policy and industrial relations', in Christopher McCrudden (ed.), *Women, Employment and European Equality Law* (London: Eclipse, 1987), p. 25.

2. Joni Lovenduski, *Women and European Politics: Contemporary Feminism and Public Policy* (Brighton: Wheatsheaf, 1986), pp. 73–4, 77.

3. Sylvia Bashevkin, 'Building a political voice: women's participation and policy influence in Canada', in Barbara J. Nelson and Najma Chowdhury (eds), *Women and Politics Worldwide* (New Haven: Yale University Press, 1994), pp. 153–4.

4. Gisela Kaplan, *Contemporary Western European Feminism* (London: Allen & Unwin, 1992), pp. 27–8.

5. Kaplan, *Contemporary Western European Feminism*, p. 185.

6. Dorothy McBride Stetson, *Women's Rights in France* (New York: Greenwood Press, 1986), pp. 142–51.

7. Rosemary Cullen Owens, *Smashing Times: A History of the Irish Women's Suffrage Movement 1889–1922*, (Dublin: Attic Press, 1984), pp. 76–7, 82; Mary Jones, *These Obstreperous Lassies: A History of the Irish Women Workers Union* (Dublin: Gill & Macmillan, 1988).

8. Hilda Tweedy, *A Link in the Chain: The Story of the Irish Housewives Association 1942–1992* ((Dublin: Attic Press, 1992), p. 28.

9. Mary Clancy, 'Aspects of women's contribution to the Oireachtas debate in the Irish Free State, 1922–1937', in Maria Luddy and Cliona Murphy (eds), *Women Surviving: Studies in Irish Women's History in the 19th and 20th Centuries* (Dublin: Poolbeg Press, 1990), pp. 217–21.

10. Irish Congress of Trade Unions, *First Annual Report* (Dublin: ICTU, 1959), p. 107.

11. Interview with Evelyn Owens, former trade unionist and member of WAC, 28 August 1996.

12. Irish Congress of Trade Unions, *Third Annual Report* (1961), p. 49.

13. Irish Congress of Trade Unions, *Fifth Annual Report* (1963), p. 64.

14. Joni Lovenduski and Vicky Randall, *Contemporary Feminist Politics: Women and Power in Britain* (Oxford: Oxford University Press, 1993), pp. 179–82.

15. Irish Congress of Trade Unions, *Third Annual Report*, p. 49.

16. Interview with Sylvia Meehan, former Chief Executive of the Employment Equality Agency and trade union activist, 22 June 1992.

17. Interview with Evelyn Owens.

18. Irish Congress of Trade Unions, *Sixth Annual Report* (1964), p. 250.

19. Irish Congress of Trade Unions, *Sixth Annual Report*, p. 254.

20. Irish Congress of Trade Unions, *Seventh Annual Report* (1965), p. 282.

21. Irish Congress of Trade Unions, *Eighth Annual Report* (1966), pp. 236–7.

22. Irish Congress of Trade Unions, *Eighth Annual Report*, p. 237.

23. Brian Hillery and Patrick Lynch, *Ireland in the International Labour Organization* (Dublin: Department of Labour, 1969), p. 19.

24. Federated Union of Employers, *Women in Employment. Implications for Equal Pay* (Dublin: FUE, 1969).

25. Irish Congress of Trade Unions, *Eleventh Annual Report* (1969), p. 216.

26. Hilda Tweedy, *A Link in the Chain*, pp. 37–40.

27. Hillery and Lynch, *Ireland in the ILO*, p. 18.

28. Commission on the Status of Women, *Report to the Minister for Finance* (Dublin: Stationery Office, December 1972), p. 8 [Prl. 2760].

29. Employer, Labour Conference, *National Agreement* (Dublin: Employer, Labour Conference, 21 December 1970), p. 5 [So. 463].
30. Commission on the Status of Women, *Report*, pp. 51–4.
31. Pat Brennan, 'Women in revolt', *Magill*, 2(7) (April 1979), 36.
32. Employer, Labour Conference, *National Agreement* (Dublin: Employer, Labour Conference, 31 July 1972), pp. 7–9.
33. *Dáil Debates*, Vol. 260, col. 576, 19 April 1972.
34. Federated Union of Employers, *Annual Report 1974* (Dublin: FUE, 1974), p. 5.
35. *Dáil Debates*, Vol. 270, col. 2032, 5 March 1974.
36. *Irish Independent*, 26 March 1974, p. 9.
37. *Irish Times*, 22 April 1974, p. 9.
38. John Dunne, 'The present position in Ireland', paper presented to a Federated Union of Employers conference on equal pay, January 1975, p. 12.
39. *Dáil Debates*, Vol. 272, col. 1592, 15 May 1974.
40. *Dáil Debates*, Vol. 273, col. 1465, 25 June 1974.
41. *Dáil Debates*, Vol. 286, col. 2021, 18 December 1975; Vol. 287, cols 1645–6, 11 February 1976.
42. Brennan, 'Women in revolt', p. 44.
43. Catherine Hoskyns, 'Give us equal pay and we'll open our own doors – a study of the impact in the Federal Republic of Germany and the Republic of Ireland of the European Community's policy on women's rights', in Mary Buckley and Malcolm Anderson (eds), *Women, Equality and Europe* (Basingstoke: Macmillan, 1988), p. 48. This was confirmed in an interview conducted on 18 March 1992 with a former civil servant in the Department of Labour, Norah O'Neill, who assisted in preparing the legislation and the amendment.
44. *Dáil Debates*, Vol. 290, col. 687, 5 May 1976.
45. Irish Congress of Trade Unions, *Fourteenth Annual Report* (1973), pp. 103, 410–20, 458.
46. *Irish Times*, 22 April 1974, p. 9.
47. Irish Congress of Trade Unions, *Seventeenth Annual Report* (1976), p. 191.
48. Employment Equality Act, 1977, section 2, p. 13.
49. *Dáil Debates*, Vol. 291, col. 152, 26 May 1976.
50. Elizabeth Meehan, 'Equal opportunity policies: some implications for women of contrasts between enforcement bodies in Britain and the USA', in Jane Lewis (ed.), *Women's Welfare, Women's Rights* (London: Croom Helm, 1983).
51. Norah O'Neill, 18 March 1992.
52. Irish Congress of Trade Unions, *Eighteenth Annual Report* (1977), p. 135.
53. *Dáil Debates*, Vol. 297, col. 1135, 9 March 1977.
54. Interview with Sylvia Meehan, 22 June 1992.
55. *Dáil Debates*, Vol. 299, col. 1056, 18 May 1977.
56. Lovenduski, *Women and European Politics*, p. 291.
57. *Dáil Debates*, Vol. 417, col. 324, 10 March 1992.

58. See, for instance, the speech by Nuala Fennell, *Dáil Debates*, Vol. 417, cols 1375–83, 10 March 1992, when she castigated the government for its lack of action on childcare provision, inadequate family planning service, low pay for women workers and the legal prohibition on non-working wives having a share in the family home.

59. Fianna Fáil and Labour, 'A programme for partnership government', in Michael Gallagher and Michael Laver (eds), *How Ireland Voted 1992* (Dublin and Limerick: Folens and PSAI Press, 1993), pp. 174–93.

60. Ireland, *Programme for Economic and Social Progress* (Dublin: Stationery Office, January 1991), para 100–2.

61. Second Commission on the Status of Women, *Report to Government* (Dublin: Stationery Office, January 1993), pp. 106–17 [Pl. 9557].

62. Press statement issued by the office of Mervyn Taylor, TD, Minister for Equality and Law Reform, 3 July 1996, pp. 2, 4.

63. Basil Chubb, *The Government and Politics of Ireland*, 3rd edition (London: Longman, 1993), p. 126.

CHAPTER 5

FAMILY LAW REFORM

'An essential part of feminism is the belief that the status of women in the family determines their status in all other areas of life.'[1] In Ireland, feminists were only too well aware of the lowly standing of women in the family. In the 1970s, they, like their counterparts in Southern European countries, politicized this issue through campaigns for family law reform. In Italy, women's equality in marriage was recognized in the family law reform bills introduced in 1975. In Portugal,[2] the adoption of a new constitution in 1976 marked a milestone in women's rights, with women being declared equal to men in all aspects of life, including marriage and the family. Similarly, in Spain, the new 1978 constitution established that discrimination within marriage was prohibited, and laws giving effect to the concept of equality between the sexes were enacted in 1981.[3] In Greece, family law was extensively overhauled between 1976 and 1982, with the abolition of the dowry system, provision for joint ownership of assets acquired during marriage and the recognition of the equal rights of both parents in respect to their children. As in the Irish case, the core question of common ownership of property within marriage was not resolved.[4]

In the case of Austria and France, much of the initiative for change in family policies came from the priorities pursued by reforming governments. Family law was extensively overhauled in Austria between 1975 and 1983. This included giving married women the right to work outside the home, providing for equality between spouses and providing for joint ownership of all family property and assets. Between 1965 and 1975, significant family law reforms were enacted in France as the old Napoleonic code was dismantled. In 1970, for instance, changes in family law stipulated that parental duties and responsibilities were to be equally divided between husband and wife. Other reforms led to the abolition of adultery as a crime and changes in the domicile law.

In contrast, reform of family law was not highlighted by modern feminists in Britain, the United States or in Scandinavian countries. The issue had been addressed in an earlier phase of feminism, when, from the end of the nineteenth century, married women in these countries were progressively granted ownership rights to their property and their earnings. These amendments to family law were in part due to the development of a widespread suffrage movement and in part to the product of a climate of political liberalism which existed in these countries at the time.[5]

This chapter examines the circumstances in which family law reform became a significant issue for Irish feminists. Indeed, during the 1970s and 1980s, the term 'family law' became closely identified in the minds of the public and of politicians with the abolition of discriminations against married women. One women's group in particular, the AIM organization, spearheaded campaigns for legal and political recognition of women's rights in marriage. The policy agenda shaped by members of the AIM group and their contribution to the development of women's rights within the family in Ireland is traced. In order to put their activities in context, I will first assess the situation of married women prior to the formation of AIM.

FAMILY LAW PRIOR TO 1972

In 1956, when introducing the first piece of modern legislation giving married women a minimal right to own property, the Minister for Justice declared that 'the progress of organised society is judged by the status occupied by married women'.[6] Hollow words indeed, considering that the family law statutes extant in Ireland until the early 1970s dated from Victorian times, when married women were afforded little legal recognition. The most significant statutes governing the legal status of married women were the Married Woman's Property Act of 1882, and the Married Women (Maintenance in Case of Desertion) Act of 1886, amended by the Irish government in 1940.[7] These acts gave minimalist property and maintenance rights to married women.

Legislation alone did not govern family policy in respect to women. The status of married women was shaped by the conservatism of both the state and the Roman Catholic Church. Clancy[8] describes the traditional view held by the post-Independence political leaders on women's role in society:

The revolutionary leaders who came to power between 1922 and 1937 were to adopt a position regarding the role of women in the new Irish state which was as remarkable for its consensus as it was for its conservatism. The function which was regularly declared to be appropriate for women was that of service in the private and domestic domain. Not only was this outlook given a ready imprimatur by the emerging political elite, but the attendant hostility to a public role for women was notably vigorous on occasion. In particular, the opposition of Kevin O'Higgins and Eamon de Valera to the public influence of women encouraged legislative measures which sanctioned such attitudes.[8]

This view of women's civic role was given constitutional status in 1937 under Articles 41 and 42. O'Connor, commenting on the constitutional implications for family policy and married women in particular, observed:

> The State in Articles 41 and 42 of the Constitution has firmly committed itself to upholding an unreservedly traditional view of the family and marriage. It recognizes the family as a moral institution, possessing inalienable and imprescriptible rights, which is regarded as the necessary basis of social order. It insists upon the indissolubility of marriage upon which the family is founded and stresses the importance of the married mother's life within the home.[9]

Indeed, as Connelly has observed, the relegation of women to the domestic sphere in a constitutional context sanctioned 'a gendered distribution of power and status which greatly favours men'.[10]

The Married Women's Status Act of 1957 gave some rights of property ownership to married women. Seven years later, in 1964, it was followed by the Guardianship of Infants Act, which recognized the equal right of a mother to both educate and have custody of her children, replacing the more traditional concept of paternal supremacy in this area.[11] In 1965, the Succession Act provided a widow with a statutory right to a share in the estate of her deceased husband. Taken together, these three acts removed some of the more glaring injustices against women in family law. Thus, when the government-appointed Commission on the Status of Women came to examine family policies for evidence of overt discrimination, it accepted that advances had been made in reforming policies in this area.[12] None the less, the Commission report recommended substantial legislative and administrative reforms to ensure the adequate protection of women in marriage. It advised that policy initiatives be taken to ensure financial security for deserted wives, restrictions to be placed on a husband's right to sell the family home without the knowledge or consent of his wife, and suggested a system of joint management and ownership of property and assets belonging to a married couple. It also sought a reciprocal enforcement of court maintenance orders between Ireland and Britain and the continuation of social welfare benefits to divorced wives.[13] These recommendations were very similar to the reform agenda developed by the Portuguese women's movement which led to the inclusion of a number of equal rights clauses in its 1976 Constitution.[14]

The Commission on the Status of Women was not alone in advocating the removal of discriminations against women within marriage. Social agencies and societies such as the Irish Society for the Prevention of Cruelty to Children (ISPCC), Alcoholics Anonymous (AA), the Free Legal Advice Centres (FLAC) and church-based organizations along with professionals involved in family counselling expressed their concerns in public about the health of Irish marriages and the status of married women. FLAC, for instance, reported that matters relating to marriage breakdown constituted the largest single category of cases dealt with by the organization.[15] The ISPCC reported that three-quarters of their cases involved wives looking for a separation or deserted wives seeking maintenance. The records of the ISPCC revealed that in the first half of 1970, it dealt with 600 cases involving desertion and provided a tracing service through its British network for the Irish local authorities.[16] In the absence of divorce, desertion was used as a way out of a failed marriage, which led to the solution being known as an Irish-style divorce. At the same time as the ISPCC were involved in tracing missing husbands, women's liberation movement activists were highlighting a series of family-related discriminations which found expression in the slogan 'Justice for widows, deserted wives and unmarried mothers'.[17]

The true scale of desertion and marriage breakdown in Ireland in the 1960s is difficult to ascertain as the absence of official statistics on the extent of marriage breakdown before 1979 has hampered formal studies attempting to quantify and analyse the issue.[18] From 1971 onwards, however, it was possible to obtain some indication of the scale of the problem from statistics made available by the Department of Social Welfare and from figures for family law cases released in Court reports. In an analysis of a compilation of this data, Duncan speculated that 'it is reasonable to assume, on the basis of the latest information, that there are at present in the Republic between five and eight thousand deserted wives, with a minimum annual increase of about five hundred'.[18] Whatever the actual figure, there was a growing public recognition of the problem of marital breakdown, heightened by the calls from welfare agencies and the women's movement for a reform of policies and practices relating to marital desertion. The Fianna Fáil administration began to tackle the problem by addressing two of its most pressing aspects – financial security for deserted wives and the scope of the courts to determine maintenance awards. In a speech on the Social Welfare Bill in July 1970, the Minister for Finance, George Colley, announced the creation of a new national assistance benefit for deserted wives, an initiative that was welcomed by the opposition parties of Fine Gael and Labour.[20] In October 1971, the Minister for Justice, Desmond O'Malley, announced changes in the legal provisions governing the award of maintenance in cases of desertion in a speech at the annual meeting of the Limerick branch

of the ISPCC.[21] The statutory maintenance payment was increased from
£4 to £15 per week for a spouse and to £5 per week for each dependent
child up to the age of 16.

While increases in the minimum maintenance awards were welcomed,
there were serious problems in the implementation of the policy. There
was no statutory obligation on a deserting husband to maintain his family,
as maintenance orders could not be enforced outside the country and the
family home could be sold without the knowledge of the wife. Free legal
aid was non-existent, presenting an obstacle to deserted wives wishing
to bring a case for maintenance to court. Furthermore, the administrative
rules under which a deserted wife's allowance could be obtained were
quite restrictive. All in all, the measures put in place prior to 1972 to
alleviate the hardship caused by marital desertion were the product of a
minimal political response to a complex and growing social problem. In
this context, AIM began to articulate a reform agenda and persisted in
highlighting inequalities in family law to successive governments.

REWRITING FAMILY LAW: THE CONTRIBUTION OF AIM

AIM was founded in 1972 by a small group composed of liberal feminists
critical of the lack of political focus in the women's liberation movement.
One founding member of the organization recalled how she was attracted
to campaigning on family law reform:

> I joined AIM as a result of a Women's Liberation meeting which was
> held in Nuala's [Fennell] house. It was my first introduction to the
> movement but I felt that there was no priority in what was being
> discussed by the women. Later, during a casual conversation, the idea
> of AIM was suggested with the intention of pressurising for maintenance
> in the home and I knew it was exactly what I needed.[22]

Another founder member remarked on the need for a group such as AIM
as a vehicle for the articulation of grievances centred on women's status
within the family:

> When the idea of AIM was first suggested its timing was exactly right.
> It coincided with the strong concern felt by many women over the
> inequalities existing in society at that time. We joined from conviction –
> or from personal experiences. We were all united in our feelings of anger
> over the lack of rights by a wife whose husband could beat her at will –
> or by the vulnerability of a woman whose family home could be sold
> over her head on the whim of her husband. One of my strongest

memories will always be our first public meeting . . . . Women stood up and told their personal histories – overwhelming stories about batterings, desertions, lack of maintenance, wives whose children were in the late teens and had never seen their fathers, women who had not been able to buy clothes for twenty years. For the first time women were standing and telling us that these things really did happen.[23]

Although group members welcomed the active support of men, AIM conveyed a woman-centred public identity. This image was further reinforced by the fact that key positions in the voluntary group – spokespersons, negotiators and administrators – were women.

The initial objective of the group was to secure the enactment of a statutory right to family maintenance and an effective enforcement procedure. Nuala Fennell, who had resigned from the women's movement to set up the AIM group (and who later became a junior minister in a Fine Gael–Labour coalition government) recalled:

once the women's liberation movement had become public and all the protests were over, letters came in, phone calls came in . . . this was really a huge cry from women in the country who were married and who had been beaten, who hadn't got homes and who were deserted wives. It was just a whole catalogue of dreadful situations. So we decided that we would work on that and that we would specifically aim for one thing at the beginning and that was to get an adequate share of maintenance for the woman.[24]

This initial single-issue agenda quickly developed to include a number of other reform objectives which fell into four broad categories. One set of reform goals sought to give married women protection within the family (such as protection from domestic violence) and rights of co-ownership to the family home. The second sought to redress discrimination that applied solely to married women and did not apply to married men or to single men and women. These included being the subject of a court action by a husband seeking financial compensation in the case of adultery and acquiring a husband's domicile, even if they were separated and living in different countries. A third set of objectives sought changes in the legal and administrative machinery which processed family disputes. AIM advocated that the state-funded free legal aid scheme, which was confined to criminal cases, be extended to encompass family law cases. It also sought the establishment of family courts and the hearing of family cases in private. The fourth area of attention consisted in pressure for reform of the laws governing marriage breakdown and later lobbying for the introduction of civil divorce. In each area, the members of AIM achieved many, if not all, of these objectives.

The AIM group did not set out to challenge the official position of the family as laid out in the Constitution. Instead, its members campaigned for specific outcomes which were intended to reform family policy and practices within existing constitutional parameters. Levine[25] notes that this group had from an early stage developed a clear strategy to guide the realization of its objectives. This consisted of a low-key, non-sensationalist campaign to raise public awareness of the problems associated with marital breakdown and with the status of women within marriage, and also involved lobbying on issues around which it could build a political consensus for reform. Assistance in the development of a strategic approach was given to the group in the early stages by a marketing expert friend of the founding members. This guidance encouraged the AIM volunteers, all of whom were new to lobbying, to direct their attention to the media and to politicians.[26]

AIM campaigners worked within the political structures from the beginning, using the media to explain the human need behind the reform proposals and building social and political acceptance of the need for change in specific areas of family policy. Group activists framed reform demands as 'issues of justice, of redress of blatant wrongs to women', and adopted an incremental approach to policy change.[27] They also sought to influence public perceptions of the injustices suffered by a sizeable number of married women. Commenting on the strategy of the group some ten years after its founding, an editorial in *AIM Newsletter* observed that:

> AIM Group's crusade over the years raised public consciousness to the level at which legislative action resulted. At the same time, through seminars, broadcasts, lectures, articles we created a climate in which deserted or separated wives no longer felt like social lepers, women were no longer ashamed to say out loud 'I'm separated' for fear that others would see them as failures. Judged over a decade, a lot has been achieved by a small band of hardworking and dedicated women. It was done without pickets or sit-ins, and every penny for the campaign and the voluntary work was raised by AIM Group.[28]

The manner in which AIM activists approached the problem of marital desertion illustrates this point. Spokespersons for the organization did not call for the introduction of divorce as a clear-cut legal solution to the extensive problem of marital desertion. Instead, they campaigned for reforms which would give women and children basic rights and a level of financial protection within a family context. In adopting a pragmatic – arguably conservative – stance on family issues, it was possible for AIM to influence a legislative agenda which built a broad consensus of legal, political and social opinion around support for policy reform. Furthermore, AIM activists did not seek to advocate policies challenging the traditional role relationships within marriage, but instead sought to bring about an equality of legal rights between men and women within this relationship.[29]

Because of the immediate, specific and reformist nature of their agenda, group leaders were able to employ standard lobbying and pressure techniques in pursuing their objectives. Indeed, AIM is a classic example of a women's group with a 'mainstream' agenda long before feminist demands found their way into mainstream politics. Its members engaged in intensive lobbying of parliamentarians, frequent discussions with the Minister for Justice of the day and had a continual presence in the media, advocating the abolition of discrimination against married women. AIM members also used their contacts among grass-roots women's groups to organize supporting political representation from sympathetic women's organizations around the country. Describing the strategy of the group, Nuala Fennell recalled:

> We selected out all the ICA guilds and branches, the Irish Housewives Association and the Federation of Women's Clubs and we visited them on a systematic basis. When we went, we brought two resolutions . . . which said that 'this branch supports the AIM organisation's proposals for reform of family maintenance legislation'. . . . We had two copies – they sent one to the minister in question and we sent one. That way you had this constant inflow of these motions on this legislation from very credible groups, which we felt was important.[30]

This strategy also served to sensitize significant social groups to the need for reforms in family law which contributed to the building of a broad social consensus on the issue. It is significant that early AIM activists recollect encountering little, if any, opposition from established social groups in their pursuit of family law reforms. AIM was to a large extent articulating a problem which had widespread recognition but no identifiable public voice.

AIM members organized regular public meetings on the subject of marital breakdown which attracted high attendances, media attention and political interest. It also published reports researched by supporters and members of the organization on subjects such as family maintenance legislation (1973) and an equitable marriage separation law (1976). Within the group, subcommittees were established as the need arose to conduct research into various aspects of family law, the findings of which contributed to the identification of reform proposals by the group. Thus AIM adopted a professional, mainstream pressure group approach from an early stage, far removed from the protest-oriented activities of the women's movement.

When we try to assess the impact of AIM, we must remember that it was working in a social and political climate in which there was a growing consensus for a redress of injustice against married women. Political leaders were responsive to the problem, and public consultations on family law reform were undertaken by the Committee on Court Practice and Procedure and the Law Reform Commission on the direction of the government. These hearings provided an official forum in which interested groups and individuals could make their views on family law reform known to policy-makers. What is noticeable about this process is the extent to which all groups contributing to these discussions on family law were in broad agreement as to the problems and the solutions required. This fact alone reinforced the political consensus on the reform agenda.

The political willingness to go along with family policy reform in property and individual rights was reflected in the policy positions of the three main parties, all of which were supportive of changes in this area. A reading of parliamentary reports during debates on any legislative proposal on family law reveals a consistent all-party consensus on the legislative measure. For instance, political sympathy with the legal and social circumstances in which deserted wives found themselves was reflected in the position adopted by the Fine Gael and Labour parties prior to the 1973 general election.[31] That the objectives of the group and those of Fianna Fáil were also at one with those stated by Fine Gael and Labour is illustrated in a Dáil speech by the opposition spokesman on Justice in 1974, David Andrews:

> There are a number of matters which the Minister could deal with urgently and they come under the three heads of deserted wives and their maintenance, matrimonial courts and free legal aid for litigants. He could also deal with a number of very serious anomalies in the law unfavourable to women – the abolition of the criminal conversation action, the clarification of the position in regard to divorces obtained in England and the abolition of the wives domicile.[32]

The strategy of the AIM group in framing its demands as issues of justice rather than as 'feminist' demands was a pragmatic articulation of the political mood.[33] It was also in keeping with the ideological orientation of the group, which was one of liberal reformism. In presenting proposals for policy change as matters of justice, AIM was seeking to ensure the maximum possibility of their acceptance by policy-makers and government advisers. Furthermore, the group was bringing political opinion around to the agenda of reforms it was proposing. For instance, in the early days of the 1973–77 Fine Gael–Labour coalition, in the course of a debate in parliament on family law reform, the role played by AIM in highlighting the problem of deserted wives was recognized by government and opposition alike.[34] However, although successive governments remained sympathetic to AIM's cause and all political parties regularly advanced arguments in favour of family law reform in parliament, the road of legislative enactment was uneven and piecemeal.

Two main factors shaping the reform process can be identified: first, the need to secure an all-party consensus in parliament on proposed reforms; second, the different priorities in the family law policy agenda of successive governments. The former was very pronounced in relation to the Family Law (Maintenance of Spouses and Children) Bill, which was finally passed by parliament in 1976. The enactment of this measure took place two years after the publication of the report of the government's advisory body, the Committee on Court Practice and Procedure, four years after the issue had been raised by AIM and six years after the problems of deserted wives were first raised in the media. The delay was occasioned by the prolonged deliberations of a special all-party parliamentary committee appointed by the Minister for Justice to discuss the draft legislation. One of the many points of contention among the committee was section 22 of the legislation which provided for the exclusion of a spouse from the home because of family violence. Reacting angrily to the delay in legislating for a maintenance policy, an AIM editorial observed that 'the Bill made one brief appearance in July 1975 as a sop to our pleading and disappeared without a trace into the committee chasm'.[35] Five months later, in May 1976, the Bill emerged from the parliamentary committee and shortly after entered the statute books. Some weeks later, the Family Home Protection Act, regulating the conditions under which the family home could be sold, was given a speedy passage through parliament.

The second factor shaping the legislative agenda on family law reform was the differing policy priorities of successive governments, clearly seen in the 1977–86 period. Around the time that the financial and property injustices against women in family law were being redressed, the government's chief law officer, Declan Costello, indicated that the Fine Gael–Labour coalition government was considering reforming the domicile law. The newly established government advisory body on legislation, the Law Reform Commission, was directed by government to 'seek the views of the general public on the question of changing the law in relation to a wife's domicile'.[36]

A short time later, the government which had set this agenda was defeated in the 1977 general election, and the 1977–81 Fianna Fáil administration set about putting into effect its own programme on married women's rights. This included the abolition of court actions for adultery and restitution of conjugal rights. These issues were already part of the political reform agenda identified by AIM and on which the group was active in making representations to government.[37] However, on the main priority issues of the AIM group at the time – the availability of free legal aid in family law cases, the establishment of family courts and the development of a conciliation service for couples with marital difficulties – there was little progress. Instead, the government chose to legislate for the least costly and least controversial options. Indeed, the frustration of AIM members at the lack of progress in these areas was evident following a round of unproductive discussions with the Minister for Justice. In the new and more extensively circulated newsletter, Women's AIM, the Editorial commented on the lack of movement on this agenda:

> Could it be that family law is the poor relation of the legislative process forever getting pushed to the back of the queue? None of these problems were new at the beginning of last year [1978] and although much investigation and discussion has taken place at government level, no positive moves have been made. At this stage, the WHY and the HOW should be obvious. So now, Mr. Collins, we say WHEN?[38]

In this period, the AIM organization received political support from Senator Mary Robinson when, in 1978 and again the following year, the liberal senator called on the government to establish a system of family courts and to introduce a comprehensive free civil legal aid scheme. In 1980 she introduced a Private Member's Bill which sought to abolish the dependent domicile of married women. These initiatives gave further political support to the campaign of AIM and, although the inbuilt government majority in the Seanad ensured that these legislative proposals would be unsuccessful, circumstances forced the government to address these issues. In 1980, political support for the repeal of the action for adultery was forthcoming from the opposition Fine Gael party in parliament. The shadow spokesperson on Justice, Michael Keating, introduced a Private Member's Bill on the issue. Introducing the proposed Bill in parliament, Keating argued that the initiative was

> essentially a commitment to rid our statute book, our way of thinking and our way of life of an act which deems a woman to be the property of her husband and which places her in a position of inferior status and restricted dignity relevant to her husband. That situation is no longer

tolerable. . . . The situation we want to change is the capacity of a husband to take an action for damages against a person who has had sexual relations with his wife.[39]

Supporting the Private Member's Bill, Labour's Eileen Desmond referred to four actions for criminal conversation heard in the High Court between 1972 and 1979. She pointed out that this legal facility was abolished in England in 1857, in Northern Ireland in 1939 and in Scotland in 1971, while no action of this kind existed in France or Germany.[40] Again, a government majority defeated the Bill, but it was obvious to AIM activists that a political consensus around this reform was emerging. The outdated laws relating to the court actions for adultery and for harbouring and enticement of a spouse were finally abolished in the Family Law Act of 1981 subsequent to the Minister for Justice holding extensive consultations with women's organizations, in particular with AIM and the NWCI.[41] This was a direct success for the AIM group[42] and was a popular reform measure with the public.

This government also introduced legislative protection for victims of domestic violence, for which again AIM activists had campaigned. The provision of barring and protection orders, involving an update of section 22 of the Family Law (Maintenance of Spouses and Children) Act 1976, was welcomed by AIM, although the organization had by now been joined by Women's Aid in campaigning for reform in the area of domestic violence. In 1980, a free civil legal aid scheme was introduced following the findings of the European Court of Human Rights that Ireland was in breach of the European Convention on Human Rights by not having this provision. In this instance, it required the intervention of an external agency to bring about this reform. Indigenous pressures such as those exerted by AIM were not sufficiently powerful to persuade politicians to introduce free civil legal aid. There were disappointments too, however. The AIM goal of establishing a system of family courts was largely ignored by the government in favour of having family law cases heard at District Court level as opposed to the High Court. This reform, which made family law a much less expensive procedure (and was also a direct outcome of the judgment of the European Court of Human Rights), was given a less than enthusiastic reception by the AIM organization.[43]

A period of government instability from June 1981 until November 1982 halted legislative progress on family policies. With the return of a Fine Gael–Labour coalition to office in 1982, the legislative agenda which these parties had set during the 1973–77 administration was resumed. With the former leader of the AIM Group, Nuala Fennell, now in a position of some power as Minister of State for Women's Affairs and Family Law Reform,

AIM spokespersons now had a political channel receptive to their agenda. The issue of domicile was reinstated as a legislative priority, finally reaching parliament in 1986 as part of a measure which gave recognition to divorces obtained outside Ireland.[44] A conciliation service for separating couples was introduced on a three-year pilot basis in early 1985. However, little progress was evident on the larger issues of the introduction of divorce legislation, a new judicial separation act and the provision for joint ownership of the family home.

AIM AND THE DIVORCE DEBATE

If AIM was influential in placing specific, narrowly defined reforms in the field of family policy on the political agenda, it had greater difficulty in finding parliamentary and government acceptance of the need to introduce divorce legislation. The group joined with the Divorce Action Group (DAG) and the Irish Council for Civil Liberties (ICCL) in lobbying for divorce from 1981 onwards. However, as this demand required a constitutional referendum if it was to be met, the process involved was necessarily much more public and highly controversial than the reform agenda pursued by AIM up to that point.

In response to the growing demand for the introduction of divorce legislation, the government brought the debate into the parliamentary arena. In 1983, in a repeat of the device used to buy political time on the issue of maintenance, an all-party parliamentary committee on marital breakdown was established with a view to obtaining all-party consensus on a family law legislative agenda including divorce. This committee received 700 written and twenty-four oral submissions, including the views of AIM, DAG, the Free Legal Aid Centres, the Catholic Marriage Advisory Council and the ICCL, the legal profession and the public. The AIM submission contained eleven sections and sought amendments to existing family legislation, an expansion of mediation services to nationwide level, a raising of the minimum age of marriage to 18 years and the introduction of divorce.[45] The consultative phase of the policy reform process was conducted within the parliamentary arena, in contrast to the process associated with many of the other legislative changes, when policy was formulated through negotiation and discussion between AIM and officials in the Department of Justice. Bringing the debate on family law reform to a parliamentary committee enabled the political parties – the opposition Fianna Fáil party in particular – to have a greater influence on the outcome of the proceedings than would have been possible in the circumstances of regular, routinized policy-making.

The parliamentary committee issued its report in 1985 following a considerable period of internal debate. The report advocated extensive legislative changes supported by all the parties. The committee was, however, divided on the introduction of divorce and stopped short of recommending the removal of its constitutional prohibition. Fianna Fáil members in the main opposed the introduction of divorce, while the measure was favoured by the government parties and the left-wing Workers' Party. The exercise did, however, serve the useful function of sensitizing parliamentarians to the problems of marital breakdown and the legislative measures required to change some policy and statutory practices in this area. This fact was acknowledged in the government's consultative document on marital breakdown published some years later in advance of plans to hold a second divorce referendum.[46]

The reform agenda promoted by the AIM group was for a period overshadowed by the more controversial divorce debate. In 1986, with little advance public or political discussion, the government announced its intention to seek a repeal of the constitutional clause providing for a ban on divorce.[47] The campaign was bitter and divisive, resulting in a defeat for the pro-divorce lobby by a majority of two to one. This result is not surprising, given that the campaign focused on the fundamental legal and moral structure of family life. In a country such as Ireland, with the continued existence of a strong Catholic ethos, such issues went well beyond the limits of tolerable policy reforms. Furthermore, the question of property ownership, in a country where land and property holding is highly valued, raised many doubts in the public mind about the equitable distribution of property in the event of divorce.

On the positive side, the divorce debate sensitized the public and the elected representatives to the requirement for extensive legislative reform of family law. In particular, the need to develop a policy which handled the issue of marital breakdown in a humane manner, making adequate financial and material provisions for wives and children in family separation cases, was highlighted during the course of the campaign. Thus, following the divorce referendum, the political debate concentrated on reforming family policies, and the policy process reverted to a routine procedure in the Department of Justice. As part of this process, AIM resumed lobbying on incremental, equality-focused issues. In 1987, the tabling of a Private Member's Bill on judicial separation in the Dáil by opposition parliamentarian Alan Shatter[48] (a politician from a legal background with an interest in family law and an adviser to AIM) served to refocus the political debate on family law reform. In an unusual move, the government adopted Shatter's initiative and passed the Judicial Separation and Family Law Reform Act in 1989. This statute broadened the grounds for judicial separation to include a 'no fault' provision and more explicit measures on financial settlements and protection for children. With the wisdom of hindsight, many commentators suggested that had this legislation been in place prior to the 1986 divorce referendum, it was likely that the constitutional question would have had a different outcome. As things stood, a second debate and national referendum on divorce was imminent.

The 1993 Fianna Fáil–Labour coalition formulated an explicit agenda for family law legislation which advanced that of the previous administration and made a specific commitment to

A major programme of family law reform, culminating in a referendum on divorce by 1994, modernisation of the law of nullity; placing a monetary value on women's work in the home for the purposes of property distribution; extension of barring order legislation; legislation to give each spouse an equal share in the family home and household belongings; increase in the age of marriage to 18; enhancement of the rights of parties in non-marital unions.[49]

In 1995, a constitutional referendum was held on divorce. This time the public supported the introduction of divorce by the narrowest of margins: 51 per cent. The first divorce in the history of the Republic of Ireland was granted in January 1997.

AIM AS A MATURE ORGANIZATION

Not all legislative efforts to redress inequalities in family law were as successful. One of the long-held objectives of AIM was to bring about joint ownership of the family home between husband and wife. Government attempts to provide for this situation in the Matrimonial Home Act of 1993 were declared unconstitutional by the Supreme Court in January 1994,[50] which means that married women do not have joint ownership of the family home with their husbands. The AIM group continues to campaign for family law reform, particularly on the joint ownership issue, but the constitutional right to private property overrides equality-seeking solutions. Yet, twenty-five years or so after its establishment, much of the AIM agenda has been realized. Taking a long-term look at the achievements of AIM, Anne O'Connor, spokeswoman for the organization, claims that:

We had a lot of input into the Family Law (Maintenance of Spouses and Children) Act which was introduced in 1976, we had a 99 per cent input into the abolition of criminal conversation – which was abolished in 1981. We had also a lot of input into the Family Home Protection Act of 1976. . . . A lot of change in the dependent domicile law was AIM policy and in 1987 there was the Judicial Separation Bill, the extension of the grounds of judicial separation. We have had a major input into all the laws that have changed.[51]

Policy-makers have repeatedly recognized the contribution made by AIM to the formulation of legislation. In the view of Richard Humphreys, special adviser to the Minister for Equality and Law Reform:

If you are talking about lobbying, if you are going about influencing the formulation of public policy by government, AIM are a reasonably good example of an effective group. They made quite a good submission on the White Paper on Marital Breakdown which I personally found quite useful [and] which had a tangible impact on the thinking within the department. It was well put together, comprehensive. It was focussed, it was specific in terms of the provisions of the White Paper and the legislation it wanted. I thought it was a good document.[52]

A general observation arising from this study is that lobby groups have a role to play in shaping legislation when they present a clear, specific and detailed argument on both the principle and technicalities of a piece of draft legislation. In this policy area, AIM has made consistent, well-researched representations to the government on specific aspects of family law since its foundation in 1972. The group also brought the discriminations against married women in family policy to the attention of the public and political representatives, revealing the human suffering behind statutory inequalities. The contribution of the voluntary activists of the AIM group to Irish society is one of bringing family policy out of the Victorian age to a respectable stage of enlightenment comparable to similar policies in most European states in the late twentieth century. As in Greece,[53] the specific demands of a pressure group campaigning for women's rights in family law provided legislators with a blueprint for reform. The existence of this symbiotic agenda-setting relationship in part explains the fact that the objectives of AIM soon found political articulation through parliamentary spokesmen within government and opposition parties. Although successive administrations did not share the same reform goals, it is noticeable that the broad agenda defined by AIM members in the early 1970s formed the basis on which various governments framed their policy proposals. After the failure of the divorce referendum in 1986, the incremental initiatives on legal separations and joint ownership of the family home reflected a return to the reform agenda articulated by AIM.

As lobby groups do not have direct political power, their capacity to influence legislation is more limited in scope than that of members of parliament or of a government. Thus in a discussion of pressure group activity, particularly when the focus is on cause-centred groups, it must be recognized that the scope available to a given group for influencing the policy process is restricted. What is notable in the case of AIM is the extent to which, given the limited opportunities for influencing decision-taking, the organization has been effective in shaping the political agenda in the area of family law.

DISCUSSION

A feature of the policy process highlighted by this study is the considerable level of incremental policy-making which, over a period of time, has altered the original policy positions in a significant fashion. It could not be said that family policy today resembles that of over twenty years ago; yet many of these changes have been accomplished with little manifestation of political conflict. This can be attributed in part to the gradual nature of the policy shifts which minimized the potential for social and political division. It can also be accounted for by the sustained consensus on the problems and solutions identified as politically feasible. While, in feminist terms, family policy has not undergone any funda-mental value restructuring, it has none the less incorporated some very real and important rights for women. The contribution of the AIM group in the policy process has played an important part in influencing this agenda.

Three factors can be identified as being of particular importance in shaping the politics of women's rights in this area: social and political attitudes, the pattern of interest representation, and the lobbying skills of the group. First, a pre-existing socio-political consensus on the need to reform family law to protect women legitimized the demands of AIM. There was a growing awareness among influential social groups, including the Catholic Church, that marital breakdown was causing severe hardship for wives and children and also gaining significant media attention. Legislators were conscious of this problem and began to develop modest initiatives to alleviate the financial difficulties caused by marital desertions. As the family law agenda developed, there was continued support both in society and in the political sphere for the rights of women within marriage. One of the reasons for this generalized sympathy for women's position came from the highlighting of anachronistic laws; another contributing factor lay in the climate of the time. In the years following the rise of modern Irish feminism, social attitudes became more accepting of women's rights. Public opinion might not have supported the introduction of divorce, but within the framework of the family recognition was given to the need to reform women's status within the institution of marriage.

Second, the pluralist set of interest relations dominating in social policy issues provided AIM with the opportunity of access to decision-makers. AIM was not facing a pre-structured policy arena in seeking political adoption of a reform agenda. The pattern of interest representation was one which was more open to a consideration of women's rights. AIM members met with and discussed issues of women's rights with successive Ministers for Justice on a regular basis and over time, AIM developed a working relationship with senior officials in the Department of Justice. This led to the relationship between the members of the AIM group, the officials and the Ministers for Justice becoming routinized. Although AIM was never given formal consultative status, it earned a *de facto* consultative position in the formulation stage of policy.

There were some family law issues which did not suit the incremental policy style of AIM, the divorce issue being a case in point. The experience of the divorce campaign shows the limits of the effectiveness of the AIM organization. Once the issue moved outside the routinized policy network and into a broader arena, other political forces dominated the policy process. In the case of the establishment of family courts and the enactment of a reform of matrimonial property, we again see the intrusion of outside agencies into the policy process and how, when the policy arena extends beyond a government department, the influence of AIM decreases. While the pattern of policy-making remains routinized, the views of AIM hold weight.

Third, the lobbying skills of the group contributed to the development of the family law agenda and to the realization of the organization's goals. From the beginning, AIM was an organization which we saw Rucht describe in Chapter 1 as a 'power-oriented' group. It was the first identifiable conventional lobby group for women's rights to emerge from the women's movement; further, it framed its demands within the structure of the dominant value system. AIM members recognized that the removal of discrimination in family law would be acceptable and that challenge to the institution of the family would not gather support. Based on this understanding, AIM maintained a high lobbying profile and developed a high level of professionalism in this activity. The group presented researched submissions to government, grew quite skilled in the use of the media and became the most visible political group advancing a feminist agenda in family law.

It is clear that the AIM group is an example of a successful cause-centred group. Over the last two decades it has succeeded in raising the issue of family law reform and in keeping it on the political agenda. It appears to have had an influence on the setting of party policy and on the development of government initiatives on family law reform. In developing specific legislative initiatives in family law, representations from AIM were treated seriously by decision-makers. In articulating a reform agenda, AIM provided a channel for an expression of a social desire for changes in family law which fed into the political process and assisted in the creation of a political and social consensus on reform measures which did not challenge the fundamental concept of the family.

Thus the secret of AIM's successful achievement of many of its goals was threefold. First, the political climate was open to the assimilation of the demands of AIM; second, the fluid interest structure assisted the group in advancing its demands; third, its professional approach to political engagement led to the demands of the organization being given serious consideration by policy-makers. However, the assessment of AIM and of its impact on family law policies must conclude with a caveat. Unlike corporatist interest structures, pluralist arrangements are open to the inclusion of new groups with a different agenda, and we must be mindful of this fact in considering the current position of AIM. Until the mid-1980s, AIM was the only group in the policy arena advocating reforms to enhance women's rights in family law. The result of the public debate on divorce was to shift the focus of the family law agenda away from women's rights within marriage and towards a resolution of the policy problems posed by the increase in the levels of marital breakdown. The extensive public and parliamentary debate on this issue gave legitimacy to the views of other groups dealing with family law issues. AIM responded by broadening its own representative function from women's interests to family interests. In doing so, it is at risk of losing its identity as the group advocating women's interests and becoming yet another pressure group in the area of family law reform. Its track record will enable AIM to hold its status as a policy influence in the short term, while its focus as a lobby group dedicated to the advancement of women's rights appears to have changed in favour of a more 'holistic' approach to family law. Women, especially married women, are still important to AIM, while men and children are becoming increasingly significant in the development of the organization's future plans. It can be argued that this priority shift reflects the success of AIM in substantially completing its original agenda and that in the 1990s the scope for policy development has broadened to include issues other than the status of married women. Indeed, this may be true. As of now, only time will allow an assessment of the impact of AIM in its capacity as a pressure group for family law reform in a broader sense.

NOTES

1. Dorothy McBride Stetson, *Women's Rights in France* (New York: Greenwood Press, 1986), p. 81.
2. For a synopsis of the major reforms relating to the status of women in Portugal, see Maria Leonor Beleza, 'Major legislation pertaining to women's rights', in Gisbert H. Flanz, *Comparative Women's Rights and Political Participation in Europe* (New York: Transnational Publishers, 1983), pp. 409–14.
3. Gisela Kaplan, *Contemporary Western European Feminism* (London: Allen & Unwin, 1992), contains information on Austria, pp. 132–3; Greece, pp. 234–5; Italy, p. 252; Norway, p. 73; Portugal, p. 186; Spain, pp. 201–5; Sweden, pp. 67–8.
4. Ann R. Cacoullos, 'Women confronting party politics in Greece', in Barbara J. Nelson and Najma Chowdhury (eds), *Women and Politics Worldwide* (New Haven: Yale University Press, 1994), pp. 317–18.
5. Joni Lovenduski, *Women and European Politics: Contemporary Feminism and Public Policy* (Brighton: Wheatsheaf, 1986), p. 20; Paul A. O'Connor, *Key Issues in Irish Family Law* (Dublin: Round Hall Press, 1988), p. 174.
6. *Proceedings of Seanad Eireann*, Vol. 47, col. 72, 16 January 1957.
7. O'Connor, *Key Issues in Irish Family Law*, p. 174. O'Connor discusses the legal implications of a policy that casts women in a traditional family role. For a broader discussion on sexual equality in the Irish constitution with an emphasis on case law, see Madeline Reid, *The Impact of Community Law on the Irish Constitution* (Dublin: Irish Centre for European Law, 1990), pp. 17–44, especially pp. 33–44.
8. Mary Clancy, 'Aspects of women's contribution to the Oireachtas debate in the Irish Free State, 1922–37', in Maria Luddy and Cliona Murphy (eds), *Women Surviving: Studies in Irish Women's History in the 19th and 20th Centuries* (Dublin: Poolbeg, 1989), p. 206.
9. O'Connor, *Key Issues in Irish Family Law*, p. 174.
10. Alpha Connelly, 'The Constitution', in Alpha Connelly (ed.), *Women and the Law in Ireland* (Dublin: Gill & Macmillan, 1993) pp. 23–4.
11. Re Tilson [1951] IR 1, quoted in Yvonne Scannell, 'The constitution and the role of women', in Brian Farrell (ed.), *De Valera's Constitution and Ours* (Dublin: Gill & Macmillan, 1988), p. 128.
12. Commission on the Status of Women, *Report to the Minister for Finance* (Dublin: Stationery Office, 1972), p. 173, paragraph 441.
13. Central Statistics Office, *Census of Population of Ireland, 1979: Vol 11, Ages and Marital Status* (Dublin: CSO, July 1981), pp. 174–83 [Prl. 9956].
14. Flanz, *Comparative Women's Rights*, pp. 224–6.
15. See, for instance, Free Legal Aid Centres, *FLAC Reports: The free legal advice centres report on their work since the organisation was founded in 1969 and make proposals for reform in our laws* (Dublin: FLAC, 1972).

16. ISPCC report quoted in *Irish Times*, 26 October 1970, p. 8, and 27 October 1970, p. 9.

17. There are many references in the literature to this aspect of discrimination against women. For the perspective of an academic who was also a feminist activist at the time, see Ailbhe Smyth, 'The Women's Movement in the Republic of Ireland, 1970–1990', in Ailbhe Smyth (ed.), *Irish Women's Studies Reader* (Dublin: Attic Press, 1993), pp. 245–69.

18. The absence of official figures on desertions, separations and foreign divorces was commented on by Kathleen O'Higgins in her 1974 study, *Marital Desertion in Ireland* (Dublin: ESRI, 1974), Broadsheet No. 9. In 1976, the National Economic and Social Council, in *An Approach to Social Policy* (Dublin: NESC, 1975), suggested the inclusion of the category of 'separated' in the census.

19. William Duncan, *The Case for Divorce in the Irish Republic*, 2nd edition (Dublin: Irish Council for Civil Liberties, 1979), pp. 12, 77–8.

20. *Dáil Debates*, Vol. 248, col. 1010, 14 July 1970; col. 1147, 15 July 1970.

21. *Irish Times*, 26 October 1971, p. 5.

22. Anne McAllister, *AIM Magazine*, Spring/Summer 1985, p. 8.

23. Deirdre McDevitt, *AIM Magazine*, Spring/Summer 1985, p. 7.

24. Interview with Nuala Fennell, founder of AIM and former Minister of State for Women's Affairs, 30 June 1992.

25. June Levine, *Sisters. The Personal Story of an Irish Feminist* (Dublin: Ward River Press, 1982), p. 231.

26. Nuala Fennell, 30 June 1992.

27. Nuala Fennell, 30 June 1992.

28. Editorial, *Women's Aim*, Issue No. 10, 1982 (10th Anniversary issue), p. 2.

29. Evelyn Mahon makes a similar point in 'Women's rights and Catholicism in Ireland', *New Left Review*, **166** (November/December 1987), 60.

30. Nuala Fennell, 30 June 1992.

31. *AIM Newsletter*, No. 2 (March 1973), p.2.

32. *Dáil Debates*, Vol. 270, col. 551, 12 February 1974.

33. Nuala Fennell, 30 June 1992.

34. *Dáil Debates*, Vol. 270, cols 511 and 550, 12 February 1974; col. 796, 14 February 1974; *Proceedings of Seanad Eireann*, Vol. 83, cols 856 and 874, 10 March 1976.

35. *AIM Group Newsletter*, No. 13, January 1976, p. 2.

36. *Irish Times*, 12 February 1976.

37. The agenda for reform identified by AIM in 1978 included domicile, legal aid, family courts, criminal conversation, loss of consortium divorce and financial support for the AIM women's centre. See *AIM Group Newsletter*, No. 20, January/February 1978, p. 1; No. 21, July 1978, p. 2.

38. *Women's AIM*, No. 3, October–December 1979, p. 2.

39. *Dáil Debates*, Vol. 318, col. 1268–80, 4 March 1980.

40. *Dáil Debates*, Vol. 318, col. 1291, 4 March 1980.

41. *Dáil Debates*, Vol. 328, cols 1026–32, 2 April 1981.

42. *AIM Magazine*, Spring/Summer 1985, p. 2.

43. *Women's AIM*, No. 7, January-March 1981.

44. *Dáil Debates*, Vol. 363, col. 3251, 19 February 1986.

45. AIM submission to White Paper on Marital Breakdown, 1990.

46. Minister for Justice, *Marital Breakdown: A Review and Proposed Changes* (Dublin: Stationery Office, 1991), p. 9 [Pl. 9104].

47. Brian Girvin, 'The divorce referendum in the Republic, June, 1986', *Irish Political Studies*, **2** (1987), 93–8.

48. *Dáil Debates*, Vol. 376, col. 1305, 9 December 1987.

49. Fianna Fáil and Labour, *Programme for a Partnership Government 1993–1997* (Dublin: Fianna Fáil and the Labour Party, January 1993), pp. 36–7.

50. *Irish Times*, 25 January 1994.

51. Interview with Anne O'Connor, AIM group spokesperson, 27 May 1992.

52. Interview with Richard Humphreys, special adviser to the Minister for Equality and Law Reform, 30 June 1994.

53. In Greece, the comparable group to AIM was known as SEGES. It did not have the longevity of AIM, disbanding in 1983. See Cacoullos, 'Women confronting party politics in Greece', p. 316.

CHAPTER 6

WOMEN AND VIOLENCE

This study of feminist politics in Ireland has identified a clear development in women's demands, from equality and rights issues to matters concerned with gender difference, specifically violence against women. This chapter focuses on the manner in which the women's movement brought the issue of violence to the attention of policy-makers and analyses the dynamics of the reform process initiated by this agenda-setting exercise. Rape and sexual violence are looked at in this context, as well as the extent to which both reformist and radical branches of the women's movement were successful in changing public policy in this area. Following this, domestic violence is considered, with a focus on the influence of the radical feminist Women's Aid group on public policy. A comparison of the effectiveness of the Rape Crisis Centre (RCC) based in Dublin (formerly known as the Dublin Rape Crisis Centre) and Women's Aid in seeking and obtaining legislative change is undertaken. I conclude by identifying the obstacles and the opportunities for feminist activity as it engaged with the State in this area.

THE BEGINNINGS OF MOBILIZATION

The issue of violence against women has been documented as being a key concern in studies of women and politics.[1] These studies record a distinct pattern of feminist political activity during the 1970s and 1980s which sought to bring about changes in the laws on violence against women. There were two aspects to this issue, the first dealing with sexual violence, the second concentrating on domestic violence. In countries where sexual violence became a political question, there was a distinct mobilization around each issue which challenged the nature and relevance of existing statutes with varying degrees of success. Rape crisis groups began to pressure for changes in the laws on sexual violence, and domestic violence issues were represented by Women's Aid groups. In Britain and France, socialist, radical and liberal feminists made common cause in seeking to change public policy in this area, while in Italy, the political experience gained by feminists during the divorce campaign encouraged the feminist movement to seek the reform of the rape and domestic violence legislation.[2] In Spain and Greece,[3] feminists campaigned for the introduction of more severe penalties for rape, while in the United States, an increase in the level of sexual assaults on women led to organized demands for reform of public policy on rape at state level.[4]

The situation in the Republic of Ireland in the 1970s and 1980s was similar to that pertaining in other countries. Violence against women emerged as an issue of concern to the women's movement from 1968 onwards; indeed, the first inkling of the problem became evident in the course of submissions to the *ad hoc* women's group which was preparing a position paper on the status of women in Ireland.[5] Activists in this area were open to the experiences of women in other countries, particularly Britain, as contact was sustained between women working on this problem in both countries.[6] Feminist networks, EU structures and international meetings provided other arenas of discussion and exchange of views with women from other countries. IU and other women's groups sent representatives to an international Tribunal on Crimes against Women, where the opportunities for informal networking were as important as the formal business of the conference.[7] Furthermore, the Committee on Women's Rights in the European Parliament provided a political forum for the debate on violence against women.[8] Just as participation in non-national and international structures had earlier assisted in the politicization of women's status in Ireland, the participation of sections of the women's movement in non-Irish meetings helped with the public politicization of the issue of violence against women in Ireland.

The laws on sexual violence in Ireland in the 1970s were very similar to those existing in other countries and were underpinned by the perception that women were seen as the exclusive sexual property of particular males.[9] Rape was a common law crime, defined under the 1861 Offences Against the Person Act as being 'unlawful carnal knowledge without a woman's consent' which was punishable by life imprisonment and could not, in law, be committed by another woman, a husband or a boy under 14 years of age. The Criminal Law (Amendment) Act of 1935 restricted the circumstances in which life imprisonment could be meted out as a punishment for sexual offences – it only applied if the victim was a girl aged under 17 or if the victim was a 'woman or girl who is an idiot, an imbecile or is feeble minded'. The rape or sexual molestation of women not in these categories was often reduced to the lesser charge of indecent assault which carried a maximum sentence of two years' imprisonment.[10]

Sexual violence was not an issue on the agenda of the political parties or the government in the 1970s, but it became politicized through the activities of both radical and moderate feminist groups. Certain conditions brought the issue to the forefront of the public mind, in particular the number of attacks on women began to escalate while the number of prosecutions remained miniscule. In 1977, for instance, there were sixty reported incidents of rape and one conviction, as compared with thirty-two incidents and five convictions in the previous year. Specific incidences of sexual violence were highlighted by some journalists and broadcasters, creating a public mood for action. Second, there was growing dis-satisfaction among the women's movement with the law and its implementation and with the attitude of much of the media in reporting crimes of sexual violence. Third, the issue of sexual violence was a political matter in Britain, where the Sexual Offences Act had been amended in 1976 following the recommendations of a government advisory group.[11] Some members of the women's movement took this legislation as an example which ought to be followed in Ireland.

The campaign to reform the law on rape was initiated almost simul-taneously but independently of each other by radical feminists and the more moderate NWCI. In 1978, around the same time as the broad feminist movement was debating the issue, the NWCI established a committee to formulate proposals on reform of the legislation on sexual violence. The motivation of the NWCI executive for examining the legislation in Ireland came from an awareness of the growing increase in sexual crimes in Ireland and observations on the reforms being introduced in Britain. The leaders of the organization were also in touch, through NCWI-affiliated groups, with attitudes among a broad spectrum of women's organizations on the issue. Executive members of the NWCI undertook a study of the laws in this area and drew up a set of recommendations for legislative reform in its report, *Rape in Ireland*, which was presented to the Minister for Justice, Gerard Collins, on 18 October 1978. Among the major reforms sought by the Council were a broadening of the definition of rape to include all forms of penetration; making rape within marriage a crime; giving the victim anonymity in newspaper reports; and introducing changes in Garda (police) procedures, in medical practices and in trial procedures. The report also recommended significant changes in the rules of evidence regarding the admissibility of a victim's previous sexual history.[12]

Some months earlier, a number of feminists had formed a group known as Campaign Against Rape to lobby for policy change in this area.[13] This action led to a broader discussion within the women's movement on the issue of violence against women.[14] As a result of this debate, feminists began to agitate on the issue. In 1978, a loose grass-roots movement known as Women Against Violence Against Women emerged, similar to the campaigning group of the same name which mobilized women into political action in Britain.[15] The campaign sought to raise public consciousness of the issue and expressed feminist anger at male violence. An early leaflet produced by this group described the general public attitude towards the crime in the following manner: 'We are told that it is our fault and that we deliberately provoke men by the way we dress, walk, talk or even because we're out on our own at night'.[16] As in Italy, France and Britain, the Women Against Violence Against Women group organized protest action to reclaim the night for women, emphasizing the interrelationship between a woman's right to move around on her own and her right to be safe from sexual abuse. On 13 October 1979, a night-time protest march in Dublin attracted an attendance of 5,000 women, including many in public life.[17] The demonstration brought the issue of sexual violence out of feminist discussion groups and into the public arena.

The Campaign Against Rape group was, in the meantime, involved in lobbying for reform of the rape laws. Within the group, however, some members had identified an urgent need for a counselling service for women who had suffered sexual assault. After some months, the majority of the activists in the Campaign Against Rape left the group to found a rape crisis centre. Although the centre initially focused on the provision of a twenty-four hour telephone counselling service, the group soon became involved in lobbying for legislative reforms, overshadowing its parent group, the Campaign Against Rape, in the process. The centre became known as the Dublin Rape Crisis Centre (DRCC) in 1979, later changing its name to the Rape Crisis Centre (RCC).

In a report on sexual violence issued in 1980 soon after the centre began to operate, the RCC highlighted a number of areas for reform. The report contained a series of recommendations including providing a statutory definition of rape which would cover the concept of marital rape, penetration by objects, oral and anal rape; the right of anonymity to be extended to the accused; the right of the victim to have her interests represented in court, and the need for a fixed date for a rape trial.[18] Many of these recommendations echoed the general tenor of the legislative reforms sought by the wider feminist movement in Ireland and in other countries. This report was also presented to the Minister for Justice and was widely distributed among politicians in an effort to provoke political awareness of the seriousness of this issue.

The agenda of the RCC was similar in many respects to that of the NWCI. Both sought a redefinition of the concept of rape to include all forms of sexual violation and were of much the same mind regarding the changes they considered necessary to the various procedures relating to the prosecution of a rape charge. Yet there is no evidence to indicate a coalition-building strategy between the two elements of the feminist movement, despite the similarity of their demands. This is a rather unusual feature of this policy process, as studies have found a pattern of feminist co-operation in pursuit of reforms on issues that generate a high level of visibility. However, in this instance, the fact that the lobbying campaigns were separate is a reflection of the lack of communication at the time between representatives of two aspects of the feminist movement in Ireland. This is, to some extent, a reflection of the position of both organizations in the political system, where the NWCI had become an integral part of conventional political processes while the RCC held the status of an outsider group within the political system. The differences in the strategic positioning of the two groups became apparent during the course of the early political debate on reform of the law on rape.

LOBBYING FOR REFORM

The first sign of political interest in the issue of women and sexual violence came in April 1978 when the Fine Gael opposition spokesperson on Justice, Jim O'Keeffe, asked a parliamentary question on the rules governing evidence in rape trials. In reply, the Minister for Justice, Gerard Collins, while 'sympathetically disposed towards doing anything that can properly be done to reduce the extent to which victims of rape are subjected to unfair cross-examination', did not indicate that he was considering changes in this area.[19] That Collins was not forthcoming about possible legislative change is not surprising, as it is not customary practice to outline new legislative proposals in response to a parliamentary question. The Minister did, however, refer to the research being carried out by the NWCI on the matter. Almost one year later, again in reply to a parliamentary question, Collins indicated that although he was unwilling to accept some of the recommendations of the NCWI report, the process of framing legislative proposals for government consideration was under way.[20]

In April 1979, a Fine Gael senator, Gemma Hussey, who identified with the women's movement on this issue and strongly advocated the need for legislative reform, succeeded in having the NCWI report debated in the Seanad.[21] The response of the Minister of State at the Department of Justice, David Andrews, to the debate was to indicate that the report of the Council was 'under the very closest and most sympathetic examination' by the Minister.[22] However, the government's delay in presenting reform proposals to the Oireachtas prompted Senator Hussey to introduce a Private Member's Bill in 1980, the Sexual Offences Bill, into the upper house. The government majority, however, ensured that the Bill was not given a second-stage reading.[23]

By November 1980, legislative preparations were sufficiently advanced to enable the new Minister of State in the Justice Department, Mr Seán Doherty, to introduce the Criminal Law (Rape) Bill. Moving the second stage of the Bill in parliament, he acknowledged the value of the submissions of both the NCWI and the RCC:

> The Minister [Gerard Collins] welcomed the submission from the Council for the Status of Women. That submission has been given very careful consideration in the course of the examination of this question. We have also had the benefit of the views of the Dublin Rape Crisis Centre and of various people experienced in the practical operation of the law as it stands at the present. The legislative proposals contained in this Bill take account of all those views.[24]

Although the government was clearly sympathetic to the victims of sexual violence and anxious to provide statutory protection and rights for women in this area, the legislation fell far short of the demands of feminist pressure groups and of the expectations of women.[25] Rape remained a common law offence, as the Minister made clear in parliament:

> Rape is a common law offence . . . the intention is not to change the law as to the meaning of rape but only to make it clear what constitutes the offence. The essence of the offence is that the woman does not consent and that the man either knows that she does not consent or is reckless as to whether she does so or not.[26]

The Bill offered a more modern restatement of the 1861 Act, substituting the words 'sexual intercourse' for 'carnal knowledge'. It also recognized that women of all ages could be raped by abolishing the application of age and mental ability criteria contained in the 1935 Act. The central question of how this crime against women was to be defined was not detailed to the satisfaction of either the NWCI or the RCC, as the legislation did not address the issue of rape within marriage and did not bring other sexual practices into the definition. Instead, the measure raised the statutory sentence for 'certain very serious and obnoxious forms of indecent assault' from two to ten years. The rules of evidence were modified to restrict the admissibility of a woman's previous sexual history and provision was made for the hearing of this aspect of a trial in private.

Doherty dealt directly with some other proposals put forward by the NWCI in the course of his parliamentary speech, giving reasons for not including the NWCI recommendations in the draft policy changes. In essence, he acknowledged the Council's report but rejected its contents.

For instance, the Bill did not provide for evidence to be heard of the character of the accused and rejected the suggestions of having gender-balanced juries and of giving legal aid to victims who sought compensation from the Criminal Injuries Tribunal.[27]

It is clear that during this stage of the reform process, the views of the NWCI were acknowledged by government representatives in preference to the representations of the RCC. This had little to do with the content of the submissions, as essentially both groups (and, indeed, the women's movement as a whole) were of one mind on the nature of reform. Instead, it threw into relief the respective relationship of each of the two women's organizations with the established political system. The NCWI had been given consultative status as the official representative of women's interests with the government, making government ministries well disposed to listen to the views of this organization. Although the demands of the NCWI in this area were, in the context of existing policy, quite radical in tone, the group was firmly based in the reformist wing of the women's movement.[28] Irish politicians appeared to be more at ease in discussing this policy issue with NWCI spokespersons than they were in dealing with representatives of the more overtly feminist RCC. Indeed, as Doherty reflected,

> The numbers of lobby groups that were around at that time were small. I met the Council for the Status of Women [NWCI] very frequently and they were the only one I met with regularity. It wasn't a militant organisation. . . .The Council for the Status of Women were the predominant force.[29]

The enactment of the Criminal Law (Rape) Act of 1981 did not fully resolve the issue of reforming the law on sexual violence. The measure was seen instead by both legislators and pressure groups alike as the first step in the process of policy reform. In this context, it is of some significance that both Fianna Fáil and the Labour Party made specific commitments to reform the law on rape and to review services and procedures in their respective programmes during the general election which followed shortly after the parliamentary passage of this Bill.[30]

REFORMING THE 1981 ACT

Once the 1981 Act had been passed, the NWCI was no longer directly involved in subsequent developments of the issue. The task of lobbying for further reforms fell to the RCC. This organization had the advantage of being able to present a case for the introduction of further legislative change with some legitimacy, given the practical experience of its members in counselling victims of sexual violence. The ability to draw on actual examples and case histories in the course of presenting an argument for change to some extent counteracted policy-makers' perception of the group as a militant feminist organization. The RCC also had the advantage of being a single-issue group, unlike the multi-issue umbrella organization of the NWCI. Although the RCC suffered from a lack of financial resources, it had committed activists with a knowledge of the political system willing to pursue the reform campaign. From this point, RCC representatives were to lead the feminist campaign for reform of the 1981 legislation. Strategically, it was decided to work within the political structures, following the example of other successful feminist reform groups.

As soon as the 1981 Act was passed, the RCC began a period of sustained political lobbying which lasted until the passage of the Criminal Law (Rape) (Amendment) Act of 1990. The purpose of the conventional pressure activity was to build support within the political parties in Ireland for legislative reform and, in doing so, RCC representatives continually advocated reform at every opportunity. They presented a case for policy changes to government advisory bodies and to parliamentary committees; raised public awareness of the need to reform the legislation through use of the media; and finally, negotiated with the Minister for Justice and government administrators on the reform proposals. Describing the group's activities between 1983 and 1987, Breda Allen, legal adviser to the Centre, recalled:

Anne O'Donnell and Olive Braiden made a written submission to the Joint Oireachtas Committee on Women's Rights and were subsequently invited to give an oral presentation to the Committee on this subject. Then we wrote to all the party leaders and all the spokespersons on Justice. When the Law Reform Commission was examining the legislation, we went down and spoke about it there. I'm a member of a political party and we spoke about it at every meeting where it was appropriate. We got people in other political parties to put in questions for their annual conference and I did the same. . . .We just talked about it all the time and if we had pull with any of the legislators, we just mentioned it over and over again. We went on deputations to see successive Ministers for Justice. . . .There were also lots of opportunities for being on radio and television and any time we were on programmes such as *Questions and Answers* we would always bring it up.[31]

From an early stage, the activists in the RCC had identified the specific aspects of the 1981 legislation which they wished to see altered and which offered the greatest likelihood of being accepted. They sought independent legal representation for the victim; an extension of the definition of rape to include marital rape and unnatural sexual acts; and a provision through which boys aged under 14 years could be charged with the crime.[32] However, the low priority accorded by the parties and government to the issue was apparent in the attitude of the Minister for Justice in the Fine Gael–Labour coalition, Michael Noonan, who expressed a reluctance to take the issue on board.[33]

The effort to bring about specific legislative changes began in earnest in 1983 when, acting on its own initiative, the RCC made a case for reform to two newly formed women-focused political agencies, the Joint Oireachtas Committee on Women's Rights and the Interdepartmental Working Party on Women's Affairs.[34] The submission highlighted the inadequacy of the 1981 Act and proposed specific policy solutions along the lines identified above. The response from the Committee on Women's Rights was to examine the 1981 Act in some detail, seeking the views of medical, legal and Garda experts along with those of the RCC.[35] In a report issued on 9 January 1987, the Committee recommended that the definition of rape should be broadened, as 'the members are convinced that the law as narrowly defined in existing legislation is too restrictive in its definition of rape and that serious sexual assaults should be included in a new and broadened definition of the crime'.[36] The report noted, however, the objections of the Garda authorities and the Law Society to the broadening of the definition.[37] Other recommendations for change included extending the charge of rape to apply to boys under 14 years of age; criminalizing rape within marriage; adequate training of doctors to deal with victims of sexual abuse; and alterations to the administrative procedures followed by the Gardai when crimes of sexual violence were reported.[38]

The Committee accepted the main arguments for reform put forward by the RCC, which is not surprising given the role of the Committee on Women's Rights as a parliamentary voice for women's demands. The chairwoman of the Committee at the time, Monica Barnes, was particularly sensitive to the case presented by the RCC, having been involved in the women's movement before entering political life. The receptivity of the parliamentary committee to RCC arguments for reform marked the start of a consensus-building exercise within the political institutions cultivated by the leaders of the RCC.

Shortly after the publication of the report of the parliamentary committee on women's rights, public pressure for legislative change in this area began to increase, which drew a response from the political establishment. The Fianna Fáil government which was returned in the February 1987 election decided in principle to amend the 1981 legislation and sought proposals to that end from the government's legislative advisory body, the Law Reform Commission.[39]

After studying the issue of rape and sexual violence for some time, the Law Reform Commission published a consultative paper on the matter on 1 December 1987, setting out its main provisional reform proposals. The publication of this paper led to a debate which engaged many feminists, reform groups, political parties and organizations as well as representatives from professional, medical and social associations. The consultative paper incorporated many of the recommendations of the RCC, including criminalizing rape within marriage, extending the law to boys aged under 14, modifying the procedures in respect of the cross-examination in court of the victim and extending full anonymity to the complainant. In addition, it proposed the creation of two new offences – sexual assault and aggravated sexual assault – to replace the old crime of indecent assault and introduced provision for financial compensation for the victim. Many of these proposals were welcomed by RCC activists and by the women's movement in general. However, on the critical issue of the legal definition of rape, the Commission did not recommend any change. As this constituted one of the key demands of RCC leaders, feminists and other interested groups, the consultative paper was seen as an inadequate response to the specific reform demands of the women's movement.

The contents of the consultative paper were discussed at a seminar on 30 January 1988 organized by the Law Reform Commission. Of the fifty participants, eleven represented women's groups, twenty-two indicated legal affiliations, seven were serving politicians and two were Garda representatives. The remaining eight represented a cross-section of medical, social, political, trade union and administrative interests. The Commission also invited comments from the public and received written submissions from twenty-eight individuals and organizations. Of these, eleven were from a broad spectrum of political, women's, trade union and reform groups and two other submissions came from individual civil servants working in the Department of Justice. Two-thirds of the written submissions were in favour of extending the definition of rape.[40]

Between the publication of the consultative paper and the submission of the final report to government in May 1988, RCC activists initiated an intensive public debate on the Law Reform Commission's proposals. This debate took the form of open meetings in cities and towns around the country; their purpose was to inform the wider public as to the general direction of the reforms being considered and to develop and reinforce a climate for change among the public at large in order to facilitate the political passage of reforms. These public debates attracted a broad audience including private citizens, members of women's organizations, feminists, representatives of professional associations and political activists. A lively national public debate ensued, generating support for a radical review of the laws on sexual violence, the message of which was not lost on either the Law Reform Commission or the government.

The content of both the written submissions and seminar discussions were significant in shaping the final legislative recommendations in the Commission's report to the government. A radical proposal was included, supported by a majority of the Commission members, to broaden the definition of rape and to apply it to both men and women as follows:

> that the crime of rape should be defined by statute so as to include non-consensual sexual penetration of the vagina, anus and mouth of a person by the penis of another person or of the vagina or anus of a person by an inanimate object held or manipulated by another person and that in this form the crime should be capable of being committed against men and women.[41]

This was a significant departure from the original position of the Law Reform Commission. It was the result of a concerted campaign by RCC leaders to shape public opinion and decision-makers' views on the need to alter the definition of the crime.

The Commission's report and the recommendations of the Joint Committee on Women's Rights constituted the basis of the draft legislation drawn up in the Department of Justice during 1988. At this stage, as the legislation was being formulated, RCC activists shifted their attention towards members of government. Olive Braiden, RCC Director, recalled her lobbying efforts at that time:

> I saw as many members of the Fianna Fáil government as I could. Máire Geoghegan-Quinn was very helpful, Mary O'Rourke, all of the women and some of the men too. Of course you always have the opposition to help you but it is better if you can get people who are in government. . . . Usually you have all the opposition with you, that's our experience, whether one is lobbying for money or for legislative change. To get people within the party in government to agree with you is more difficult. They may personally say they support you but it's what the party says that counts.[42]

Many of the reforms sought by RCC leaders were included in the Criminal Law (Rape) (Amendment) Bill when it was introduced in the Seanad on 15 December 1988. Rape within marriage was given statutory recognition. The law was extended to apply to boys aged under 14. Other sexual crimes which did not involve penetration, such as aggravated sexual assault, were recognized and defined in the draft legislation. Some slight advance was made in relation to independent legal representation for the victim, although the principle was not in itself included in the draft legislation. However, there was some controversy around an appropriate definition of rape. The Minister for Justice, Gerard Collins, had chosen to reject the majority recommendation of the Law Reform Commission in favour of the more conservative minority view which suggested that the definition of the crime should not be changed.[43] This decision attracted significant criticism from opposition parliamentarians and from spokespersons for the RCC, but it was the preferred option of the Law Society and the Garda, as stated in their respective submissions to the Oireachtas Committee on Women's Rights.[44] Little progress was made on this front.

In July 1989, Ray Burke was given the Justice portfolio in a cabinet reshuffle. In the meantime, pressure had been building up within the Oireachtas and among the public as a result of the activities of the RCC leadership for a broadening of the definition of the crime. The two chief spokespersons for the RCC, Olive Braiden and Breda Allen, had a series of meetings with Burke and his senior officials, during which, according to both sides, a constructive working relationship developed between the issue representatives and the policy-makers.[45]

The Minister was unwilling at first to change the draft legislation. However, negotiations between RCC representatives and senior administrators in the Department of Justice resulted in a compromise which was satisfactory to both sides. Olive Braiden recollected the discussions with the Minister for Justice and the officials in his Department on this point:

> We wanted a broadening of the definition of rape. They were not prepared to look at it at all, but after a few meetings with him [the Minister for Justice] and his team they came up with the idea of putting in rape under section 4, which covers all offences that before had been indecent assault.[46]

In effect, the solution on offer was to provide for two broad categories of rape: the first which encompassed the conventional understanding of the crime; and the second which categorized other offensive acts of penetration as rape, but placed them in a different section of the legislation. The definition of the crime was therefore broadened, while the original understanding of rape remained in place. However, the demand for separate legal representation for the victim was firmly opposed by individual lawyers and representatives of the profession. Instead, the right to free legal aid for advisory purposes was extended to the victim. This was largely a meaningless gesture, given the underfunded condition of the free legal aid services. It was rendered even less relevant by the legal context in which rape cases were conducted, with the victim acting as a witness for the state prosecution.

Although the reforms passed in parliament in 1990 constituted a significant improvement for women, some outstanding issues remain to be resolved. The need for separate legal representation for the victim when crimes of sexual violence are being prosecuted has emerged as an important issue. The judiciary's sentencing policy for such crimes has come in for some sustained criticism since 1990. RCC leaders continue to campaign for an explanation from the Director of Public Prosecutions when cases of sexual violence are not prosecuted. Reforms in these areas are seen as being essential in refining the law and in giving further formal recognition to the seriousness of this crime and its effects on the victim.[47]

One incident above all others served to highlight many of the deficiencies in the 1990 legislation. The rape of a young teenage girl in 1991, the conviction of a businessman for the crime and his subsequent successful appeal to have his sentence reduced drew an angry reaction from the public and the women's movement.[48] The case gave the women's movement a focus for a co-ordinated campaign on women and violence. In 1995, representatives from the NWCI, RCC, Women's Aid and the ICA met with the Minister for Justice Nora Owens (a former voluntary worker with Women's Aid) to discuss the manner in which the judicial process handled rape and sexual crimes against women. The Minister agreed to fund a report on the matter and a working party was established by the NWCI to that end. Within a year, on 1 November 1996, the working party presented its report containing eighty-four recommendations for changing the legal and judicial process in respect to crimes of violence against women and children to the Justice Minister.[49] Ten days later, the need for changes in judicial practices was again highlighted when a man convicted of abusing his niece from when she was 6 years of age and who was given a five-year term in prison had his sentence reduced to six months.[50]

THE INFLUENCE OF THE RAPE CRISIS CENTRE

In questioning the perceptions of both feminists and legislators informing the 1990 Act, Fennell criticizes the mainstreaming of the issue and of its feminist advocates. She makes the point that in participating in the law reform process, feminists argued in terms of the existing legislation and its defects rather than constructing an alternative woman-centred analysis of sexual violation:

Women, by participating in the law reform process, culminating in the 1990 Act, created the impression of a shared definition of rape which may long be with us. . . . In defining the abnormal or deviant, without addressing the vision of the normal, women have left the legislators and the judiciary with their vision intact. . . . The legal construction of rape has once again been stymied by those assumptions which are shared by men rather than men and women. From this perspective reform of the crime is not in a woman's voice but drowned in the male chorus.[51]

While Fennell raises many useful and provocative questions about the current legislation and its operation, it is clear that in an Irish context the nature of policy reform is one which inevitably involves compromise between the participants. In this case, the 1990 Act strikes a delicate balance. The RCC representatives did not get all the reforms they sought to achieve, yet they succeeded in bringing about considerable changes in the 1981 Act. As a consequence of the political and public debate on sexual violence in the 1980s provoked by the women's movement, significant procedural and administrative changes have taken place, resulting in a greater sensitivity in the handling of reported rapes by the police authorities and the medical profession. The campaign for legislative reform sustained by the RCC resulted in a piece of legislation for which there was broad approval both within the women's movement and Irish society.

It is arguable as to whether these reforms would have been enacted without the campaigning efforts of the RCC over a seven-year period. It appears from a study of this particular policy process that the sustained lobbying of this group around a set of clearly identified reform proposals led to a relatively early review and significant reform of the 1981 Act. Parliamentary debates and media reporting of the reform process refer to the agenda-setting and lobbying activities of the Centre's activists. The group also participated extensively in the policy formulation process, leading to a substantial realization of its reform goals. Thus at the end of the process, the *Irish Times* carried a report which stated that

Amendments to the existing rape legislation which are expected to be debated and passed by the Senate on Wednesday evening have been welcomed by the Opposition, by members of the Oireachtas All Party Women's Rights Committee and by the organisation which has campaigned most vigorously for change, the Rape Crisis Centre.[52]

As in the case of family law reform, we can see the building of all-party consensus around the legislation. This was brought about through the persistent lobbying efforts of the RCC, and was assisted at various stages by parliamentary support, legal reports and by the mobilization of the public in favour of change. The outcome is one which can be seen as a sign that, within a decade, the attitude of policy-makers on matters of sexual violence had modified to incorporate a greater understanding of the complexities of the crime.

DOMESTIC VIOLENCE

Domestic violence was for many years a hidden social issue, and the feminist organization Women's Aid was the 'cinderella' of women's movement groups in terms of gaining political attention. It therefore comes as no surprise to find that legislation dealing with domestic violence was given a lower political priority than other, more visible women's rights issues. Yet, by 1996, the issue of women and domestic violence was seen as part of government business. The story of how domestic violence came from the margins to the centre of the political stage is a tale of how one women's group learned to play the political game.

Representations on the policy changes required to give women protection from the violent behaviour of a spouse were made initially by the AIM group. While Women's Aid was an offshoot of AIM, it concentrated on providing a voluntary service for battered wives and their children and left the politicization of this issue to the AIM group. The rationalization of the refuge service in the 1980s gave Women's Aid leaders time and space to become advocates for political reform in this area of law. The transition of the organization from a voluntary service to a professional research and lobbying agency took place from 1990 onwards. As with other women's organizations with a focus on political reform, the issue and its representatives have become part of the mainstream political process. None the less, the Women's Aid organization, probably the largest single-issue women's group in the country in 1996, continues to identify itself as a radical feminist organization.[53]

CHANGING THE LAW

Prior to 1976, a woman seeking protection from her husband's violence could bring charges under the Victorian law, the Offences Against the Person Act of 1861. The protection afforded by this method was the same as that given to an individual assaulted by a stranger. Judicial interpretations of the Married Women (Maintenance in Case of Desertion) Act of 1886, led to the concept of 'constructive desertion' including desertion arising from domestic violence. The Committee on Court Practice and Procedure explained this concept as follows:

Where a husband, without cause, makes life intolerable for his wife and children, so that she, for her own or her children's protection, is forced to leave the husband, a court will treat the husband as having 'constructively' deserted his wife, and may make a maintenance order against him if he fails to make provision for maintenance of his family. Habitual drunkenness, violence, adultery and cruelty to children have been treated as 'constructive desertion'.[54]

The problem of domestic violence, although well recognized in court proceedings, was not a matter of general public concern. The issue remained hidden from public discussion until 1969 when it was raised within the *ad hoc* committee lobbying for the establishment of a commission on the status of women. The chairwoman of the group, Hilda Tweedy, recalled:

It was during this period [1969] that the question of battered wives was first brought to our attention in a memorandum from a country branch of one of our organisations. Until then women had been reluctant to speak about the violence in their homes.[55]

The report of the Commission on the Status of Women in 1972, which provided legislators with a blueprint for women's rights reforms, did not refer to domestic violence. Gradually, public attention was brought to bear on family matters through the efforts of AIM, and incidences of domestic violence were reported by the media on a regular basis from 1974 onwards as newspaper articles and television programmes brought the issue into the open.[56] In April 1974, Women's Aid was founded in Dublin to provide a refuge for women who suffered from abuse modelled on the service in London established by Erin Pizzey. Nuala Fennell, a founder member of both organizations, drew a distinction between the priorities of AIM and Women's Aid at the time:

The only reason why Women's Aid was set up was because the problem presented itself in such numbers and with such intensity that you couldn't ignore it. You couldn't wait until legislation came in. That was the difference between Women's Aid, which was service-centred and AIM. AIM group wasn't.[57]

In contrast to the experience in Britain, where Women's Aid became organized on a nationwide basis, the provision of emergency shelter accommodation in Ireland was organized in an unco-ordinated manner. The name 'Women's Aid' was given to the first refuge in Dublin and, while other shelters established subsequently around the country were not offshoots of the Dublin group, some shared the same feminist self-help philosophy as Women's Aid. AIM group members were often instrumental in establishing these refuges: in Galway, members of AIM were associated with the setting up of a women's refuge in the city and in Dundalk, AIM members provided a counselling service for women victims of violence, and worked closely with the police authorities in the town. In Limerick, members of the local branch of ADAPT, the support group for separated and deserted wives, established a women's refuge.

While Women's Aid concentrated on the provision of an emergency service for abused women and their families, raising public and political awareness of this issue continued to be part of the agenda for family law reform being pushed by AIM. The initial response of legislators was, as we have seen, to insert a clause (section 22) in the Family Law (Maintenance of Spouses and Children) Act of 1976 which gave women who were suffering from or threatened with violence some statutory protection. This Act made provision for the issuing of a barring order by the District Court against a violent spouse, preventing him (usually) from entering the home for a period of three months. Although the measure was a limited one, it did provide some level of redress for women suffering from violence in their homes.

During the course of the implementation of this Act, the effective enforcement of barring orders proved to be problematic. Representations were made on repeated occasions by AIM leaders to the Minister for Justice, who responded by requesting the Garda, as the law enforcement authority, to tighten procedures in this area.[58] The issue was also highlighted in the media.[59] In the meantime, abusive matrimonial relationships were the subject of extensive discussion at the feminist conference on violence held in Galway in May 1978, where it became clear that refuge workers would need to adopt a more pro-active political strategy if reform were to ensue:

> This meeting of women from all the refuges in Ireland was seen as very important. The lack of contact and lack of co-ordination in working out philosophy and ways of pressurising the government, etc., were discussed. It was decided that one immediate pressure for change should be to get barring orders made effective. They are totally ineffective at the moment because if the husband breaks the barring order there is no provision for arrest on the spot. All the woman can do is go back to the court and in the meantime she is usually beaten up several times.[60]

In 1979, the shelter groups formed a federation 'in order to have a more effective voice in policy-making'.[61] Although the federation remained in place, the political initiative soon dissipated under the pressure of providing an emergency voluntary service for victims of domestic violence. By 1981, pressure was mounting for a strengthening of the barring order mechanism, and AIM members organized a public meeting which discussed the implementation of the family law legislation. The Fine Gael opposition spokesman on Justice, Michael Keating, raised the issue in parliament, and Women's Aid called for the introduction of a number of specific legislative and administrative reforms.[62]

The government responded with the introduction of the Family Law (Protection of Spouses and Children) Bill in the Dáil in 1981. The Minister of State at the Department of Justice, Seán Doherty, admitted that there had been problems in implementing the measures in the 1976 legislation as highlighted over a period of time by AIM and later by Women's Aid. The 1981 measure was designed to redress this problem, as the Minister explained in parliament:

> I have received various representations, mainly from some women's organisations, that their experience suggested that the system needed strengthening. Initially it was thought the problems might be solved by a more active involvement of the Garda Síochána in the issuing of summonses for breaches of barring orders. Unfortunately while an improvement was achieved in this way, it has been found not to be enough and that is why we have this bill now.[63]

The demand for reform was not solely confined to women's pressure groups. Senior civil servants in the Department of Justice had independently assessed the enforcement of the 1976 legislation and were of the opinion that this area required significant policy reforms. Through the Minister, Gerard Collins, they obtained government approval to begin drafting a bill on domestic violence.[64] Commenting on the drafting process, Patrick Terry, a former senior civil servant, recalled:

> At the time there was a great deal of talk about protecting women in situations of domestic violence. . . . The Secretary of our Department at the time, Andy Ward, took a very great interest in it. The 1981 Bill introduced protection orders for the first time. We improved the situation for getting a barring order and we made it a criminal offence to breach the barring order. We gave the power of arrest without warrant to the Gardaí. And side by side the police were instructed to try to get over their traditional reluctance to become involved in rows between husband and wife. We really did a bit of new thinking. The protection order was something new. In a sense the concept would have come from lobbying

groups but my understanding is that we went further than women's groups expected.[65]

The novel component in the legislation was the protection order – a court order restraining a man from abusing or threatening his wife during the interim period before a barring order was obtained. In parliament, Doherty acknowledged the contributions made by members of the judiciary, police officers and the women's interest groups, AIM, Women's Aid and the NWCI in formulating the legislation.[66] In the process of policy formulation, consideration was also given to the laws in the United Kingdom and the United States dealing with domestic violence. Assessing the legislation, Terry noted that

> There was a real commitment inside the Department to get something done and we led the way there in the British Isles on it. The bill we brought in at the time was a tremendous advance on the British position and the Northern Ireland one . . . there was a commitment to make it as good as we possibly could, and I think the lobby groups were surprised that so much came out so quickly.[67]

The opposition parties welcomed the Bill and the measure passed all stages in the Dáil on the same day. In a comment on the new legislation, members of the AIM group recognized the progressive nature of the legislation at that time:

> This Act will unquestionably improve the lot of the battered wife. After perhaps years of domestic violence three months was a ridiculously short time to be delivered from the menace of a battering husband. . . . Barring orders of twelve months are therefore to be welcomed. . . . The Act actually goes beyond what many reformers had demanded. The principal change is that District Court barring orders will now exclude a violent spouse for twelve months instead of the previous three months. . . . Also new are the measures for dealing with those who break barring and protection orders. . . . Similarly, the introduction of protection orders is an improvement, applying as they do to the critical period between application for a barring order and the Court hearing of the case.[68]

Throughout this reform process the representations of Women's Aid were clearly overshadowed by those of the AIM group, which had developed effective lobbying skills and was clearly part of the family law process. Women's Aid was, in terms of interest representation, still on the margins of politics. Within the women's movement, the specific groups concerned with domestic violence were satisfied with the 1981 statute and the need to campaign for legislative reform receded.

The enactment of this legislation did more than provide legal protection for women in violent home circumstances; it also brought domestic violence into the ambit of family law reform. The 1985 Report of the Joint Committee on Marriage Breakdown dealt in some detail with issues arising from the implementation of the 1981 Act.[69] Women's Aid was not among the lobby groups with an input into the deliberations of the committee,[70] although representatives from the AIM group were consulted. However, Women's Aid representatives were making their views known in bureaucratic circles and the significance of their contribution was, in return, recognized by administrators.[71]

During the 1980s, the funding and staffing of refuges became a highly charged issue, culminating in a strike of voluntary workers at the Women's Aid refuge in a city suburb of Dublin. This particular problem, which stemmed from personality factors among the staff of the refuge and from disagreements over policy direction, led to a rethink by state officials of the funding and support services for victims of domestic violence. The State intervened to provide funding and professional staff for the Dublin service through the Eastern Health Board, a blueprint that was followed by other health boards. By 1985, twelve groups located in the main urban centres in the country were receiving a modest amount of financial support from the State.[72] Now, a moderate level of financial security gave the voluntary staff of the Dublin refuge, many of whom were campaigning feminists, the opportunity of concentrating on the politicization of the issue. Commenting on this change in orientation, the director of Women's Aid, Roisín McDermott noted:

> We have moved away from providing the emergency service. We firmly believe that is the responsibility of the Health Board and we would sooner put our energy into something like a second stage refuge which the government are never going to provide, because they would see it as a luxury. So we divide our time into three parts – using our political power to put pressure on government to create more refuges, providing a service which women need and working on providing a helpline and a second stage refuge.[73]

An indication of a new level of professionalism in the approach of Women's Aid to the political management of domestic violence was illustrated in the commissioning by the organization of the first piece of research on domestic violence in Ireland. This consisted of a survey of public attitudes towards family violence in Ireland as part of a common European Social Fund research project on domestic violence and child sexual abuse with the Women's Aid group in Northern Ireland and a childcare organization in Britain.[74] Some time later, a study commissioned by the Federation of Women's Refuges was published which built up a profile of the nature and frequency of domestic violence and assessed the response of the agencies from which battered women sought help. The study made a series of recommendations on the measures necessary for a more effective implementation of existing policies.[75]

Following the publication of these studies, the Minister for Justice, Gerard Collins,[76] introduced a bill amending the 1981 legislation to 'enable the court to grant a protection order as an alternative to, and separately from, a barring order'. The Minister referred to the submissions of the AIM group and the commitment in the Fianna Fáil election manifesto as being significant considerations in bringing forward this legislation:

> I might mention that this Bill was prepared in response to representations made by a number of interest groups concerned with family law reform, notably the AIM group, to the effect that a less drastic remedy should be available to victims of domestic violence, as an alternative to a full barring order. . . . I should like to point out also that the Bill follows the commitment in the Fianna Fáil *Programme for National Recovery* to amend the law to protect women against domestic violence.[77]

The opposition spokesperson on Justice, Alan Shatter, drew extensively on the recommendations in the Women's Aid research in responding to this Bill. However, the legislation did not proceed. Women's groups were unhappy with one aspect of the Bill, which provided that a judge would decide on which protective measure was appropriate, rather than the woman bringing the application.[78] Extensive representations were made to the Minister on this point. In withdrawing the Bill, the Minister recognized the opposition of the women's movement to its contents:

> opposition to it grew among women's organisations – including the body which had originally campaigned for the Bill – based on their fear that if the Bill were enacted the courts might almost invariably take the 'soft option' of granting a protection order instead of a barring order, thus diminishing the existing legal protection for wives and children who are the chief victims of family violence.[79]

By now, Women's Aid was beginning to gain recognition from politicians as a legitimate interest group sharing a similar agenda on domestic violence to AIM. In January 1991, the group held a meeting with the Oireachtas Joint Committee on Women's Rights, at which they sought increased funding for the refuge service; further research into the problem of domestic violence; legislative protection for all people living with a violent partner; and greater resources for the legal aid service.[80] At the same time, the AIM group began to campaign to have the 1981 Act amended to include cohabitees. This agenda was supported by Women's Aid which also sought a greater commitment on the part of the police authorities in following up breaches of barring orders.[81] As with the NWCI and the RCC, both organizations developed their respective political campaigns with little disagreement on the overall reform agenda and from this time onwards, Women's Aid activists were to give considerable attention to the political aspect of their business.

In a submission to the Commission on the Status of Women in February 1991, Women's Aid reiterated the three specific areas in which it sought reforms: that police be given powers of arrest when called to domestic dispute cases; the inclusion in the legislation of cohabitees; and improvements in the legal aid scheme. The Report to Government of the Second Commission on the Status of Women made recommendations similar to those presented by Women's Aid.[82] The Commission also recommended more effective procedures for police intervention in cases of domestic violence, an issue which was subsequently taken up by the Fianna Fáil–Labour government.[83] The media began to give regular attention to domestic violence and to the underfunded state of the refuge service.[84] However, while emergency funding was allocated by the government to individual refuges on an *ad hoc* basis, the issue did not gain further political attention until early in 1994.

The 1993 programme for government agreed between Fianna Fáil and the Labour Party contained a low-level commitment to reform the laws on domestic violence. Although there was no great public demand for reform, the Minister for Equality and Law Reform, Mervyn Taylor, gave domestic violence some priority and recognized Women's Aid spokespersons as offering a legitimate perspective in this policy area. Richard Humphreys,[85] the Minister's special adviser, described the manner in which Women's Aid representatives moved to the centre of the policy-formulating process:

When we came in to office in 1992 the issue of domestic violence legislation was only a bit of an idea, really. No tangible work had been done since the failed government bill in 1987. It wasn't really high on the agenda and Mervyn Taylor wanted to add a bit of impetus to it. We consulted with Women's Aid and the Rape Crisis Centre and the Minister went to visit the Women's Aid refuge for the specific purpose of getting views from people who would benefit from new legislation. They put forward very clear views, very helpful suggestions. Obviously we already had some material in the form of the Commission on Women report, the Kilkenny incest investigation and the Law Reform Commission report. But all the same it was very valuable and useful to have Women's Aid's point of view especially as they're the main organisation on the scene.[85]

Legislation was prepared in the Department of Equality and Law Reform before the collapse of the Fianna Fáil–Labour government in November 1994 which met the demands of Women's Aid. The draft legislation survived the government upheavals of the time and was brought before parliament in 1995. The Domestic Violence Bill of 1995 received general consensus in parliament on 6 December and was passed into law effective from 27 March 1996. The Act contained a series of wide-ranging reforms including strengthening the powers of arrest of police authorities in domestic violence incidents; extending the law to give cohabitees protection from a violent partner and giving parents protection from violent children over 18 years of age; making safety orders available as an alternative to barring orders, and providing health boards with the powers to apply for protection orders on behalf of adult and child victims of domestic violence.[86] A safety order could last for five years and the life of a barring order was extended to up to three years.

This new legislation has been welcomed by all concerned with domestic violence. However, Women's Aid continues to campaign for adequate resources for the District Court system which will ensure the implementation of the legislation and to press for adequate monitoring of the legislation. Roisín McDermott's reaction to the Act reflects these concerns:

> The legislation is very good, but the resources were not given to the courts. And since the legislation was enacted, applications to the District Court within two months rose by 131 per cent. So that's the Department of Justice's problem, not Equality and Law Reform. Now we are lobbying for the resources to deal with it.[87]

The mainstreaming of domestic violence did not end with the enactment of the Domestic Violence Act of 1996. Drawing on a comprehensive study[88] commissioned by the organization in 1995, Women's Aid representatives presented a case to government for the development of an overall government policy on domestic violence by an interdepartmental committee. McDermott commented on the manner in which Women's Aid set about convincing government of the necessity of developing an integrated policy on domestic violence:

> One of the recommendations of the research was that an inter-departmental committee be set up because we have noticed over the years that a woman may have to go to five or six government Departments in her attempts to deal with an abusive man. The

Departments are not speaking to each other, and we are speaking to all of them individually. And interestingly enough, through our affiliation with Women's Aid in Britain we heard about Leeds interface project. We have been over there twice or three times to research the project. So we have been trying to sell this to government. We started lobbying on 1st November 1995. We had our first meeting with officials from the Department of Health and we've been at it ever since. It is now ready to be set up in three weeks' time. It will be overseen by the Department of the Tanaiste [deputy Prime Minister]. It's a huge, huge step forward because it will finally mean that the Departments are speaking to each other. Health, Social Welfare, Justice, Education, Environment are involved. . . .We have senior policy-makers on it. We're happy about that. We're hoping they will draw up a plan within three years of how that group can actually be mirrored at local level. I think it's a really important step. So we are very pleased we managed to do it.[89]

On 15 October 1996, the first meeting of the government's working group on violence against women was held with a brief to report to the government by February 1997. The membership of the working party was broadened from that envisaged by Women's Aid to include representatives of the police force, health boards and experts from the voluntary sector as well as government officials. The task set for the working party was twofold: to examine the most effective methods of delivering a quality service and support to women and children who were victims of violence, and to recommend ways of reducing the incidence of violence through education and through work with violent men.[90]

Women's Aid is now clearly recognized by policy-makers as a group with a valuable contribution to make to the drafting of legislation in view of its extensive experience in the area of domestic violence. While the AIM group also continues to promote policy reforms in this area, the focus of media and political attention has shifted towards Women's Aid. McDermott has no illusions as to the relevance of Women's Aid to decision-makers:

The reason governments meet us is because they know we have actually some pull, we have some say and we have a following. It's not that any of them have a conscience about domestic violence. They literally weigh up the situation and ask themselves 'what will happen if I meet them, what will they say if I don't'. We have a very strong media profile. I think we have managed to carve out a niche for ourselves and we are seen as experts in this area, so if anything does happen the media automatically come to see us. Politicians take notice of strong voices, because they simply cannot afford not to.[91]

When it comes to securing political gains, Women's Aid leaders have learned to play the game by the conventional rules of pressure politics. So far, the formula has worked.

DISCUSSION

This chapter has shown how two women's groups, initially quite peripheral to the political process, lobbied to secure a measure of protection for women from sexual and domestic violence. The study also shows how two other more established groups, the NWCI and AIM, were largely responsible for putting the issue on to the political agenda in the first place and obtaining a response from policy-makers. The initial demands of both the NCWI and AIM groups were met to differing degrees. The Criminal Law (Rape) Act of 1981 did not go far enough in addressing the issue as analysed by the women's movement in general and women's interest representatives and thus it was to be a campaigning issue for some considerable time. The Family Law (Protection of Spouses and Children) Act of 1981 went further than women's groups expected it to go, so that demands were satisfied and there was no evidence of pressure for reform building up for some time.

These two differing policy outcomes led to the newer women's interest representatives, the RCC and Women's Aid, following different campaigning routes and the issue of sexual violence was returned to the political agenda through the efforts of the RCC. The group was largely responsible for defining the terms on which the debate on rape and sexual assault took place in government, parliament and associated arenas. In contrast, domestic violence did not feature in public discussion until 1991, when AIM and Women's Aid separately began to define specific areas for reform and sought to bring these changes about. From this time onwards, Women's Aid made the transition from being a pressure group on the periphery of the policy network to one given recognition by policy-makers.

Both the RCC and Women's Aid are involved in providing a voluntary social service. The dual burden of the demands of service provision and active campaigning has been felt within both organizations, exacerbated in both cases by lack of funding. The resolution of these internal tensions was accompanied by a major restructuring of each organization and the availability of increased government funding on more flexible terms. This reflects a growth in the professionalization of the service aspect of both groups and is also seen in the more active and focused campaigning strategies of each organization. This in some respects echoes the conclusion of Stedward,[92] who, following May and Nugent, claims that the internal tensions of a group are an important variable in determining group relations with policy-makers.

The above study of the politics of women and violence shows a very striking pattern: that of an older, more established women's group being replaced as the women's interest representative in a particular policy area over a period of time by an organization with a more radical view. This occurred in the case of the NWCI and the RCC in the area of sexual violence and between AIM and Women's Aid in the area of domestic violence. The newer representatives of women's interests were not accepted by policy-makers solely on the basis of their lobbying skills, but because both had the legitimacy of experience and expertise in the policy area of violence against women. In more recent years, both groups have been perceived by the public, the media and government as being spokespersons for the women's movement on the issue of women and violence and, through the campaigns of activists in both organizations, the issue has become part of mainstream politics and government business. Significantly, in both cases, the commitment to legislative reform from within the administration was an important element in shaping a satisfactory policy outcome. This continued commitment is indicated by regular conferences organized by government agencies,[93] government-led working parties on violence and consistent political attention to the problem of violence against women. A Domestic Violence and Sexual Assault Unit was opened in the national headquarters of the police force in 1993 and police training programmes now include the study of sexual violence. Both Women's Aid and the RCC have played a significant role in the educational development of the police force in this area. More recent events suggest a trend towards breaking the isolationist mould in which these feminist organizations have worked to date and there is evidence of increasing co-operation with other feminist organizations and with state agencies in the development of a more coherent public policy approach to the issue of women and violence. The effects of this new development in main-streaming the issue of violence against women is bearing fruit, with a greater awareness of the complexities of the issue evident among professional bodies, state agencies and the judiciary.

NOTES

1. See, for instance, Joni Lovenduski and Vicky Randall, *Contemporary Feminist Politics: Women and Power in Britain* (Oxford: Oxford University Press, 1993),

pp. 302–51; Dorothy McBride Stetson, *Women's Rights in France* (New York: Greenwood Press, 1986), pp. 161–73.

2. Joni Lovenduski, *Women and European Politics: Contemporary Feminism and Public Policy* (Brighton: Wheatsheaf, 1986), p. 267; Gisela Kaplan, *Contemporary Western European Feminism* (London: Allen & Unwin, 1992), refers to the situation in Italy, pp. 251–3, and in France, p. 169.

3. Maria Teresa Gallego Mendez, 'Women's political engagement in Spain', in Barbara Nelson and Najma Chowdhury (eds), *Women and Politics Worldwide* (New Haven: Yale University Press, 1994), p. 669; Ann R. Cacoullos, 'Women confronting party politics in Greece', in Nelson and Chowdhury (eds), *Women and Politics Worldwide*, p. 319.

4. McBride Stetson, *Women's Rights in France*, p. 168.

5. Hilda Tweedy, *A Link in the Chain: The Story of the Irish Housewives Association 1942–1992* (Dublin: Attic Press, 1992).

6. *WICCA*, Issue 1 (1978), pp. 7–8.

7. *Banshee*, Issue 1, p. 11.

8. Socialist Group, *Sexual Violence against Women and Girls* (Brussels: Socialist Group, 1986).

9. Council for the Status of Women, *Submission on Rape in Ireland* (Dublin: CSW, 1978), p. 6.

10. Dublin Rape Crisis Centre, *First Report* (Dublin: DRCC, 1979), p. 6.

11. Lovenduski, *Women and European Politics*, p. 261; *Proceedings of Seanad Eireann*, Vol. 91, cols 1121–2, 4 April 1979.

12. Council for the Status of Women, *Submission on Rape in Ireland*.

13. Dublin Rape Crisis Centre, *First Report*, p. 9. This report gives 26 July 1977 as the date on which the decision by feminists to campaign for legislative change was made.

14. The issue was discussed at a national women's conference in January 1978 and at a special conference in Galway in May 1978. *WICCA*, Issue 1, p. 2.

15. Lovenduski and Randall, *Contemporary Feminist Politics*, p. 318.

16. Women Against Violence Against Women, Leaflet, October 1978.

17. Women Against Violence Against Women, Press statement, 13 October 1978.

18. Dublin Rape Crisis Centre, *First Report*, p. 8.

19. *Dáil Debates*, Vol. 305, cols 1709–11, 27 April 1978.

20. *Dáil Debates*, Vol. 311, col. 1141, 14 February 1979.

21. *Proceedings of Seanad Éireann*, Vol. 91, cols 1078–1132, 4 April 1979.

22. *Proceedings of Seanad Éireann*, Vol. 91, col. 1118, 4 April 1979.

23. *Proceedings of Seanad Éireann*, Vol. 94, cols 679–88, 17 June 1980; cols 955–62, 19 June 1980.

24. *Dáil Debates*, Vol. 323, col. 1453, 4 November 1980.

25. The support among women for the reforms advocated by the NWCI was evident from the resolution on rape passed at a national women's forum in November 1980. A summary of the debate noted that 'the introduction of a Government Bill on Rape was long overdue and must include all forms of rape to cover those who had been forced to engage in abnormal sexual practices, and that rape within marriage should be recognized as a crime'.

Council for the Status of Women, *Irish Women Speak Out: A Plan of Action* (Dublin: Co-op Books, 1981), p. 73.

26. *Dáil Debates*, Vol. 323, col. 1454, 4 November 1980.

27. *Dáil Debates*, Vol. 323, col. 1463, 4 November 1980.

28. Yvonne Fitzsimons, 'Women's interest representation in the Republic of Ireland: the Council for the Status of Women', *Irish Political Studies*, **6** (1991), 37–52.

29. Interview with Seán Doherty, former Minister for Justice, 27 July 1994.

30. *Labour '81 Election Programme* (Dublin: Labour Party, 1981), p. 52; Fianna Fáil, *Our Programme for the '80s* (Dublin: Fianna Fáil, June 1981), p. 63.

31. Interview with Breda Allen, legal adviser to the Rape Crisis Centre, 2 July 1992.

32. Breda Allen, 2 July 1992.

33. Interview with Michael Noonan, former Minister for Justice, 14 July 1994.

34. *Irish Times*, 10 December 1990, p. 2; *The Report of the Joint Committee on Women's Rights on Sexual Violence* noted that 'it was an earlier written submission from this group [Dublin Rape Crisis Centre] calling for amendments to the Act which initiated the Joint Committee's examination' (Dublin: Stationery Office, 1987), p. 8.

35. The Oireachtas Committee invited members of the Garda Síochána, the Law Society, the Sexual Assault Treatment Unit as well as the Rape Crisis Centre to give formal evidence on the operation of existing legislation governing sexual violence.

36. Joint Committee Report, *Sexual Violence*, pp. 44–5.

37. Joint Committee Report, *Sexual Violence*, pp. 10–11.

38. Joint Committee Report, *Sexual Violence*, pp. 45–9.

39. Law Reform Commission, *Rape and Allied Offences* (Dublin: Law Reform Commission, May 1988), p. v [LRC24–1988]. This gives 6 March 1987 as the date on which the Attorney General requested the Law Reform Commission to formulate proposals for the reform of the 1981 Act.

40. Law Reform Commission, *Rape and Allied Offences*, pp. 33–4.

41. Law Reform Commission, *Rape and Allied Offences*, p. 8.

42. Interview with Olive Braiden, Director of the Rape Crisis Centre, 29 June 1992.

43. *Proceedings of Seanad Éireann*, Vol. 121, col. 1477, 15 December 1988.

44. *Proceedings of Seanad Éireann*, Vol. 121, col. 1912, 1 February 1989.

45. Olive Braiden, 29 June 1992; Breda Allen, 2 July 1992; and James Martin, a civil servant in the Department of Justice with responsibility for preparing the rape legislation, 8 August 1994.

46. Olive Braiden, 29 June 1992.

47. Olive Braiden, 25 September 1996.

48. This was the famous 'X' case which led to a complex referendum on abortion in 1992 and mobilized public sympathy for victims of rape and sexual assault. For an account of the 'X' case and the referendum, see Brendan Kennelly and Eilis Ward, 'The abortion referendums', in Michael Gallagher and Michael Laver (eds), *How Ireland Voted 1992* (Dublin and Limerick: Folens and PSAI Press, 1993), pp. 115–34.

49. *Irish Times*, 2 November 1996, p. 6.

50. *Irish Times*, 11 November 1996, p. 1.

51. Caroline Fennell, 'Criminal law and the criminal justice system: woman as victim', in Alpha Connelly (ed.), *Gender and the Law in Ireland* (Dublin: Oak Tree Press, 1993), pp. 168–9.

52. *Irish Times*, 10 December 1990, p. 2.

53. Interview with Roisín McDermott, Chairperson of Women's Aid, 9 September 1996.

54. Committee on Court Practice and Procedure, *Desertion and Maintenance* (Dublin: Stationery Office, 12 February 1974), p. 10 [Prl. 3666].

55. Hilda Tweedy, *A Link in the Chain*, p. 40.

56. See, for instance, articles in the *Irish Independent* such as 'What protection for battered wives?', 6 March 1974, p. 10; *Irish Times*, 'Finding a refuge for beaten wives', 4 April 1974, p. 15, and 'In the shadow of violence', 28 January 1976. See also Maeve Casey, *Domestic Violence against Women: The Women's Perspective* (Dublin: Federation of Women's Refuges, 1987), p. 7.

57. Nuala Fennell, 30 June 1992. Similar sentiments are recorded in various newsletters of the AIM group. Issue no. 6 in March 1974 contained the following statement: 'Just as ADAPT was formed as a result of the persistent incidence of desertion and the problems it creates similarly our next major project is being undertaken because of the many cases we are meeting of wife brutality . . . this is a very serious problem, again, in all income groups and in city and country areas.'

58. *Women's AIM*, 3 (October–December 1979), 2; *Women's AIM*, 4 (January–March 1980), 9.

59. *Magill*, January 1978.

60. *WICCA*, 2 (Summer 1978), pp. 7–8.

61. Adapt Refuge, Limerick and Mid Western Health Board, *Seeking a Refuge from Violence, the Adapt Experience* (Dublin: Policy Research Centre, 1993), Vol. 1, p. 10.

62. Women's Aid documentation, untitled (February 1981), pp. 19–20.

63. *Dáil Debates*, Vol. 328, col. 2385, 7 May 1981.

64. Interview with Patrick Terry, former civil servant in the Department of Justice with responsibility for preparing the legislation, 28 July 1994.

65. Patrick Terry, 28 July 1994.

66. *Dáil Debates*, Vol. 328, col. 2417, 7 May 1981.

67. Patrick Terry, 28 July 1994.

68. *Women's AIM*, 9 (Autumn 1981), 12.

69. Joint Committee on Marriage Breakdown, *Report* (Dublin: Stationery Office, 27 March 1985) [Pl. 3074], pp. 66–70.

70. Joint Committee on Marriage Breakdown, *Report*, pp. 129–30.

71. Interdepartmental Working Party on Women's Affairs, *Irish Women: Agenda for Practical Action* (Dublin: Stationery Office, February 1985), pp. 157–8 [Pl. 3126].

72. Interdepartmental Working Party on Women's Affairs, *Agenda for Practical Action* (Dublin: Stationery Office, February, 1985), p. 182.

73. Roisín McDermott, 11 July 1992.

74. Women's Aid Refuge, *Findings of a Common Research Project Between Women's Aid, Dublin, Boys and Girls Welfare Society, Cheshire, Northern Ireland Women's Aid, Belfast* (Dublin: Women's Aid, 1986).

75. Maeve Casey, *Domestic Violence Against Women.*

76. *Dáil Debates*, Vol. 375, col. 1300, 19 November 1987.

77. *Dáil Debates*, Vol. 375, col. 1302, 19 November 1987.

78. Interview with Anne O'Connor, spokeswoman for the AIM group, 8 August 1994.

79. Minister for Justice, *Marital Breakdown: A Review and Proposed Changes* (Dublin: Stationery Office, 1991), p. 40 [Pl. 9104].

80. *Irish Times*, 24 January 1991.

81. *Irish Times*, 29 January 1991.

82. Second Commission on the Status of Women, *Report to Government* (Dublin: Stationery Office, January 1993), pp. 44–7 [Pl. 9557].

83. *Irish Times*, 9 March 1994, p. 4.

84. *Irish Times*, 10 June 1991, p. 10; 16 July 1991, p. 10; 20 December 1993, p. 17.

85. Interview with Richard Humphreys, special adviser to the Minister for Equality and Law Reform, 30 June 1994.

86. *Irish Times*, 18 May 1994, p. 8; 27 May 1994, p. 2.

87. Roisín McDermott, 9 September 1996.

88. Kelleher and Associates and Monica O'Connor, *Making the Links: Towards an Integrated Strategy for the Elimination of Violence against Women in Intimate Relationships with Men* (Dublin: Women's Aid, 1995).

89. Roisín McDermott, 9 September 1996.

90. *Irish Times*, 16 October 1996, p. 5.

91. Roisín McDermott, 9 September 1996.

92. Gail Stedward, 'Entry to the system: a case study of Women's Aid in Scotland', in A. G. Jordan and J. J. Richardson (eds), *Government and Pressure Groups in Britain* (Oxford: Oxford University Press, 1987), p. 222.

93. See, for example, the Safety for Women Conference organized by the Garda Síochána and Department of Justice with the assistance of the NWCI in October 1992.

CHAPTER 7

CONTRACEPTION

In 1973, Mary McGee, a 27-year-old mother of four children and the wife of a fisherman, made legal history when she established her right in law to import into Ireland a contraceptive jelly for her own use. It was to take another six years before the Dáil passed legislation decriminalizing contraception and twenty-one years in total before all prohibitions on the availability of contraceptives were lifted. Few countries in the Western world experienced controversies around contraception in the late twentieth century, Ireland being an exception to this general rule. The public and political debate on the sale and availability of contraceptives lasted for a decade, and it involved a sustained challenge to a confessional state by a highly political family planning organization, campaigning feminists, a number of liberal politicians and a single courageous woman.

Liberalizing the ban on contraceptives was a key aim of the women's liberation movement and was sustained as a feminist issue in subsequent years. Yet, in contrast to the other policy concerns discussed in this book, it cannot be seen solely as a concern of the women's movement. The legalization of contraception was on the political agenda of social reformers who, although sympathetic to and supportive of the feminist cause, were not necessarily involved in women's movement politics.

The contraception controversy can be taken as a reflection of the changing nature of Irish society in the course of a generation. It represented a visible weakening of restrictive social norms and religious orthodoxy and it became a focus for liberal voices in parliament and public life. Significantly, it mirrored a silent revolution on the part of women, changing in a fundamental way the nature of women's relationship with society.

The story of the Irish contraceptive debate began in 1935, with the passage of the Criminal Law (Amendment) Act. This piece of legislation sought to regulate prostitution and, in the process, proscribed the sale, importation, advertisement and distribution of contraceptives.[1] The Censorship of Publications Acts of 1929 and 1946 reinforced this ban on all recognized methods of family planning. Section 7 of the 1929 Act prohibited all literature which advocated 'the unnatural prevention of conception or the procurement of abortion or miscarriage, or the use of any method, treatment or appliances for the purpose of such prevention or procurement'. As Jackson points out, the intention informing these statutes was to restrict sexual mores, not to develop pro-natalist policies.[2]

However, state laws alone did not bring about a climate in which contraception was not an issue open to public discussion: the conservative attitude of the Roman Catholic Church to such matters encouraged a climate of sexual repression and denial. Michael Solomons, a Jewish gynaecologist and founder of the first Family Planning Centre in the country, observed:

> The strict moral guide-lines on sex and sex-related matters that were upheld by the Catholic Church had instilled a fear of sex in many people and created a climate in which it was unlikely that a frank discussion about sex would take place. Although there was no law preventing people from talking about family planning or the use of contraception, for the majority of men and women there was no one to discuss it with.[3]

Catholic clergy advocated the practice of 'natural' family planning through the use of the Billings method and the rhythm method, as alternatives to abstinence from sexual relations within marriage. Legal prohibitions were reinforced by the moral teaching of the Roman Catholic Church, which forbade the use of artificial methods of birth control: indeed, the contraception issue vividly illustrates the close and interlocking relationship between policy decisions in the Irish State and Catholic social teaching.

Ireland, though, was not unique in experiencing a close collaboration between the Catholic Church and the State on such matters. In other European countries with an institutionalized Roman Catholic Church, legislation allowing for the practice of birth control was introduced relatively late in the twentieth century. In France,[4] for instance, laws to legalize contraception were introduced in parliament in 1967 and passed in 1974, while the Italian parliament decriminalized contraception in 1968,[5] followed by the Spanish parliament in 1978.[6] In Chile,[7] the Philippines[8] and other non-European Catholic countries, Catholic teaching and state laws combine to restrict access to contraception to the present day.

There is a suggestion that the perpetuation of a climate of repressive sexual mores in Ireland stemmed from national economic circumstances. In a survey of the literature on social practices in late nineteenth-century Ireland, O'Higgins[9] concluded that economic deprivation after the 1845–48 Famine led to a pattern of postponed marriages and a high level of permanent celibacy. This Malthusian[10] approach to population control required a strict moral code if it was to be effective. Inglis gave an insight into the mutual reinforcement of economic requirement and Catholic social teaching when he observed that

The temptations that years of celibacy imposed on [the unmarried Irish] could obviously only be resisted with the help of a powerful moral code; priests felt it necessary to push sexual licence to the head of the ordinary sins against which they preached; and also to seek in every possible way to remove the occasion of sin, such as mixed gatherings for dancing and other relaxations, which elsewhere would have been thought innocent enough.[11]

These social attitudes, which led Solomons to observe that 'the word contraception was missing from the national vocabulary',[12] persisted until the 1960s. This resistance to social change was noted by Kirk, who declared:

Éire has been for decades resistant to particular changes in social attitudes, and in family and welfare law, which have become common-place in many European countries during the post-war years. . . .There is hardly another European country in which a single religion so completely dominates the culture.[13]

Apart from some isolated questions in parliament, contraception did not become a political issue until around 1970. None the less, demographic and attitudinal trends were developing which were to underpin the intense public debate on birth control during the 1970s. As we have seen, Ireland experienced a boom in marriage and a decrease in the age of marriage for both men and women during the 1960s. Given the high degree of commitment to religious practice in the community, one would expect a consequent rise in overall fertility, yet this did not happen. Instead, from 1963 onwards, when the contraceptive pill became available in Ireland, family size began to decline. Given the legal prohibition on contraception, the pill was prescribed as a 'cycle regulator', and Mary Henry, an outspoken liberal doctor, observed that 'The Pill was a God-send for both Irish doctors and women because it is perfectly obvious that it had nothing to do with sex.'[14]

The personal decision by many fertile women to engage in sexual relations without fear of pregnancy was an issue which Irish governments ignored during the 1960s, although on an international level the government was aware of moves to liberalize contraception laws. Ireland was one of fifty-six nations to subscribe to a resolution which considered 'that couples have a basic human right to decide freely on the number and spacing of their children and a right to adequate education and information in this respect'. This resolution was passed at the United Nations Conference on Human Rights in Tehran in 1968.[15] The following year, 1969, the government supported a similar resolution at the General Assembly of the United Nations.[16] Contraception was not, however, on the political agenda of the Irish government.

In early 1969, the first family planning clinic was opened in Dublin by a group of doctors, trading under the name of the Irish Family Planning Association (IFPA) and modelled on the lines of British family planning organizations. The IFPA conducted its business in a low-profile manner, relying on personal and medical networks for publicity. Solomons, in describing the early days of the family planning clinic, conveys a sense of the conservative attitude in Irish society towards contraception:

> Our main fear was not being raided by the Gardaí but that the phone would not ring. In fact only 167 new patients visited the clinic in 1969, and we spent most evenings chatting and drinking cups of tea. Here lay the rub. It was a difficult business putting the word about that a family planning clinic had set up shop in Dublin. We had agreed during meetings that we should keep a low profile in order to avoid possible legal challenge. We were relying on discreet disclosures from doctors, nurses and between friends to alert people to our existence. We told clients about all methods of contraception that were available to us at the time; this included the rhythm method, the pill and diaphragms. It was then up to the client to make up her mind. At this time the majority were middle class. We regretted that the so-called 'blue card' holders, the majority of whom were working class, were not turning up to any great extent. It revealed a problem with our information networks and customer targeting practices but it also revealed the extent to which conservative teaching continued to dominate people's lives. Even in 1969 the majority of Irish people would have been unwilling to visit a family planning clinic, believing the use of 'unnatural' methods of family planning to be a sin.[17]

This low profile was not to continue. In 1970, the Irish Medical Union held a public meeting on family planning which was packed to capacity. One of the speakers was a young senator, Mary Bourke (who shortly afterwards married and changed her name to Mary Robinson), a specialist in constitutional law.[18] The meeting attracted widespread media coverage and effectively sparked a lively public debate on birth control. The issue of legalizing contraception remained topical and widely debated in the country during the remainder of 1970. In 1971, the public debate on contraception was further enlivened, assisted by the coincidence of a number of events.

The politicization of the family planning question came about in March 1971 when three Senators – Mary Robinson, John Horgan and Trevor West – sought to introduce a bill repealing the existing legislation.[19] Arguing for publication of the Bill, Mary Robinson noted that the subject has been discussed widely in the Press and debated around the country. . . . We feel that to be allowed to publish the Bill would curtail a great deal of misleading talk. It would mean that the debate would be centred on the relevant subject matter of the Bill, on the strict control of distribution of contraceptives which it now contains, and on the same issue, which is a civil rights issue, whether we, as an Irish community, can tolerate the practices of others in relation to practices which we might not condone for moral reasons.[20]

This attempt to introduce a Private Member's Bill reforming the family planning laws failed, as did three further efforts in the following five months, as the Fianna Fáil government displayed implacable opposition to the introduction of legislation of this kind.[21]

Action to change the laws was not confined to the parliamentary arena: the women's liberation movement began to hold a number of public protests on the issue. Protests which demanded a removal of the restrictive laws on contraception took place outside Roman Catholic churches during Mass on Sundays, pickets were placed on political party offices and regular demonstrations were mounted outside the gates of Leinster House. At the Labour Party Annual Conference in 1971, a motion was passed supporting the legalization of contraception in Ireland.[22] The issue raised divisions within the party between the reformers and those from rural areas who were strongly opposed to change: indeed, after the issue was debated at the conference, delegates on opposing sides spat at one another as they made their way out of the conference hall.[23] However, over time, Labour Party leaders sought to amend these divisions, and Labour was to remain the only party advocating this reform for many years. Perhaps the most colourful protest of all was the 'contraceptive train' – an event which in hindsight can be seen as a defining moment in the campaign to legalize contraceptives in Ireland. The succinct description offered by Solomons captures the event and its implications for the law:

On 22 May 1971 members of the Irish Women's Liberation Movement travelled to Belfast on what became known as 'the contraception train'. The women bought condoms and other contraceptives in Belfast and returned with their illegal imports to challenge the customs officials at the Dublin terminus. The authorities let them pass without question. As a media event the contraceptive train was a great success. Highlighting the fact that in some respects Irish law was an ass, the women got huge press coverage.[24]

This event caused considerable embarrassment for the government. In reply to a Dáil question on the incident, the Minster for Finance, George

Colley,[25] sought to defend the legal position by denying that there had been any importation of contraceptives. He declared that 'none of the customs officials is aware of the incidents of the kind alleged'. The Catholic Church continued to hold that contraception was an immoral act and totally forbidden by Church teaching, and Church leaders referred to the 1968 papal encyclical, *Humanae Vitae*, to support this position. Yet there were some signs of more liberal thought within the Catholic Church; for instance, a confidential report to the Irish Theological Association recommended that

Section 17 of the Criminal Law (Amendment) Act be amended to remove the restriction of freedom of methods of family planning; this has become an obviously divisive piece of legislation especially when so many people regard contraception not only as permissible, but even as a duty in certain circumstances. The social good which the law is seeking to promote can and should be promoted in other ways. Consequential amendments of the 1929 and 1946 censorship Acts are also recommended.[26]

However, the Irish hierarchy continued to oppose any attempt to legalize the importation and use of contraceptives. In the meantime, family planning clinics (which were still operating outside the law) were being established in other parts of Dublin in order to cope with the increasing demand for their services, and one large state-funded maternity hospital began to provide a family planning service for patients. The status quo on contraception was being eroded.

On 19 December 1973, a single event made reform inevitable. Some years earlier, acting on medical advice, Mrs Mary McGee ordered a quantity of contraceptive jelly for her personal use from England. The contraceptive was confiscated by the Revenue Commissioners, in response to which, Mrs McGee took her case against the State and the Revenue Commissioners, testing the legality of the actions of the State in impounding the jelly. Following a two-year legal battle, Mrs McGee made legal and constitutional history when the Supreme Court found that she had a right to import contraceptives into Ireland for personal use.[27]

Although this legal finding placed the issue back into the parliamentary arena, the anti-contraception lobby was preparing to challenge any liberalization of the law. Immediately following the issuing of the Supreme Court judgment, on 20 December, officials of the IFPA were charged with selling, offering and advertising contraceptives and the distribution of a book containing family planning advice.[28] The summons came about as a result of a complaint made to the police authorities by John O'Reilly, a member of the Irish Family League (IFL), a conservative

Catholic organization, who was later to become the mastermind behind the successful campaign to place a ban on abortion in the constitution in 1983. IFPA members were found guilty of the charge and fined.

Early in 1974, following the Supreme Court decision in the McGee case, Mary Robinson proposed the second stage of another Family Planning Bill in the Seanad. She called for a repeal of the prohibition on the sale of contraceptives, arguing that the Supreme Court judgment made it necessary for legislators to act on this issue, that the situation lacked coherent regulation and that the government commitments to inter-national human rights declarations required an amendment of national law.[29] This view was opposed by other senators who favoured support for the status quo, as 'the law regarding the sale of contraceptives is clearly concerned with public morality as part of the common good'.[30] Opponents of the Family Planning Bill supported the position of the Catholic Church on the use of contraceptives. They advocated a more widespread use of natural family planning methods and suggested that when these methods of fertility control failed, more children were a welcome addition to any family.[31] Some speakers warned of the consequences of liberalizing the contraception laws in apocalyptic terms, envisaging that 'the mail order companies were going to fly in and had already hired squads of women who were recruited to distribute contraceptives'.[32]

At this point, there were clearly two opposing positions reflecting the divisions in society on the issue. One, in favour of reform, sought to provide for the family planning needs of heterosexual couples and saw this reform as part of the process of building a pluralist Ireland. Opponents of reform argued that contraception would lead to abortion and was against the teaching of the Roman Catholic Church and against the morality of 90 per cent of the population. These positions were not to change in the coming years: what *was* to change was the level of support for either side.

The lively Seanad debate was brought to an end when the Minister for Justice, Patrick Cooney, announced in the upper house that the government was poised to introduce its own Family Planning Bill. Commenting on the government measure some weeks later, Mary Robinson noted it to be a

> very, very restrictive and unacceptable measure for those of us who would like to promote the right to family planning in this country . . . it is aspects such as the confining of contraceptives to married people, the licensing of the venues, the licensing of those who wish to manufacture, sell or have contraceptives which make the Government Bill unworkable.[33]

The coalition government's measure (entitled The Control of Importation, Sale and Manufacture of Contraceptives Bill, 1974) proved to be a divisive piece of legislation. Conservative members of the larger of the two coalition parities, Fine Gael, did not support its passage in the Dáil. Indeed, parliamentary history was made when the Taoiseach, William Cosgrave and the Minister for Education, Dick Burke, were two of the seven government politicians who crossed the floor of the house to join the Opposition in voting down the measure. The Bill was defeated by seventy-four votes to sixty-one.[34] With victory going to political conservatives, Ireland was once again spared the 'dangers from sex speculators and legalized brothels'.[35]

In December 1974, contraception was once again raised in the Seanad by Mary Robinson through a Private Member's Bill. While a majority in the Seanad agreed to publish the Bill, parliamentary timetabling tactics were used to block further progress of the measure. Two years later to the day, the issue was brought before the upper house again as a Labour Party Private Member's Bill by Mary Robinson and John Horgan, both of whom had joined the Labour Party in the interim. The legislative measure came shortly after the Censorship of Publications Board had banned the IFPA booklet *Guide to Family Planning* on the grounds that it was 'indecent and obscene'.[36]

Although the ban was ruled as invalid by the High Court on 1 July 1977, Irish attitudes towards contraception were still quite conservative, if changing; for instance, an opinion poll taken in 1971 showed that only 34 per cent favoured a change in the law to make contraceptives publicly available.[37] Although over 40,000 women were using the pill by 1975, opinion polls showed that supporters of reform had increased to 47 per cent.[38] Professor Quinlan, a conservative member of the Seanad, tapped into the mood of the majority when he asked whether the Irish people were prepared to legalize contraception and 'to follow the road of mother England, to follow along the road to decadence which has so quickly and so drastically overtaken Great Britain in the past two decades?'[39]

Although this legislative initiative was again doomed to failure, public attitudes towards changing the law on contraception were to change quickly. Early in 1976, the women's movement and members of the women's section of the Labour Party joined with the IFPA in forming a pressure group to work for a change in the law. The committee, with a national base, became known as the Contraception Action Programme (CAP), and directed its campaigning efforts to raising public awareness of the issue. Two of CAP's most successful strategies were the collection of signatures on a nationwide petition calling for the legalization of contraception and the holding of a public meeting in Dublin on

30 November 1976. According to a feminist magazine which carried a report of the campaign, 'Before the public rally organized by CAP held in the Mansion House on November 30th last, contraception was not a live issue according to the various journalists and TV people CAP approached. How wrong they were!'[40] The efforts of the CAP campaign began to pay dividends when support for the cause of the group began to come from a range of different organizations. Trade union and student organizations, women's groups, the NWCI, community associations along with small left-wing political parties supported the reform movement spearheaded by CAP.[41] In April 1977, the membership of the NWCI gave an overwhelming majority vote for change, while the Irish Medical Association and the Irish Association of Social Workers also favoured reform of the law.[42] Public opinion was slowly changing to support a reform in the contraceptive laws.

This swing in the public mood did not go unnoticed by politicians: in the course of the 1977 general election, Fianna Fáil gave a commitment to introduce legislation on contraception within a year of being in office, one promise among many in a manifesto with a highly populist appeal. The party won the general election with a significant majority. Party leaders were reminded of their promise some seventeen months after taking office by Mary Robinson in the course of moving her seventh Private Member's Bill on the issue in the Seanad.[43] Although assured that the government was about to introduce a measure to that effect, Robinson and other opposition members of the Seanad stepped up the pressure on Fianna Fáil to deliver on its commitment. The Health (Family Planning) Bill was published by the Minister for Health, Charles Haughey, on 13 December 1978.

This Bill was a complex and conservative one; although it contained some of the Robinson proposals, it was essentially a minimalist response to the situation where couples were increasingly using birth control methods without concern for the law. The Bill charged the regional health boards with the provision of a comprehensive natural family planning service. It restricted the availability of contraceptives to a prescription when a doctor was 'satisfied that the contraceptives are sought *bona-fide* for the purpose of family planning or for adequate medical reasons and in appropriate circumstances'.[44] Chemists with ethical objections to stocking contraceptives would not be obliged to do so, while the advertising and importation of contraceptives was to be restricted to licensed wholesalers and chemists.

This 'Irish solution to an Irish problem', as the Bill was described by the Minister for Health, provoked a strong response from all sides. Conservatives pointed out the loopholes in the Bill such as a failure to include a definition of an abortifacient, no prohibition on teenage sexual activity or no proof of marriage needed by doctors in prescribing contraceptives.[45] Liberal parliamentarians were equally opposed to the measure on the grounds that it did not go far enough in reforming the law. The Bill and the views it provoked did not take women into account, according to a Labour Party member of parliament, Eileen Desmond:

> We are still a very paternalistic society. We think that adults must have their mind made up for them and their morals decided for them on a matter like this. We decide that the personal decisions of women, the people who are most concerned, should be disregarded. This Bill and much of the debate has been mindless and brutal towards women and their problems. As a woman TD I must protest at the blatant disregard for women as persons which has been displayed in this Bill. Male lobbies have been vocal on this matter and have submitted their views, which they are entitled to do, but they have no right to dictate to the many harassed, overburdened, often underweight and sometimes battered young mothers whom I meet during my constituency work.[46]

Amid accusations from the opposition parties in parliament of secret meetings and clandestine deals between the Minister for Health and the Roman Catholic hierarchy, the measure passed all stages and became law in 1979. Thus, a demand initially voiced by the women's movement, given practical effect by the spread of family planning clinics and stridently opposed by conservative forces eventually found its way on to the statutes of the land, in the process of which the coalition of liberals and feminists that formed around contraceptive reform was opposed by both Church and State. However, the extent of conservative opposition to changing the status quo was such that governments had little room to manoeuvre when seeking to give effect to the Supreme Court judgment in the McGee case.

Indeed, the story of family planning in Ireland became a story of a struggle for dominance between the views of liberals and conservatives and between secular and denominational forces. Just as in the case of abortion politics reform in Italy, the feminist perspective was lost in the conflict between other, longer established and more entrenched politically polar opposites. With the wisdom of hindsight, one can see that the struggle to bring about reform of the laws on contraception was the first expression of a tension which was to recur at regular intervals during the 1980s and 1990s – a conflict between the status quo and the forces of change around sexual matters and morality.

The limited access to contraception permitted in the 1979 Act (which came into effect on 1 November 1980) defused the grass-roots CAP campaign and the committee disbanded. However, it soon became apparent that the intention of the Act to control the sale of condoms and restrict their supply to married couples who wished to use them for *bona fide* family planning purposes was proving unworkable, as in the months following the enactment of the law, various ways of skirting the restrictions in the statute were found. Family planning clinics set up chemists' shops on their premises to enable them to sell contraceptives; student leaders began to install contraceptive vending machines in colleges in breach of the law. None the less, government turned a blind eye to these breaches of the law, and it was estimated that from 1980 onwards, around ten million condoms were sold each year. However, conservative opponents of the legislation remained vigilant: in 1983, a doctor and a leading member of the IFPA, Andrew Rynne, was fined £500 for supplying condoms to a patient at a weekend when chemists' shops were closed. This event once again drew the attention of elected representatives to the unresolved problems surrounding the family planning legislation. In 1984, in a similar action, members of the family planning clinic in Dun Laoghaire, the south Dublin constituency of the Minister for Health, were prosecuted for selling condoms.[47]

On return to office in 1982, the Fine Gael and Labour government promised to review the family planning legislation and provide a full family planning service where required. Early in 1985, the Minister for Health, Barry Desmond, introduced a Bill which sought to amend the 1979 Act so as to provide 'an acceptable framework for the provision of a comprehensive family planning service for all those who require such service'.[48] An assessment of the availability of family planning services had found that there were significant areas of the country where chemists were unwilling to stock condoms. Doctors, too, had difficulty in operating the Act: some refused to do so on grounds of conscience, others argued that it was not the function of a doctor to prescribe non-medical contraceptives. The lack of a nationwide family planning service was also highlighted in the departmental review: of the fifteen family planning clinics in the country at the time, only five were located outside the Dublin area. The Health (Family Planning) Bill of 1985 brought to government by Desmond sought to address these two central issues by extending the sale of condoms to health board clinics, doctors' surgeries, maternity hospitals and family planning centres and by making them available without a prescription to anyone over 18 years of age. Strong objections to the Bill were expressed by the Roman Catholic hierarchy on the grounds that the Bill encouraged immorality; it was also opposed by Fianna Fáil, who were accused of political opportunism by parliamentarians from the government side. Opposing the Bill in parliament, the Fianna Fáil spokesman on health, Dr Rory O'Hanlon, argued that 'There is nothing to stop a young girl of 15 or 16 years of age from going into a chemist's shop wearing high-heeled shoes and asking for contraceptives. How is the chemist to know her age?' Conservative politicians on the government side also opposed the amendment and called for a free vote as in 1974. Fears that the Bill would 'open the sluice gates to widespread promiscuity', of increased sexual activity among teenagers, of 'the spectre of serious, detrimental moral change' and 'a growth in venereal diseases' formed the basis of conservative objections within and outside parliament.[49]

The parliamentary debate took place in a highly charged atmosphere. The bruising 1983 constitutional referendum banning abortion was still fresh in the minds of the public and parliamentarians alike. The mobilization of political forces which characterized that political event was easily repeated by tightly organised groups opposing the Bill, and the intimidation to which supporters of the Bill were subject, including threats of kidnapping and burning, was raised by the Minister for Health and echoed by other speakers. Desmond O'Malley, a Fianna Fáil parliamentarian supporting the Bill, described it thus:

> the most extraordinary and unprecedented extra-parliamentary pressure [that] has been brought to bear on many Members of the house. This is not merely ordinary lobbying. It is far more significant. I regret to have to say that it borders at times almost on the sinister.[50]

Women's views were represented by Gemma Hussey, Monica Barnes and Nuala Fennell, three Fine Gael politicians with backgrounds in feminist politics. They pointed out that women were unhappy with the existing law which led many to depend on the rhythm method and other forms of natural family planning for birth control. The NWCI sought the support of all parliamentarians for the 1985 Bill and after a short, intense debate, the amendments to the 1979 Act were carried by a narrow majority. The practical effect of the 1985 reforms was to regularize and increase the availability of condoms, but it did not fill the voids in the provision of comprehensive family planning facilities in the country as a whole; nor did it legalize the sale of condoms from vending machines and other sources. It did, however, mark a success for the liberal supporters of a reform agenda in family policy, just as it marked the fulfilment of a central aim of the women's movement. For many, the passage of the 1985 Act brought to an end a campaign which had lasted for almost fifteen years.

Yet this reform bill did not finally put the contraception issue to rest. Unfinished business remained as to the question of the outlets where condoms could be sold and their supply to those under 18 years of age. With a growing realization of the public health problem of the spread of the AIDS virus, the availability of condoms once again became a focus of attention. Public interest was sparked by the prosecution of the IFPA for breaking the law by selling condoms in a music shop, Virgin Megastore, in Dublin city centre. In defence of their actions, IFPA representatives argued that their reason for having an outlet in a public place was motivated by their commitment to fight the spread of infectious diseases, in particular HIV and AIDS. Although the IFPA lost the case, and was subject to a fine of £500 (paid on their behalf by the rock band U2), the controversy served to place the availability of condoms back on to the political agenda. The government was clearly embarrassed at having to deal with this no-win issue, and the Minister for Health, Rory O'Hanlon, responded by introducing the Health (Family Planning)(Amendment) Bill to parliament in 1991. The Bill gave the responsibility to the health boards to decide on the availability of condoms in their area, and drew an irate reaction from the members of the health boards, many of whom were government parliamentarians and local councillors, who criticized their ministerial colleague for his lack of political leadership.[51] However, in a cabinet reshuffle some months later, this contentious piece of legislation was discarded in favour of an alternative version proposed by his successor in the Department of Health, John O'Connell. In his second-stage speech, the Minister firmly defined the proposed law as a preventive medical matter and not a contraceptive issue when he declared that 'the prevention of transmission of these diseases is a matter of serious concern not only to my Department, but also to the wider community. The wider availability of condoms, coupled with educational initiatives, has a major role to play in this endeavour'.[52]

Criticism from the opposition parties that the Bill was a restrictive one, failing to make a full and comprehensive national family planning service available to all, was accepted by the Minister at committee stage.[53] Having agreed to institute a service of this kind, the measure passed quickly into law; however, it was to be revisited just one year later by O'Connell's successor, Brendan Howlin. The prohibition on the sale of condoms from vending machines and the difficulty of enforcing the age limit of seventeen years for condom purchasers – two provisions in the 1992 Act – had proved difficult to enforce. Furthermore, officials in the Department of Health remained concerned about the public health risks associated with unprotected sexual activity, and in response to these concerns Howlin introduced the Health (Family Planning)(Amendment) Bill in 1993. In doing so, he isolated this measure even more from the need to provide a national comprehensive family planning service, with public health considerations given priority and family planning to be given attention 'as part of an overall strategy for health which is currently being developed in the Department'.[54] The Bill legalized the sale of condoms from vending machines, abolished the age criteria for their purchase and removed all controls over the sale and supply of condoms. Although the measure was generally welcomed by legislators, Liz O'Donnell of the opposition Progressive Democrat Party pointed out that women's rights to control their fertility were once again being ignored:

> Tubal ligation is still only available in a very restricted way in public hospitals. Indeed the right of women not to have children has never been conceded yet in this state. One of the first frontiers of the women's movement was the right to have true reproductive freedom for women. The battle goes on.[55]

The provision of a comprehensive contraceptive and family planning service continues to exercise the minds of women and administrators. In the wake of the 1992 referendum on the right to travel for abortion and the right to access to information on abortion services in other countries,[56] the provision of a comprehensive family planning service had been given some attention by officials in the Department of Health and by individual health boards. On instruction from the Minister for Health, Michael Noonan, all health boards have assessed their family planning services[57] and most surveyed their women patients with regard to the adequacy of medical services for women. One typical response[58] was that 40 per cent of women viewed family planning services in their area as inadequate. In 1996, it was obvious that a political commitment was forthcoming to ensure the provision of an adequate family planning service throughout the country. This included providing services for male and female sterilization; medical contraceptives such as the pill and spermicides; non-medical contraceptives such as condoms, IUDs and diaphragms; natural methods and education, counselling and advice on all legal methods of contraception. Given the political and religious sensitivities on the issue of abortion in Ireland, it remains to be seen how 'comprehensive' that service will be.

DISCUSSION

The issue of contraception is an interesting example of a feminist issue being mainstreamed and in the process being redefined by legislators. It also illustrates the difficulties faced by the women's movement in retaining ownership of an issue which excites public controversy and mobilizes opposing political forces. The campaign for the reform of the laws on contraception was first begun by the women's movement and feminists engaged with other liberal groups, notably the IFPA, in campaigning for reform. The issue was introduced into the legislative arena by liberal politicians sympathetic to the feminist demand. None the less, the weight of conservative opinion in society and political life ensured that this issue would find difficulty in advancing past the introductory stage in the political process. The one catalyst to the progress of this issue was the judicial finding in the McGee case, which forced legislators to consider ways of introducing reforms of the contraceptive laws.

The six-year time lapse between the ruling of the Supreme Court and the enactment of a modest family planning law indicates the marginal nature of this issue as a political concern. Political decision-makers, who in other circumstances were advocates of protective policies for women, did not feel obligated to legislate for reproductive control; indeed, the time lag could have been longer were it not for the public support for reform demonstrated by the activities of the CAP campaign. This organization succeeded in building a grass-roots coalition of diverse groups and individuals around the need for reform which could not be ignored by decision-makers. Other factors, too, contributed to forcing political attention on the issue. The continual civil disobedience campaign waged by the IFPA which at certain times prompted police action highlighted the inadequacy of family planning laws, and the concern for public safety as knowledge of HIV and AIDS grew among the medical and political community also focused attention on prevention through the use of condoms. Yet at no time during the entire period of the campaign was the nature of a fully comprehensive family planning service ever defined by legislators or debated in parliament, thus preventing an acrimonious discussion on abortion, a political issue which polarized the country in 1983. From a politician's perspective, there were few votes in advocating that abortion be part of a comprehensive state family planning policy; instead, contraception became narrowly defined as a policy for the sale of condoms. This understanding of contraceptive practice facilitated a public health interpretation of the issue which accompanied a progressive liberalizing of the contraceptive laws in the 1990s. However, the health in question was not defined in terms of women's health and reproductive control needs: although condoms became available without restriction, women's needs in the area of fertility control failed to be met. There was a political consensus around the need to contain the AIDS crisis in spite of the objections of the Roman Catholic Church to the practice of homosexual relations, yet no such consensus was forthcoming around the contraceptive needs of women. At the present time, this issue is being handled in a low-profile manner, with a focus on the health requirements of women. However, the implementation of a fully comprehensive family planning service remains the responsibility of each of the eight regional health boards, which offers eight different sites for future controversy on this issue.

Ultimately, feminist agitation on contraception was subsumed into a general liberal campaign to reform the law. While the women's movement played a significant part in the public campaign to pressure for legislative change, particularly in 1971 and again in the 1976–79 period, the control of the issue lay chiefly with Irish legislators. Feminist activists failed to form an identifiable pressure group dedicated to the reform of family planning laws. In this instance, the pattern of successful exclusively feminist lobbying, which we have seen take place in other policy areas, did not occur, partly because of the lack of feminist leadership on this issue, but also because of the existence of the IFPA. This organization, while incorporating feminist activists, was liberal in its ethos, had considerable legitimacy as a medically dominated group and was perceived as the voice of reform. In addition, feminist and IFPA demands were aired in parliament by liberal politicians. There was little room for the development of a parallel independent feminist campaign on this issue in the already crowded liberal space occupied by other supporters; nor was it possible to contain the issue and the controversy it engendered to a single government department, unlike other feminist policy arenas. The reform of the contraception laws proved too visible and divisive an issue for the exercise of controlled political management by feminists or legislators. Once parliament had ratified the 1979 and 1985 Acts, contraception as an issue of reproductive right was no longer on the political agenda. Abortion and contraception were kept separate by CAP activists and political reformers alike, while those opposed to the extension of contraceptive freedom linked both issues. Gradually, a state contraception policy as a multi-dimensional response to women's reproductive needs became defined in narrow terms when it became a matter of the sale of condoms rather than a question of the provision of counselling, educational, medical and surgical facilities for women's fertility control. This latter question is the one the Minister for Health, Michael Noonan, has only recently, in 1995, begun to hesitantly recognize. It has taken the Irish political system one whole generation to accept the feminist demand for reproductive control. Given the strong representation of conservative interests on many of the country's hospital and health boards, it may take another generation before this demand is implemented in full.

NOTES

1. Section 17(1) of the Criminal Law (Amendment) Act, 1935 provided that: 'It shall not be lawful for any person to sell, or expose, offer, advertise, or keep for sale or to import or attempt to import into Saorstat Eireann, for sale any contraceptive.'

2. Pauline Conroy Jackson, 'Women's movement and abortion: the criminalization of Irish women', in Drude Dahlerup (ed.), *The New Women's Movement: Feminism and Political Power in Europe and the USA* (London: Sage, 1986), p. 51.

3. Michael Solomons, *Pro-Life? The Irish Question* (Dublin: Lilliput Press, 1992), p. 15.

4. J. Cohen, 'France: a change of policy', in E. Ketting (ed.), *Contraception in Western Europe: A Current Appraisal* (Carnforth, Lancs: Parthenon Publishing Group, 1990), pp. 13–17.

5. G. Benagiano, 'Italy: contrasts in family planning', in E. Ketting (ed.), *Contraception in Western Europe*, pp. 51–6.

6. J. Linhard, 'Spain: ten years of progress', in Ketting, E. (ed.), *Contraception in Western Europe*, pp. 29–35.

7. Lezak Shallat, 'Rites and rights: Catholicism and contraception in Chile', in Judith Mirsky and Marty Radlett (eds), *Private Decisions, Public Debate: Women, Reproduction and Population* (London: Panos, 1994), pp. 149–62.

8. Malou Mangahas, 'The oldest contraceptive: the lactational amenorrhea method (LAM) and reproductive rights', in Judith Mirsky and Marty Radlett (eds), *Private Decisions, Public Debate*, pp. 57–68.

9. Kathleen O'Higgins, 'Family planning services in Ireland with particular reference to minors', in Hyman Rodman and Jan Trost (eds), *The Adolescent Dilemma: International Perspectives on the Family Planning Rights of Minors* (New York: Praeger, 1986), p. 107.

10. Orest and Patricia Ranum (eds), *Popular Attitudes Toward Birth Control in Pre-industrial France and England* (London: Harper & Row, 1972), pp. 2–3, 118–22.

11. Brian Inglis, *The Story of Ireland* (London: Faber and Faber, 1966), quoted in O'Higgins, 'Family planning services in Ireland', p. 108.

12. Michael Solomons, *Pro-Life?*, p. 6.

13. Maurice Kirk, 'Law and fertility in Ireland', in Maurice Kirk, Massimo Livi Bacci and Egon Szabady (eds), *Law and Fertility in Europe: A Study of Legislation Directly or Indirectly Affecting Fertility in Europe*, Vol. 2 (Liege, Belgium: European Coordination Centre for Research and Documentation in Social Sciences, 1975), pp. 387–8.

14. *Proceedings of Seanad Éireann*, Vol. 92, col. 656, 13 July 1979.

15. Solomons, *Pro Life?*, p. 23.

16. *Proceedings of Seanad Éireann*, Vol. 69, col. 1355, 31 March 1971.

17. Solomons, *Pro-Life?*, pp. 29–30.

18. Solomons, *Pro-Life?*, p. 32.

19. *Proceedings of Seanad Éireann*, Vol. 69, col. 1151, 10 March 1971.

20. *Proceedings of Seanad Éireann*, Vol. 69, col. 1356, 10 March 1971.

21. *Proceedings of Seanad Éireann*, Vol. 70, col. 168, 12 May 1971; cols 705–9, 30 June 1971; cols 964–70, 7 July 1971.

22. Interview with Mary Freehill, Labour Party Councillor and a founding member of the Contraception Action Programme, 26 January 1997.

23. *Sunday Tribune*, 7 July 1991, p. 13.

24. Solomons, *Pro-Life?*, p. 33.

25. *Dáil Debates*, Vol. 254, col. 881, 2 June 1971; cols 1345–9, 9 June 1971.

26. McDonough Report, quoted in Maurice Kirk, 'Law and fertility in Ireland', in Kirk *et al.*, *Law and Fertility in Europe*, p. 395.

27. For a brief legal outline of this case, see Maurice Kirk, 'Law and fertility in Ireland', in Kirk *et al.*, *Law and Fertility in Europe*, pp. 395–6.

28. Maurice Kirk, 'Law and fertility in Ireland', in Kirk *et al.*, *Law and Fertility in Europe*, p. 396, and Solomons, *Pro-Life?*, p. 37.

29. *Proceedings of Seanad Éireann*, Vol. 77, col. 205–18, 20 February 1974.

30. *Proceedings of Seanad Éireann*, Vol. 77, col. 245, 21 February 1974.

31. *Proceedings of Seanad Éireann*, Vol. 77, cols 267–89, 21 February 1974.

32. *Proceedings of Seanad Éireann*, Vol. 77, col. 377, 21 February 1974.

33. *Proceedings of Seanad Éireann*, Vol. 77, col. 655–7, 21 March 1974.

34. *Dáil Debates*, 16 July 1974.

35. Quote from Dáil speech of noted conservative politician, Oliver J. Flanagan, referred to in Solomons, *Pro-Life?*, p. 38.

36. Solomons, *Pro-Life?*, p. 41; *Proceedings of Seanad Éireann*, Vol. 85, col. 1074, 16 December 1976.

37. *Sunday Tribune*, 7 July 1991, p. 13.

38. Hibernia poll, quoted in *Proceedings of Seanad Éireann*, Vol. 85, col. 1078, 16 December 1976.

39. *Proceedings of Seanad Éireann*, Vol. 85, col. 1113, 16 December 1976.

40. *Banshee*, 6 (January 1977), 6.

41. *WICCA*, Issue 8, 1978, pp. 15–16.

42. *Proceedings of Seanad Éireann*, Vol. 86, cols 799–85, col. 1078, 16 December 1976.

43. *Proceedings of Seanad Éireann*, Vol. 90, col. 223, 22 November 1978.

44. *Proceedings of Seanad Éireann*, Vol. 92, col. 603, 3 July 1979.

45. *Proceedings of Seanad Éireann*, Vol. 92, col. 607–22, 3 July 1979.

46. *Dáil Debates*, Vol. 313, cols 1299–1300, 5 April 1979.

47. *Irish Times*, 19 September 1984.

48. *Dáil Debates*, Vol. 355, col. 2582, 14 February 1985.

49. *Dáil Debates*, Vol. 355, col. 2589, 14 February 1985; Vol. 356, col. 191, 19 February 1985.

50. *Dáil Debates*, Vol. 355, col. 2591, 14 February 1985.

51. *Dáil Debates*, Vol. 356, col. 275, 20 February 1985.

52. *Irish Times*, 2 August 1991, p. 2.

52. *Dáil Debates*, Vol. 422, col. 741, 8 July 1992.

54. *Dáil Debates*, Vol. 422, col. 1231, 9 July 1992.

55. *Dáil Debates*, Vol. 431, col. 1727, 3 June 1993.

56. *Dáil Debates*, Vol. 431, col. 1743, 3 June 1993.

57. Brendan Kennelly and Eilis Ward, 'The abortion referendums', in Michael Gallagher and Michael Laver (eds), *How Ireland Voted 1992* (Dublin and Limerick: Folens and PSAI Press, 1993), pp. 115–34.

58. *Irish Times*, 24 March 1995, p. 1.

59. Midland Health Board Report, quoted in *Irish Times*, 19 March 1996, p. 3.

CHAPTER 8

CONCLUSION

In this book, I have discussed the emergence and evolution of many issues which characterize modern feminist politics in the Republic of Ireland. Modern Irish feminism has evolved since the 1970s. One notable feature of the feminist agenda is the extent to which it has expanded to incorporate a wide and complex range of issues. The original demand for equal rights in a number of specific issue areas has grown to include issues of difference and identity, and from a short-lived period of protest, feminism has spread its roots into the institutional political process. Although the heady days of mass mobilization passed quickly, the experience of women working together for change has been repeated around specific issues, some of which are included in this book. Irish feminists of today may not choose to have a picnic with their children on the lawn of Leinster House to draw attention to inadequate family policies and they do not often need to adopt protest strategies. In 1992, Irish women were sufficiently powerful to threaten the ratification of the Maastricht Treaty, and in 1996, they held the career of the Minister for Health in their hands as he mismanaged the hepatitis C scandal.

Although the visible signs of feminist mobilization were few and far between during the course of the last twenty-five years, feminism left a lasting mark on Irish politics. That legacy found a space and a voice within the political system when feminist organizations won a place at the negotiating table on specific issue areas. The involvement of feminist representatives in the policy process is growing all the time: one of the most recent developments has been the inclusion of NWCI representatives with the social partners in a national economic and social forum. We see also that feminism has left a mark on Irish political institutions which have evolved to incorporate a number of feminist policy agencies at national level. Political parties now take women's issues more seriously than before, although they have some way to go in addressing issues of gender representation within their organizations. We can say with some certainty that feminists have found a foothold in the policy-making process and that their concerns have become part of mainstream politics; yet their numerical representation in positions of influence in Irish politics and society is still inadequate. This remains a real challenge for Irish feminists now that their agenda is no longer a marginal one. That is the work of another day. In the meantime, they can take comfort from the knowledge that Irish feminists have become experienced and professional in their political dealings which will stand them in good stead in the future.

In writing this book, I began from the premise that the activities of Irish feminists made a difference to the development of women's rights policies from the 1970s onwards. I was not sure how that had happened, nor was I certain of the process involved. I now see that opening up a space for women-centred policies took place in the context of a traditional, socially conservative society. Yet Irish society was changing. The extent of this change can be seen in the comprehensive dismantling of gender-related discriminations since 1970. Through group activity, feminists sought to realize certain goals which would improve the status of women. The strategies used by some of these groups in order to achieve their policy objectives are documented in the book. Some have been more successful than others. Five case studies later, I am in a slightly better position to offer comments on the obstacles and opportunities which confronted feminist representatives as they negotiated policy reforms with the State. It was also noted that the issues around which women in Ireland constructed campaigns were not specific to this country; in fact, there was considerable similarity in the grievances of women across the European Union. The general cross-fertilization of ideas in European and international arenas contributed to the politicization process of women in Ireland.

So why did women's groups engage so closely with the political system in a classic interest group style? Why did they, in the terminology of interest group studies, seek to become 'insiders' rather than remaining as 'outsiders'? The answer lies in part with the nature of the women's movement in Ireland, in part with the pragmatism of the power-oriented movement leaders, and finally with the restricted range of strategic options available to women's rights activists. Together, these three factors led the women's movement towards institutionalization almost before the protest phase had ended.

Feminism in Ireland was largely a liberal rather than a radical phenomenon which offered a weak manifestation of feminist challenge compared with the mobilization of women in Britain and Italy. The movement demands were similarly weak, concentrating on equal rights issues rather than issues which challenged the role relationships between women and men in society; in other words, the women's movement of its own accord defined its grievances in role equity terms. Again, this is not surprising, given the dominance of conservative social values and attitudes in Ireland, and is a neat illustration of the point that social movements, being products of a specific political system, shape their demands in accordance with their perception of the tolerance of that system.

Second, while the women's movement was a tame manifestation of feminist protest found in other countries, it still found itself outside the parameters of conventional politics. However, the movement had neither the personal nor the organizational resources to sustain a challenge from the periphery of the established political process. With some notable exceptions, feminist protests were sporadic, unco-ordinated and lacking in a clear overall focus. It was impatience with this marginalization that led many Irish activists to reconsider their commitment to a movement of social protest. The celebrated case of the resignation of one of the founder members of the movement, Nuala Fennell, encapsulated the impatience of Irish women with marginal political action. In her own words, Fennell described the movement as 'anti-American, anti-clergy, anti-government, anti-ICA, anti-police, anti-men'.[1] It again comes as no surprise to find that Fennell went on to found the first contemporary women's rights pressure group, AIM, a short time later. Other politicized women shared Fennell's views and, eschewing the politics of protest, focused on becoming familiar with the established exchanges of routine politics in order to achieve equality for women.

Third, given the lack of support within society for radical politics, given the moderate reform demands of the women's movement and given the close, almost intimate style of Irish politics, the strategy offering the best potential for success lay in engaging in interest representation. Women, as we have seen, had no voice within the political or decision-making structures; thus their grievances were not heeded when expressed outside the structures of conventional political participation. The only viable alternative was to represent women's demands through the adoption of assimilative strategies such as lobbying, research and other conventional pressure group activities, a fact which gives relevance to the role of the NWCI as the representative voice of women in Ireland. It also explains the significance of the two government Commissions on the status of women and the political acceptance of their respective reports.

It seems as if the articulation of women's politics has relevance for decision-makers as long as it is conducted within establishment politics. In this, the Irish women's movement has more in common with Greek and possibly Portuguese feminist politics than with that of other European countries. Even in Spain, a country which shares many social patterns with Ireland, the politics of the women's movement followed a different path to that in Ireland. It involved co-option, without doubt, but the co-option into the political system did not take the form of a high level of interest group representation. Instead, as Mendez[2] shows, the women's movement was absorbed by the political forces striving for the creation of a democratic state. Feminism became part of the socialist political agenda, where it has remained ever since.

On the surface, the interest-group style of politics engaged in by women's representatives in Ireland has parallels with women's politics in the United States, but there is a significant difference. Interest-group politics is highly institutionalized in the American political system, where the main women's groups are well funded, have considerable resources at their disposal and operate as full-time professional lobbying organizations. In the Irish case, the representatives of women's interests often work on a voluntary or part-time basis, have few resources and often have funding problems which go so far as to threaten the continuance of the public service side of their activities.[3]

The point of addressing the issues of theory and practice in relation to the women's movement in Ireland is to show how social movement theories have a certain, if limited, value in explaining how and why the women's movement developed in the manner in which it did. In order to follow the story to its next stage, we need to turn to the interest-group literature, as the women's rights agenda was given political expression through the activities of women's groups engaging in standard interest representation. Social movements often adopt conventional interest-group structures and strategies in order to further their goals. This, as Offe[4] points out, is necessary if a movement is to continue, and is seen as a sign of institutional maturity. These groups are identified as social movement organizations and they can be seen as a subset of the cause-centred groups recognized in the theoretical work on interests, but undifferentiated by interest-group researchers. This diffuse pattern of social action is, according to Rouchon,[5] a characteristic of new social movements. However, if interest group strategies are adopted by a social movement, it follows that the theoretical analysis of power relations between groups and the State as supplied by interest-group researchers could provide a framework for constructing an analysis of group success. This book has addressed the group–government relationship in pluralist and corporatist contexts; this approach was found to be useful in determining a range of variables which appeared to occur with some frequency in studies of interest-group politics. It was not surprising to find that, in the application of social movement theories to specific case studies, these variables also occurred.[6]

In the introduction, I asked the question 'What do Irish women's groups do in order to influence public policy decisions?' From an extensive reading of the literature, I suggested that five factors were significant in facilitating or hindering the acceptance of feminist demands by the political system: the existing policy position; the pattern of interest intermediation; the attitude of the public and elected representatives; the lobbying skills of women's groups; and the capacity of government to initiate and support new policies. The application of these factors to the issues showed that combinations of the above variables interacted to assist or inhibit opportunities for the development of policy changes sought by feminist groups.

From the study, issue by issue, of the major sites of feminist mobilization in Ireland, one can conclude that the five factors chosen from the literature contributed to shaping the engagement of organized women with the political system. While most of the factors were present in each case, we have seen that some were more significant than others, and we are now in a position to draw some conclusions about the general operation of these factors.

The first conclusion to be drawn is the significance attaching to the structure of interest relations in a given policy area. Women's groups can press demands with greater facility in an open, pluralist context than in a policy arena characterized by a closed, corporatist pattern of interest representation. In other words, the agenda-setting of women's concerns is less problematic in pluralist policy environments. This is, of course, a general feature of interest-group relations and is well documented in the case of interest groups in other policy areas and political systems. Women campaigning for equal pay faced resistance from a corporatist policy network, where employers, unions and government were slow to acknowledge the presence of WAC and the demand for equal pay. In contrast, it was seen that members of the AIM, NWCI and RCC groups had easier access to policy-makers and a greater scope for representation of their agenda, although it was also seen that there are limits to the openness of pluralist politics in addressing issues from a feminist perspective. The contraception debate is a case in point. Here we can see clearly that the dominance of liberal interests in the contraceptive law reform campaign had the effect of constructing this debate in a narrow, legalistic fashion which inhibited the articulation of a feminist critique of reproductive control policies. Of course, although there were other factors influencing the shape of the contraception debate, it is interesting to observe the silence from feminists within the liberal constituency as to the scope and content of the controversy.

The second conclusion is that the opportunities for policy reform in a closed policy system are more limited than those occurring in a policy sector in which pluralist relations dominate. This is because feminist groups can exploit alternative institutional routes to decision-makers in open policy sectors, whereas in closed systems, it is difficult for feminist representatives to locate alternative channels of access to political agencies. As this study of the politics of employment equality shows, women's interest representatives had to go outside the conventional interest group framework in order to gain political attention for their demands. Similarly, in the contraception debate, the issue was placed on the political agenda by the Supreme Court. The government ignored the demand for legal reform expressed by liberal parliamentarians, the women's movement and the IFPA up until this point, in effect preventing the opening of this policy area to discussion through refusing to recognize that reform was required.

However, it has also been observed that not all feminist groups within open policy systems have the same access to policy-making arenas. This highlights my third conclusion, that the development of sophisticated lobbying and public relations skills are important for the successful representation of women's demands. Both AIM and the RCC groups stand out in this regard, while the maturing of Women's Aid is an example of an organization developing politically attuned lobbying skills over time. However, the best lobbying and public relations skills are to no avail unless there is a certain level of acceptance among the public and policy-makers that reform in a particular area is desirable. In the focus on a range of feminist demands it was found that the nature of the relationship between groups and the State was conditional on the level of social and political acceptance of these demands. Issues around which a broad consensus either existed or was generated were more likely to receive political attention than those without a generalized level of support. As was seen from the study of family law reform and sexual violence, the manifest public support for reform in these policy areas strengthened the position of feminist representatives in their discussions with decision-makers. It must be remembered, though, that in both instances, feminist groups played a pro-active role in generating that consensus and in bringing it to the fore and that, in the case of equal pay, the controversy surrounding the implementation of the policy witnessed a latent public support for the issue which feminists successfully mobilized. In contrast, my analysis of the contraception controversy points to the difficulties experienced by women's representatives in gaining a foothold in the policy arena, where even liberal parliamentarians found their initiatives blocked time and again by a political consensus opposing reform in this area. It took some time before moves to change the policy position were initiated.

Fifth, the general policy review that takes place within the bureaucratic system has a role to play in the advancement of women's rights, and this routine process can lead to policy outcomes which have the potential to be comprehensive and progressive. This illustrates an equally important fact: the extent to which public officials are willing to take a pro-active approach to policy-making in the area of women's rights. This proved to be a critical element in the creation of a satisfactory outcome for all participants concerned with protecting women from sexual and domestic violence. The extensive family law reforms introduced over a twenty-year period also indicate the willingness of the State to be active in shaping significant policy changes.

Although each issue area contained its own specific combination of factors, one can detect a pattern in which some factors assisted and others acted to inhibit the production of policy outcomes favourable to the women's groups in this study. The political engagement of women's groups will now be examined in this light.

STRUCTURAL OPPORTUNITIES FOR CHANGE

One clear variable facilitating a policy outcome which accords with the goals of the women's interest groups is the development of lobbying skills by women's representatives. This involves the acquisition of a deep knowledge of how the political system operates, the significant actors in a policy area, knowing the value of and utilizing various pressure points in the system, and mounting a consistent, reasoned and sustained campaign for policy change. In this study, the AIM group and the RCC are examples of groups which have learned how to lobby in a professional and organized manner. The AIM group built up regular contacts with successive Ministers for Justice, opposition spokespersons on Justice and with sympathetic parliamentarians. It argued for reform using the instruments of rationality, sustainable research and logical presentation of facts. It pointed to anomalies and flaws in existing policies and sought public and political support for their removal and replacement by policies which enhanced women's rights.

The RCC also used its knowledge of the political process to bring about a specific policy outcome by building parliamentary support for reform through the Oireachtas Committee on Women's Rights and through the political parties. It also gained support for its goals among the membership of the powerful government advisory body, the Law Reform Commission. A further factor was the promotion of a positive working relationship between public officials and the RCC representatives. This was as much dependent on the interpersonal dynamics of both groups as it was on objective assessments of the merits of policy change.[7]

In both cases, the lobbying skills of the group representatives overcame other obstacles such as the changing priorities of successive governments in the case of family law reform and the resistance to policy change by the government in the case of policies on sexual violence. In the case of AIM, it had the advantage of operating in a political and social environment which was open to a sympathetic consideration of family law reform. Indeed, the prevailing social attitude towards the need for reform in this area is graphically summed up by Levine:

> In retrospect it seems obvious that Irish society would accept the distressed wife as a charitable cause. The important thing was that *marriage* was not being questioned. No one was being blamed except 'the law'. The deserted wife became an institution. She wasn't asked to fight. She would be rescued. Poor woman. After all, what could she do if himself abandoned her? Besides, what about the unfortunate children?[8]

On the other hand, the RCC had to mobilize general support among women for legislative change in the policy on sexual violence, and there is evidence to show that such support existed. National gatherings of women identifying as feminists were concerned with the existing laws, and disquiet with the legislation was evident among women whom the NWCI sought to represent.[9] However, the skill of both AIM and the RCC was to harness this general dissatisfaction to support the reform agenda being sought in their respective policy areas by both groups. Thus, with the weight of public support behind them, representatives could hold discussions with public officials on government reform proposals from a position of strength. The AIM group and the RCC can be seen as particularly successful at the agenda-setting phase of policy-making.

The pattern of political engagement experienced by Women's Aid prior to 1990 stands in contrast to that of the above groups. Despite the existence of general support among women for amendments to the policies on domestic violence, Women's Aid was not in a position to capitalize on this support base as it did not have effective lobbying systems in place. Instead, the organization was enmeshed in the role of service delivery, which prevented it from concentrating on the policy aspect of its activities. By the time Women's Aid was in a position to focus on the national policy process, the agenda for reform had been co-opted by a left-of-centre government. None the less, the professionalization of Women's Aid as a representative organization during the 1990s has paid dividends, and it is now recognized by the government as a significant representative agency in this issue area.

The case of employment equality calls for a different analysis to that of the other issues. This is because, as we have seen, the pattern of interest relations in this policy sector were more highly structured and less permeable than those existing in the social policy arena. The feminist trade union group, WAC, did not play a major part in setting the equal pay agenda – this had been done by the EU and by the Commission on the Status of Women. Nor did it make a significant contribution to the formulation of equal pay proposals. WAC had, however, a significant role in keeping the issue alive in trade union politics. As an organization, it came to the fore in public terms at the stage of policy implementation when it organized a broad campaign under the umbrella of the Equal Pay Committee which mobilized popular support for the full implementation of the equal pay legislation. This mobilization has much in common with the strategies followed by challenging or 'outsider' groups. Given the closed nature of the policy sector, the choice open to the women's group was limited. None the less, this strategy paid off, and, allied to the ruling from the EU, had the desired policy effect; the spin-off effect in terms of group–government relations was the recognition of the views of the WAC in the subsequent formulation of the employment equality legislation. For a brief period, WAC succeeded in breaking into the tripartite policy network governing economic relations once it had shown that it could command alternative sources of political support for its goals.

OBSTACLES TO THE POLITICAL ADOPTION OF A FEMINIST AGENDA

The most persistent obstacle to the achievement of the goals of women's groups in this study is the resistance of the government to policy change. In each issue area discussed, there is evidence of the government's reluctance to advance on the terms of feminist policy positions. The contraception debate is probably the most visible example of the government's refusal to entertain a reform agenda. Another instance was government reluctance to revisit the 1981 law on sexual violence. The attitude of government to reform was probably most successfully managed by the AIM group: as its agenda was a wide-ranging one, it was able to accommodate its own goals to that of the government of the day. Hence, the changing political ideology of successive governments led to the enactment of varying pieces of the family law reform agenda in which AIM was an active participant.

The discussions on the politics of employment equality have shown how successive governments were largely indifferent to representations on equal pay. However, as already noted, this indifference was reinforced by a reluctance of both employer and trade union interests to see the policy enacted. In the case of the reform of the rape legislation, there was a conscious attempt by government to ignore the issue until the pressure for reform had grown too great to be ignored. In the context of domestic violence, the comprehensive policy changes, introduced largely through the commitment of senior public officials, served to defuse demands for reform, yet, as the implementation process highlighted inadequacies in the legislation, the government's response to pressures to amend the legislation was perceived by women's groups as inadequate. Thus, government's lack of interest, or indeed outright opposition, blocked the way for the enactment of policy change. Again, this finding emphasizes the general significance of government commitment which has been identified in the broad interest group studies.

MAINSTREAMING FEMINIST POLITICS

In sum, then, we can say that AIM and RCC organizations appear to have been the most successful in having their demands accepted by policy-makers as each group was closely involved in shaping the detail of legislation. This co-operative effort by feminist representatives and decision-makers ultimately produced policies that proved acceptable to all concerned. WAC witnessed the enactment of equal pay as an 'outsider' rather than as an 'insider' in the policy process since, although it had the ear of decision-makers as employment equality policies were being shaped, this was not as potent a political issue as equal pay. Indeed, the overall success of women's groups in bringing about change in the field of employment equality has been limited. Women's Aid has developed a considerable lobbying expertise and is recognized by the government as a significant voice for change in the area of domestic violence. While the history of politics in this area has been one in which administrative officials and government took the political initiative, this has now been superseded by the pro-active approach of Women's Aid leaders. Of late, too, is the emerging coalition between elite women's organizations on the issue of violence against women. In the reform of the contraception laws, the failure of feminists to articulate a distinct agenda meant that a woman-centred policy outcome was unlikely.

In terms of the pattern of group–government relations, we have seen that when policy issues were managed within a confined network, a generally satisfactory outcome was obtained for women. The main participants in this area were usually the relevant government minister, senior administrative officials answerable to the minister and interest group representatives directly involved with a particular issue. While other political and social groupings participated in the process, their involvement was largely in supportive or legitimizing roles rather than in making a direct contribution to shaping the detail of legislation. The politics of women's rights involved negotiation and compromise between a small group of individuals in each area, a pattern that can be seen to replicate the 'segmented pluralism' pattern identified by Jordan as being characteristic of policy-making in liberal democracies. Issues which provoked a wider debate, such as that of divorce and contraception, enlarged the policy-making arena, while the high visibility that accompanied debates on these issues and the degree of controversy they provoked made policy solutions more difficult to frame.

While there appears to be little space for protest-oriented groups in the Irish policy system, the use of protest-style politics was found to be necessary on occasions to bring home to the government the level of popular support among women for a particular demand. However, the pattern of conventional interest politics is reasserted once the point has been made, making the politics of women's rights in Ireland highly institutionalized, and resulting in limited substantive outcomes framed in terms of equality and the extension of protective rights. The radical agenda which incorporates a reappraisal of gender roles offered by autonomous feminism in other countries has, as yet, found no place in the interaction between women and politics in Ireland.

Finally, this study suggests a modification of a conventional wisdom often cited in the literature on women and politics. Lovenduski notes that 'if a policy has a low visibility, fits in with prevailing values and involves narrow concerns, its chances of adoption are greater than if it is controversial, wide ranging and conspicuous'.[10] The policies considered in this book were at one time challenging, high-visibility issues. Their political management by both feminist advocates and the State eventually brought them into the conventional policy network, in the process of which activists in these feminist organizations have been admitted to the routinized policy process. Feminist issues and women's organizations have now become part of mainstream politics in Ireland.

NOTES

1. June Levine, *Sisters: The Personal Story of an Irish Feminist* (Dublin: Ward River Press, 1982), p. 231.

2. Maria Teresa Gallego Mendez, 'Women's political engagement in Spain', in Barbara Nelson and Najma Chowdhury (eds), *Women and Politics Worldwide* (New Haven: Yale University Press, 1994), pp. 661–73.

3. In the case of AIM, the RCC and Women's Aid, the need to seek funding from the State and to raise money through voluntary fund-raising activities has placed a considerable strain on the energy of volunteer activists and has, by the admission of spokespersons, limited their capacity to act as effective lobbyists for policy reforms.

4. Claus Offe, 'Reflections on the institutional self-transformation of movement politics: a tentative stage model', in Russell J. Dalton and Manfred Kuechler (eds), *Challenging the Political Order: New Social and Political Movements in Western Democracies* (Cambridge: Polity Press, 1990), pp. 239–41.

5. Thomas R. Rouchon, 'The West European peace movement and the theory of new social movements', in Dalton and Kuechler (eds), *Challenging the Political Order*, pp. 105–6.

6. From a social movement perspective, Joyce Gelb, for instance, looks at feminist activity in Britain, Sweden and the US using a similar range of variables in *Feminism and Politics: A Comparative Perspective* (Berkeley: University of California Press, 1989). Coming from an interest-group approach to the study of women and politics, Boneparth and Stoper offer a selection of environmental, systemic and political variables along with a discussion of policy characteristics as a model for analysing women's engagement with the policy process. These are similar to the political opportunity structure model used by Gelb. See Ellen Boneparth and Emily Stoper, 'Introduction: A framework for policy analysis', in Ellen Boneparth and Emily Stoper (eds), *Women, Power and Policy: Towards the Year 2000* (New York: Pergamon Press, 1988), pp. 1–19.

7. This factor was mentioned by all participants involved in the discussions on changing the rape laws.

8. Levine, *Sisters*, p. 237.

9. See, for example, Bernadette Barry, *Women at Home: A Report on Nationwide Get-togethers* (Dublin: Council for the Status of Women, 1983), p. 9, and Mary Ena Walsh, *Women in Rural Ireland* (Dublin: Council for the Status of Women, 1983), p. 37.

10. Joni Lovenduski, *Women and European Politics: Contemporary Feminism and Public Policy* (Brighton: Wheatsheaf Books, 1986), p. 249.

BIBLIOGRAPHY

BOOKS, ARTICLES AND REPORTS

Adapt Refuge, Limerick, and Mid Western Health Board (1993) *Seeking a Refuge from Violence, the Adapt Experience*. Dublin: Policy Research Centre.

Bachrach, P. and Baratz, M. (1962) 'Two faces of power', *American Political Science Review*, **56**(4), 947–52.

Baker, Susan (1988) 'The nuclear power issue in Ireland: the role of the Irish anti-nuclear movement', *Irish Political Studies*, **3**, 3–17.

Baker, Susan (1991) 'Public policy agenda setting; the use of Northern Ireland's lignite deposits', *Administration*, **39**(2), 147–66.

Barry, Bernadette (1983) *Women at Home: A Report on Nationwide Get-togethers*. Dublin: Council for the Status of Women.

Barry, David (1989) 'The involvement and impact of a professional interest group', in D. G. Mulcahy and Denis O'Sullivan (eds), *Irish Educational Policy – Process and Substance*. Dublin: Institute of Public Administration, pp. 133–62.

Barry, Ursula and Jackson, Pauline (1988) 'Women on the edge of time: part-time work in Ireland, North and South', in Mary Buckley and Malcolm Anderson (eds), *Women, Equality and Europe*. Basingstoke: Macmillan, pp. 78–94.

Bashevkin, Sylvia (1994) 'Building a political voice: women's participation and policy influence in Canada', in Barbara J. Nelson and Najma Chowdhury (eds), *Women and Politics Worldwide*. New Haven: Yale University Press, pp. 142–60.

Beale, Jenny (1986) *Women in Ireland, Voices of Change*. Dublin: Gill & Macmillan.

Beleza, Maria Leonor (1983) 'Major legislation pertaining to women's rights', in Gisbert H. Flanz, *Comparative Women's Rights and Political Participation in Europe*. New York: Transnational Publishers Inc, pp. 409–14.

Benagiano, G. (1990) 'Italy: contrasts in family planning', in E. Ketting (ed.), *Contraception in Western Europe: A Current Appraisal*. Carnforth, Lancs: Parthenon, pp. 51–6.

Blackwell, John (1986) *Women in the Labour Force*. Dublin: EEA.

Blackwell, John (1989) *Women in the Labour Force*. Dublin: Employment Equality Agency & Resource & Environmental Policy Centre, UCD.

Boneparth, Ellen (1982) *Women, Power and Policy*. New York: Pergamon Press.

Boneparth, Ellen (1982) 'A framework for policy analysis', in Ellen Boneparth (ed.), *Women, Power and Policy*. New York: Pergamon Press, pp. 1–19.

Boneparth, Ellen and Stoper, Emily (1988) *Women, Power and Policy: Towards the Year 2000*. New York: Pergamon Press.

Boneparth, Ellen and Stoper, Emily (1988) 'Introduction: a framework for policy analysis', in Ellen Boneparth and Emily Stoper (eds), *Women, Power and Policy: Towards the Year 2000*. New York: Pergamon Press, pp. 1–19.

Breen, Richard, Hannan, Damien F., Rottman, David B. and Whelan, Christopher T. (1990) *Understanding Contemporary Ireland*. Dublin: Gill & Macmillan.

Brennan, Pat (1979) 'Women in revolt', *Magill*, **2**(7), 34–46.

Brown, Alice and Galligan, Yvonne (1993) 'Views from the periphery: changing the political agenda for women in the Republic of Ireland and Scotland', *West European Politics*, **16**(2), 165–89.

Buckley, Mary and Anderson, Malcolm (1988) *Women, Equality and Europe*. Basingstoke: Macmillan Press.

Cacoullos, Ann R. (1994) 'Women confronting party politics in Greece', in Barbara J. Nelson and Najma Chowdhury (eds), *Women and Politics Worldwide*. New Haven: Yale University Press, pp. 312–25.

Callan, Tim and Farrell, Brian (1991) *Women's Participation in the Irish Labour Market*. Dublin: National Economic and Social Council [Pl. 8449].

Casey, Maeve (1987) *Domestic Violence Against Women – The Women's Perspective*. Dublin: Federation of Women's Refuges.

Chubb, Basil (1992) *The Government and Politics of Ireland*. London: Longman.

Clancy, Mary (1989) 'Aspects of women's contribution to the Oireachtas debate in the Irish Free State, 1922–37', in Maria Luddy and Cliona Murphy (eds), *Women Surviving: Studies in Irish Women's History in the 19th & 20th Centuries*. Dublin: Poolbeg, pp. 206–32.

Clemens, Elizabeth S. (1993) 'Organizational repertoires and institutional change: women's groups and the transformation of U.S. politics, 1890–1920', *American Journal of Sociology*, 98(4), 755–98.

Coakley, John (1993) 'Society and political culture', in Coakley and Gallagher (eds), *Politics in the Republic of Ireland*. Dublin and Limerick: Folens and PSAI Press, pp. 25–48.

Coakley, John and Gallagher, Michael (1993) *Politics in the Republic of Ireland*. Dublin and Limerick: Folens and PSAI Press.

Cochrane, Allan and Clarke, John (1993) *Comparing Welfare States: Britain in International Context*. Milton Keynes: Open University Press.

Cohen, J. (1990) 'France: a change of policy', in E. Ketting (ed.), *Contraception in Western Europe: A Current Appraisal*. Carnforth, Lancs: Parthenon Publishing Group, pp. 13–17.

Commission of the EC (1992) *Women in the European Community*. Luxembourg: Commission of the European Communities.

Connelly, Alpha (1993) *Gender and the Law in Ireland*. Dublin: Oak Tree Press.

Connelly, Alpha (1993) 'The constitution', in A. Connelly (ed.), *Gender and the Law in Ireland*. Dublin: Oak Tree Press, pp. 4–27.

Connelly, Alpha and Hilliard, Betty (1993) 'The legal system', in A. Connelly (ed.), *Gender and the Law in Ireland*. Dublin: Oak Tree Press, pp. 212–38.

Connolly, Linda (1996) 'The women's movement in Ireland, 1970–1995: a social movement analysis', *Irish Journal of Feminist Studies*, 1(1), 43–77.

Conroy Jackson, Pauline (1987) 'Women's movement and abortion: the criminalization of Irish women', in Drude Dahlerup (ed.), *The New Women's Movement: Feminism and Political Power in Europe and the USA*. London: Sage, pp. 48–63.

Coulter, Carol (1993) *The Hidden Tradition: Feminism, Women and Nationalism in Ireland*. Cork: Cork University Press.

Council for Social Welfare (1974) *A Statement on Family Law Reform*. Dublin Council for Social Welfare.

Council for the Status of Women (1978) *Submission on Rape in Ireland*. Dublin: CSW.

Council for the Status of Women (1985) *Who Makes the Decisions?* Dublin: CSW.

Council for the Status of Women (1991) *Submission to the Commission on the Status of Women*. Dublin: CSW.

Cullen Owens, Rosemary (1984) *Smashing Times: A History of the Irish Women's Suffrage Movement, 1889–1922*. Dublin: Attic Press.

Curtin, Chris, Jackson, Pauline and O'Connor, Bernadette (1987) *Gender in Irish Society*. Galway: Galway University Press.

Dahl, R. A. (1961) *Who Governs?* New Haven: Yale University Press.

Dahlerup, Drude (1987) *The New Women's Movement: Feminism and Political Power in Europe and the USA*. London: Sage.

Dalton, Russell J. and Kuechler, Manfred (1990) *Challenging the Political Order: New Social and Political Movements in Western Democracies*. Cambridge: Polity Press.

Dalton, Russell J., Kuechler, Manfred and Burklin, Wilhelm (1990) 'The challenge of new movements', in Dalton and Kuechler (eds), *Challenging the Political Order: New Social and Political Movements in Western Democracies*. Cambridge: Polity Press.

Daly, Mary E. (1995) 'Women in the Irish Free State, 1922–1939: the interaction between economics and ideology', *Journal of Women's History*, 6(4)/7(1), 99–116.

Davies, P. L. (1987) 'European Community legislation, UK legislative policy and industrial relations', in Christopher McCrudden (ed.), *Women, Employment and European Equality Law*. London: Eclipse, pp. 23–51.

Donnelly, Seán (1992) *Poll Position: An Analysis of the 1991 Local Elections*. Dublin: Seán Donnelly.

Dowse, Robert E. and Hughes, John A. (1986) *Political Sociology*. New York: John Wiley & Sons.

Dublin Rape Crisis Centre (1979) *First Report*. Dublin: DRCC.

Duncan, William (1979) *The Case for Divorce in the Irish Republic*. Dublin: Irish Council for Civil Liberties.

Dunne, John (1975) 'The present position in Ireland', paper presented to a conference of the Federated Union of Employers on equal pay.

Eager, Clare (1991) 'Splitting images – women and the Irish civil service', *Seirbhis Phoibli*, 12(1), 15–23.

Employer, Labour Conference (1970) *National Agreement*. Dublin: Employer, Labour Conference [So. 463].

Employer, Labour Conference (1972) *National Agreement*. Dublin: Employer, Labour Conference.

Employment Equality Agency, *Annual Reports*, 1977–93.

Employment Equality Agency (1995) *Women in the Labour Force*. Dublin: EEA.

Eurostat (1995) *Women and Men in the European Union: A Statistical Portrait*. Luxembourg: Office for Official Publications of the European Communities.

Farrell, Brian (1988) *De Valera's Constitution and Ours*. Dublin: Gill & Macmillan.

Farrell, David M. (1992) 'Ireland', in Richard S. Katz and Peter Mair (eds), *Party Organizations: A Data Handbook on Party Organizations in Western Democracies, 1960–90*. London: Sage, pp. 389–457.

Federated Union of Employers (1969) *Women in Employment. Implications for Equal Pay*. Dublin: FUE.

Federated Union of Employers (1974) *Annual Report 1974*. Dublin: FUE.

Fennell, Caroline (1993) 'Criminal law and the criminal justice system: woman as victim', in Connelly (ed.), *Gender and the Law in Ireland*. Dublin: Oak Tree Press, pp. 151–70.

Fianna Fáil (1981) *Our Programme for the '80s*. Dublin: Fianna Fáil.

Fianna Fáil and Labour (1993) *Programme for a Partnership Government 1993–1997*. Dublin: Fianna Fáil and Labour.

Fitzsimons, Yvonne (1991) 'Women's interest representation in the Republic of Ireland: the Council for the Status of Women', *Irish Political Studies*, 6, 37–52.

Flanz, Gisbert H. (1983) *Comparative Women's Rights and Political Participation in Europe*. New York: Transnational Publishers.

Free Legal Aid Centres (1972) *FLAC Reports: The free legal advice centres report on their work since the organisation was founded in 1969 and make proposals for reform in our laws*. Dublin: FLAC.

Freeman, Jo (1982) 'Women and public policy: an overview', in Boneparth (ed.), *Women, Power and Policy*. New York: Pergamon Press, pp. 41–65.

Freeman, Jo (1983) *Social Movements of the Sixties and Seventies*. New York: Longman.

Freeman, Jo (1983) 'A model for analyzing the strategic options of social movement organizations', in Freeman (ed.), *Social Movements of the Sixties and Seventies*. New York: Longman, pp. 193–210.

Freeman, Jo (1983) 'On the origins of social movements' in Freeman (ed.), *Social Movements of the Sixties and Seventies*. New York: Longman, pp. 8–32.

Gallagher, Michael (1983) *The Irish Labour Party in Transition 1957–82*. Manchester: Manchester University Press.

Gallagher, Michael and Laver, Michael (eds) (1993) *How Ireland Voted 1992*. Dublin and Limerick: Folens and PSAI Press.

Gallagher, Michael, Laver, Michael and Mair, Peter (1992) *Representative Government in Western Europe*. New York: McGraw-Hill.

Galligan, Yvonne (1993) 'Party politics and gender in the Republic of Ireland', in Joni Lovenduski and Pippa Norris (eds), *Gender and Party Politics*. London: Sage, pp. 147–67.

Galligan, Yvonne (1997) 'Ireland', in Beate Hoecker (ed.), *Handbuch Politische Partizipation von Frauen in Europa*. Leverkusen: Leske & Budrich.

Gamson, William (1975) *The Strategy of Social Protest*. Homewood, IL: Dorsey Press.

Gardiner, Frances (1992) 'Political interest and participation of Irish women 1922–1992: the unfinished revolution', *Canadian Journal of Irish Studies*, 18(1), 15–39.

Geier, Karsten D. (1990) 'Peace movements and the struggle within: a reply to L. Martin Overby', *West European Politics*, 13(1), 275–9.

Gelb, Joyce (1989) *Feminism and Politics: A Comparative Perspective*. Berkeley: University of California Press.

Gelb, Joyce (1990) 'Feminism and political action', in Dalton and Kuechler (eds), *Challenging the Political Order*. Cambridge: Polity Press, pp. 137–55.

Gelb, Joyce and Palley, Marian Lief (1987) *Women and Public Policies*. Princeton, NJ: Princeton University Press.

Girvin, Brian (1987) 'The divorce referendum in the Republic, June, 1986', *Irish Political Studies*, 2, 93–8.

Hansard Society Commission (1990) *Women at the Top*. London: Hansard Society for Parliamentary Government.

Hesketh, Tom (1990) *The Second Partitioning of Ireland: The Abortion Referendum of 1983*. Dun Laoghaire: Brandsma Books.

Hillery, Brian and Lynch, Patrick (1969) *Ireland in the International Labour Organization*. Dublin: Department of Labour.

Hoecker, Beate (1997) *Handbuch Politische Partizipation von Frauen in Europa*. Leverkusen: Leske & Budrich.

Hoskyns, Catherine (1988) 'Give us equal pay and we'll open our own doors – a study of the impact in the Federal Republic of Germany and the Republic of Ireland of the European Community's Policy on women's rights', in Buckley and Anderson (eds), *Women, Equality and Europe*. Basingstoke: Macmillan, pp. 33–55.

Inglis, Brian (1966) *The Story of Ireland*. London: Faber and Faber.

Institute of Public Administration (1994) *Yearbook*. Dublin: IPA.

Irish Congress of Trade Unions, *Annual Reports 1959–75*.

Irish Congress of Trade Unions (1992) *Implementation of Equality Report 'Programme for Progress'*. Dublin: ICTU.

Jackson, Pauline Conroy (1987) 'Women's movement and abortion: the criminalization of Irish women', in Dahlerup (ed.), *The New Women's Movement: Feminism and Political Power in Europe and the USA*. London: Sage, pp. 48–63.

Jensen, Jane and Sineau, Mariette (1994) 'The same or different? an unending dilemma for French women', in Barbara Nelson and Najma Chowdhury (eds), *Women and Politics Worldwide*. New Haven: Yale University Press, pp. 244–60.

Jones, Mary (1988) *These Obstreperous Lassies: A History of the Irish Women Workers Union*. Dublin: Gill & Macmillan.

Jordan A. G. (1990) 'The pluralism of pluralism: an anti-theory?', *Political Studies*, **38**, 286–301.

Jordan, A. G. and Richardson, J. J. (1987) *Government and Pressure Groups in Britain*. Oxford: Clarendon Press.

Kaplan, Gisela (1992) *Contemporary Western European Feminism*. London: Allen & Unwin.

Katz, Richard S. and Mair, Peter (1992) *Party Organizations: A Data Handbook on Party Organizations in Western Democracies, 1960–90*. London: Sage.

Kelleher Associates and O'Connor, Monica (1995) *Making the Links: Towards an Integrated Strategy for the Elimination of Violence against Women in Intimate Relationships with Men*. Dublin: Women's Aid.

Kelso, William (1978) *American Democratic Theory – Pluralism and Its Critics*. London: Greenwood Press.

Kennedy, Finola (1989) *Family, Economy and Government in Ireland*. Dublin: Economic and Social Research Institute.

Kennedy, Liam (1994) *People and Population Change*. Belfast: Co-operation North.

Kennelly, Brendan and Ward, Eilis (1993) 'The abortion referendums', in Gallagher and Laver (eds), *How Ireland Voted 1992*. Dublin and Limerick: Folens and PSAI Press, pp. 115–34.

Ketting, E. (1990) *Contraception in Western Europe: A Current Appraisal*. Carnforth, Lancs: Parthenon Publishing Group.

King, Deborah (1976) *Women at Work*. Dublin: An Gúm.

Kirk, Maurice (1975) 'Law and fertility in Ireland', in Kirk *et al.* (eds), *Law and Fertility in Europe: A Study of Legislation Directly or Indirectly Affecting Fertility in Europe*, Vol. 2. Liege, Belgium: European Coordination Centre for Research and Documentation in Social Sciences.

Kirk, Maurice, Bacci, Massimo Livi and Szabady, Egon (1975) *Law and Fertility in Europe: A Study of Legislation Directly or Indirectly Affecting Fertility in Europe*, Vol. 2. Liege, Belgium: European Coordination Centre for Research and Documentation in Social Sciences.

Kitschelt, Herbert P. (1986) 'Political opportunity structures and political protest: anti nuclear movements in four democracies', *British Journal of Political Science*, **16**(1), 57–85.

Klandemans, P. Bert (1990) 'Linking the "old" and "new": movement networks in the Netherlands', in Dalton and Kuechler (eds), *Challenging the Political Order*. Cambridge: Polity Press, pp. 122–36.

Knoke, David (1990) *Organizing for Collective Action – The Political Economies of Associations*. New York: Aldine de Gruyter.

Kriesberg, Louis (1981) *Research in Social Movements, Conflict and Change*. Vol. 4. Greenwich, CT: JAI Press.

Labour Party (1981) *Election Programme*. Dublin: Labour Party.

Law Reform Commission (1988) *Rape and Allied Offences*. Dublin: Law Reform Commission [LRC24–1988].

Levine, June (1982) *Sisters. The Personal Story of an Irish Feminist*. Dublin: Ward River Press.

Lewis, Jane (1983) *Women's Welfare, Women's Rights*. London: Croom Helm.

Lindblom, Charles E. (1965) *The Intelligence of Democracy*. New York: Free Press.

Lindblom, Charles E. (1980) *The Policymaking Process*. Englewood Cliffs, NJ: Prentice-Hall.

Linhard, J. (1990) 'Spain: ten years of progress', in E. Ketting (ed.), *Contraception in Western Europe: A Current Appraisal*. Carnforth, Lancs: Parthenon Publishing Group, pp. 29–35.

Lovenduski, Joni (1986) *Women and European Politics: Contemporary Feminism and Public Policy*. Brighton: Wheatsheaf Books.

Lovenduski, Joni and Norris, Pippa (1993) *Gender and Party Politics*. London: Sage.

Lovenduski, Joni and Randall, Vicky (1993) *Contemporary Feminist Politics: Women and Power in Britain*. Oxford: Oxford University Press.

Luddy, Maria and Murphy, Cliona (1989) *Women Surviving: Studies in Irish Women's History in the 19th & 20th Centuries*. Dublin: Poolbeg.

McBride Stetson, Dorothy (1986) *Women's Rights in France*. New York: Greenwood Press.

McCann, Dermot (1993) 'Business power and collective action: the state and the confederation of Irish Industry 1970–1990', *Irish Political Studies*, 8, 37–54.

McCarthy, John D. and Zald, Mayer N. (1977) 'Resource mobilization and social movements: a partial theory', *American Journal of Sociology*, 82, 1212–41.

McCrudden, Christopher (1987) *Women, Employment and European Equality Law*. London: Eclipse.

MacCurtain, Margaret and O'Corrain, Donncha (1978) *Women in Irish Society*. Dublin: Arlen House.

McLaughlin, Eugene (1993) 'Ireland: Catholic corporatism', in Cochrane and Clarke, *Comparing Welfare States: Britain in International Context*. Milton Keynes: Open University Press.

Mahon, Evelyn (1987) 'Women's rights and Catholicism in Ireland', *New Left Review*, 166.

Maier, C. S. (1987) *Changing Boundaries of the Political: Essays on the Evolving Balance Between State and Society, Public and Private in Europe*. Cambridge: Cambridge University Press.

Mangahas, Malou (1994) 'The oldest contraceptive: the lactational amenorrhea method (LAM) and reproductive rights', in Judith Mirsky and Marty Radlett (eds), *Private Decisions, Public Debate*. London: Panos, pp. 57–68.

Manning, Maurice (1978) 'Women in Irish national and local politics 1977–77', in MacCurtain and O'Corrain (eds), *Women in Irish Society*. Dublin: Arlen House, pp. 92–102.

Manning, Maurice (1988) 'Women and the elections', in Howard R. Penniman and Brian Farrell (eds), *Ireland at the Polls 1981, 1982 and 1987: A Study of Four General Elections*. Durham NC: Duke University Press, pp. 156–66.

Meehan, Elizabeth (1983) 'Equal opportunity policies: some implications for women of contrasts between enforcement bodies in Britain and the USA', in Lewis (ed.), *Women's Welfare, Women's Rights*. London: Croom Helm, pp. 170–92.

Meehan, Elizabeth (1990) 'British feminism from the 1960s to the 1980s', in Harold L. Smith (ed.), *British Feminism in the Twentieth Century*. Aldershot: Edward Elgar, pp. 189–204.

Meehan, Elizabeth and Sevenhuijsen, Selma (1991) *Equality Politics and Gender*. London: Sage.

Mendez, Maria Teresa Gallego (1994) 'Women's political engagement in Spain', in Barbara Nelson and Najma Chowdhury (eds), *Women and Politics Worldwide*. New Haven: Yale University Press, pp. 661–73.

Meulders, Daniele, Plasman, Robert and Stricht, Valerie Vander (1993) *Position of Women on the Labour Market in the European Community*. Aldershot: Dartmouth.

Mirsky, Judith and Radlett, Marty (1994) *Private Decisions, Public Debate: Women, Reproduction and Population*. London: Panos.

National Economic and Social Council (1975) *An Approach to Social Policy*. Dublin: NESC.

Nealon, Ted (1977) *Guide to the 21st Dail and Seanad*. Dublin: Platform Press.

Nealon, Ted (1987) *Guide to the 25th Dail and Seanad*. Dublin: Platform Press.

Nealon, Ted (1989) *Guide to the 26th Dáil and Seanad*. Dublin: Platform Press.

Nelson, Barbara J. and Chowdhury, Najma (1994) *Women and Politics Worldwide*. New Haven: Yale University Press.

Norris, Pippa (1988) 'The gender gap: a cross-national trend?', in Carol M. Mueller (ed.), *The Politics of the Gender Gap: The Social Construction of Political Influence*. London: Sage, pp. 217–34.

O'Connor, Paul A. (1988) *Key Issues in Irish Family Law*. Dublin: Round Hall Press.

O'Dowd, Liam (1987) 'Church, State and women: the aftermath of partition', in Curtin et al. (eds), *Gender in Irish Society*. Galway: Galway University Press, pp. 3–36.

O'Halpin, Eunan (1993) 'Policymaking', in Coakley and Gallagher (eds), *Politics in the Republic of Ireland*. Dublin and Limerick: Folens and PSAI Press, pp. 190–206.

O'Higgins, Kathleen (1974) *Marital Desertion in Ireland*. Dublin: ESRI.

O'Higgins, Kathleen (1986) 'Family planning services in Ireland with particular reference to minors', in Hyman Rodman and Jan Trost (eds), *The Adolescent Dilemma: International Perspectives on the Family Planning Rights of Minors*. New York: Praeger.

O'Leary, Cornelius and Hesketh, Tom (1988) 'The Irish abortion and divorce referendum campaigns', *Irish Political Studies*, 3, 43–62.

Oberschall, Anthony (1973) *Social Conflict and Social Movements*. Englewood Cliffs, NJ: Prentice-Hall.

Offe, Claus (1987) 'Challenging the boundaries of institutional politics: social movements since the 1960s', in C. S. Maier (ed.), *Changing Boundaries of the Political*. Cambridge: Cambridge University Press, pp. 63–105.

Offe, Claus (1990) 'Reflections on the institutional self-transformation of movement politics: a tentative stage model', in Dalton and Kuechler (eds), *Challenging the Political Order*. Cambridge: Polity Press, pp. 239–41.

Overby, L. Martin (1990) 'West European peace movements: an application of Kitschelt's political opportunity structures thesis', *West European Politics*, **13**(1), 1–11.

Pisciotta, Elenore Eckmann (1987) 'The strength and powerlessness of the new Italian women's movement: the case of abortion', in Dahlerup (ed.), *The New Women's Movement*. London: Sage, pp. 26–47.

Randall, Vicky (1987) *Women and Politics: An International Perspective*. Basingstoke: Macmillan Education.

Randall, Vicky and Smyth, Ailbhe (1987) 'Bishops and bailiwicks: obstacles to women's political participation in Ireland', *Economic and Social Review*, **18**(3), 189–214.

Ranum, Orest and Patricia (1972) *Popular Attitudes Toward Birth Control in Pre-industrial France and England*. London: Harper & Row.

Regan, Marguerite C. and Wilson, Frank L. (1986) 'Interest group politics in France and Ireland: comparative perspectives on neo-corporatism', *West European Politics*, **9**(3), 393–411.

Reid, Madeline (1988) *The Impact of Community Law on the Irish Constitution*. Dublin: Irish Centre for European Law.

Rootes, C. A. (1991) 'The new politics and the new social movements in Britain', Paper presented to the Political Studies Association Conference, Lancaster, 15–17 April.

Rouchon, Thomas R. (1990) 'The West European peace movement and the theory of new social movements', in Dalton and Kuechler (eds), *Challenging the Political Order*. Cambridge: Polity Press, pp. 105–21.

Rucht, Dieter (1990) 'The strategies and action repertoires of new movements', in Dalton and Kuechler (eds), *Challenging the Political Order*. Cambridge: Polity Press, pp. 156–75.

Rudig, Wolfgang (1988) 'Peace and ecology movements in Western Europe', *West European Politics*, **11**(1), 27–39.

Sapiro, Virginia (1987) 'The women's movement, policy and politics in the Reagan era', in Dahlerup (ed.), *The New Women's Movement*. London: Sage, pp. 122–39.

Scannell, Yvonne (1988) 'The constitution and the role of women' in Brian Farrell (ed.), *De Valera's Constitution and Ours*. Dublin: Gill & Macmillan, pp. 123–36.

Schattschneider, E. E. (1975) *The Semi-Sovereign People – A Realist's View of Democracy in America*. Hinsdale, IL: Dryden Press.

Schmitter, Philippe C. and Lembruch, Gerhard (1979) *Trends Towards Corporatist Intermediation*. London: Sage.

Schmitter, Philippe C. (1979) 'Still the century of corporatism?' in Schmitter and Lembruch (eds), *Trends Towards Corporatist Intermediation*. London: Sage, pp. 7–52.

Shallat, Lezak (1994) 'Rites and rights: Catholicism and contraception in Chile', in Mirsky and Radlett (eds), *Private Decisions, Public Debate*. London: Panos, pp. 149–62.

Skocpol, Theda, Abend-Wein, Marjorie, Howard, Christopher and Lehmann, Susan Goodrich (1993) 'Women's associations and the enactment of mothers' pensions in the United States', *American Political Science Review*, **87**(3), 686–97.

Smelser, Neil (1962) *Theory of Collective Behaviour*. London: Routledge & Kegan Paul.

Smith, Harold L. (1990) *British Feminism in the Twentieth Century*. Aldershot: Edward Elgar.

Smith, Martin J. (1990) 'Pluralism, reformed pluralism and neopluralism: the role of pressure groups in policy-making', *Political Studies*, **38**, 302–22.

Smith, Martin J. (1993) *Pressure Power and Policy: State Autonomy and Policy Networks in Britain and the United States*. London: Harvester Wheatsheaf.

Smyth, Ailbhe (1992) *The Abortion Papers: Ireland*. Dublin: Attic Press.

Smyth, Ailbhe (1992) 'A sadistic farce', in Smyth (ed.), *The Abortion Papers: Ireland*. Dublin: Attic Press, pp. 7–23.

Smyth, Ailbhe (1993) *Irish Women's Studies Reader*. Dublin: Attic Press.

Smyth, Ailbhe (1993) 'The women's movement in the Republic of Ireland 1970–1990', in Smyth (ed.), *Irish Women's Studies Reader*. Dublin: Attic Press, pp. 245–69.

Socialist Group, European Parliament (1986) *Sexual Violence Against Women and Girls*. Brussels: Socialist Group.

Solomons, Michael (1992) *Pro-Life? The Irish Question*. Dublin: Lilliput Press.

Stedward, Gail (1987) 'Entry to the system: a case study of Women's Aid in Scotland', in Jordan and Richardson (eds), *Government and Pressure Groups in Britain*. Oxford: Oxford University Press, pp. 211–33.

Truman, David B. (1971) *The Governmental Process*. New York: Alfred Knopf.

Turner, Ralph (1981) 'Collective behaviour and resource mobilization as approaches to social movements: issues and continuities', in Louis Kriesberg (ed.), *Research in Social Movements*, Vol. 4. Greenwich, CT: JAI Press, pp. 1–24.

Tweedy, Hilda (1992) *A Link in the Chain: The Story of the Irish Housewives Association 1942–1992*. Dublin: Attic Press.

Walker, Brian M. (1992) *Parliamentary Election Results in Ireland, 1918–92*. Dublin: Royal Irish Academy.

Walsh, Brendan M. (1993) 'Labour force participation and the growth of women's employment, Ireland', *Economic and Social Review*, 24(4), 369–400.

Walsh, Mary Ena (1983) *Women in Rural Ireland*. Dublin: Council for the Status of Women.

Ward, Margaret (1989) *Unmanageable Revolutionaries: Women and Irish Nationalism*. Dingle: Brandon Press.

Wilcox, Clyde (1991) 'Support for gender equality in west Europe – a longitudinal analysis', *European Journal of Political Research*, 20(2), 127–47.

Williamson, P. J. (1989) *Corporatism in Perspective: An Introductory Guide to Corporatist Theory*. London: Sage.

Women's Aid Refuge (1986) *Findings of a Common Research Project Between Womens Aid, Dublin, Boys and Girls Welfare Society, Cheshire, Northern Ireland Women's Aid, Belfast*. Dublin: Women's Aid.

Yishai, Yael (1993) 'Public ideas and public policy: abortion politics in four democracies', *Comparative Politics*, 25(2), 207–28.

GOVERNMENT PUBLICATIONS

Acts of the Oireachtas.

Central Statistics Office, *Census of Population of Ireland, 1979. Volume 11, Ages and Marital Status* (July 1981) [Prl. 9956].

Central Statistics Office, *Economic Series* (December 1993).

Commission on the Status of Women, *Report to the Minister for Finance* (December 1972) [Prl. 2760].

Committee on Court Practice and Procedure, *Nineteenth Interim Report, Desertion and Maintenance* (February 1974) [Prl. 3666].

Dáil Éireann, *Debates*, 1969–96.

Department of Health, *Tuarascail an Ard-Chlaraitheora* (1951).

Department of Health, *Vital Statistics* (1951, 1971, 1991).

Department of the Environment, *General Election 1992: Election Results and Transfer of Votes* (1993).

First Progress Report of the Monitoring Committee on the Implementation of the Recommendations of the Second Commission on the Status of Women (May 1994) [Pn. 0798].

Interdepartmental Working Party on Women's Affairs, *Irish Women: Agenda for Practical Action* (February 1985) [Pl. 3126].

Joint Oireachtas Committee on Women's Rights, *Sexual Violence* (1987).

Joint Oireachtas Committee on Women's Rights, *Changing Attitudes to the Role of Women in Ireland: Attitudes Towards the Role and Status of Women 1975–1986* (May 1988) [Pl. 5609].

Joint Oireachtas Committee on Women's Rights, *Motherhood, Work and Equal Opportunity – A Case Study of Irish Civil Servants* (July 1991) [Pl. 8249].

Labour Force Survey 1991 (June 1992).

Marital Breakdown: A Review and Proposed Changes (September 1992) [Pl. 9104].

Proceedings of Seanad Éireann, 1969–96.

Programme for Economic and Social Progress (January 1991) [Pl. 7829].

Report of the Joint Committee on Marriage Breakdown (27 March 1985) [Pl. 3074].

Second Commission on the Status of Women, *Report to Government* (January 1993) [Pl. 9557].

Second Progress Report of the Monitoring Committee on the Implementation of the Recommendations of the Second Commission on the Status of Women (March 1996) [Pn. 2489].

Statistical Abstract (1992).

The Development of Equal Opportunities, March 1987–September 1988: Coordinated Report (1988) [Pl. 6056].

Women's Representative Committee, *Second Progress Report on the Implementation of the Recommendations in the Report of the Commission on the Status of Women* (December 1978).

NEWSPAPERS, JOURNALS, PERIODICALS AND PAMPHLETS

AIM Newsletter, 1973–79.

Banshee, March–August 1976.

Irish Independent, 1970–90.

Irish Times, 1970–96.

Irishwomen United, 1976.

Magill, 1976, 1978.

WICCA, 1978.

Women Against Violence Against Women, pamphlets and statements, 1978.

Women's Aid documents, February 1981.

Women's AIM, 1979–85.

INDEX